Kim Hughes GC is a warrant officer in the British Army and is the most highly decorated bomb disposal operator serving in the British Armed Forces. He was awarded the George Cross in 2010 following a gruelling six-month tour of duty in Afghanistan, during which he defused 119 improvised explosive devices, survived numerous Taliban ambushes and endured a close encounter with the Secretary of State for Defence. He is an acclaimed public speaker and a trustee of the Victoria Cross and George Cross Association.

Praise for *Painting the Sand*

'Breathtaking. Kim Hughes is the man who stands between us and oblivion.' Andy McNab, author of *Bravo Two Zero*

'An uplifting and enlightening account of the personal courage and dedication required to do a very lonely job in the most extreme of conditions.' John Nichol, *Mail on Sunday*

'A heart-pounding behind-the-scenes look at one of the most dangerous trades in the military.' *Soldier* Magazine

'Though Hughes is self-deprecating in his book, it is genuine heroism and honesty that endear him to the reader.' *The Australian*

D0263295

PAINTING THE SAND

One Man's Fight Against the Taliban
Bomb-makers of Helmand

KIM HUGHES GC

**SIMON &
SCHUSTER**

London · New York · Sydney · Toronto · New Delhi

A CBS COMPANY

First published in Great Britain by Simon & Schuster UK Ltd, 2017
This paperback edition published by Simon & Schuster UK Ltd, 2018
A CBS COMPANY

1 3 5 7 9 10 8 6 4 2

Simon & Schuster UK Ltd
1st Floor
222 Gray's Inn Road
London WC1X 8HB

www.simonandschuster.co.uk
www.simonandschuster.com.au
www.simonandschuster.co.in

Simon & Schuster Australia, Sydney
Simon & Schuster India, New Delhi

The author and publishers have made all reasonable efforts to contact copyright-
holders for permission, and apologise for any omissions or errors in the
form of credits given. Corrections may be made to future printings.

A CIP catalogue record for this book
is available from the British Library

Paperback ISBN: 978-1-4711-5672-4
eBook ISBN: 978-1-4711-5673-1

Typeset in the UK by M Rules
Printed and bound by CPI Group (UK) Ltd, Croydon, CR0 4YY

MIX
Paper from
responsible sources
FSC
www.fsc.org   FSC® C020471

Simon & Schuster UK Ltd are committed to sourcing paper that is made from
wood grown in sustainable forests and support the Forest Stewardship Council,
the leading international forest certification organisation. Our books
displaying the FSC logo are printed on FSC certified paper.

For Mum

Contents

Foreword

Improvised explosive device – IED – the preferred weapon of terrorist groups around the world for over forty years. The IED can kill you two ways. A big bomb, say twenty-plus kilos, will blow you to pieces. Quick and painless. But if you're unlucky, I mean really unlucky, the blast will cut you in half, take away your legs and leave you disembowelled. You might survive but not for long, not unless you've got immediate access to a fully equipped trauma hospital with highly qualified battle-hardened war surgeons.

In Afghanistan in 2008, the Taliban began making IEDs by the thousand. The bombs weren't sophisticated – in fact the quality was crap. But that wasn't the issue. The problem was the number. By 2009 there were an estimated 10,000 IEDs buried in the ground in Helmand at any one time. British soldiers were being killed and injured every day. Morale was low and for a few brief months over that summer the Taliban were winning.

The best weapon against the IED is the bomb disposal operator. That was my job. When I flew into Helmand on the 6 April 2009 I was expected to hit the ground running, to tackle everything the Taliban could throw at me. I thought I was ready but, in reality, I wasn't.

A couple of decades earlier when the Troubles in Northern Ireland were at their height a bomb disposal operator could be expected to deal with six to eight complex bombs in six months and in the busier parts of the province sometimes a lot more. By the end of my six months in Helmand I had defused more than a hundred IEDs.

What you will read over the next few hundred pages will tell you how I and my team helped beat the Taliban and lived to tell the tale. It was often a close-run thing. We made mistakes, casualties were taken, but in the end we were lucky. It's a tough read. I haven't pulled any punches. The book has been written so that you will know what it's like to get up close and personal to an IED. How an IED is put together and what it's like to defuse a bomb in a minefield when you're surrounded by the dead and the dying.

Today, right now, in towns and cities across the UK, would-be terrorists are designing a new generation of IEDs – more deadly than anything seen in Afghanistan. It's a game of cat and mouse and at the moment we're ahead, but for how long?

I

First Op – Boots on the Ground

13 May 2009

Ten minutes to landing. Thank fuck. The longer we were airborne, the greater the risk. The Chinook was an easy target,
even at night and the Taliban were gunning for a big prize.
Burning alive in Afghan wasn't the way I wanted to sign off.

My arse was aching like you wouldn't believe and my legs felt
like they belonged to someone else. My body was screaming
with cramp and the heat was unbelievable. I was sitting down on
the Chinook's shiny, steel deck, unable to move, straitjacketed
by my own equipment. My body armour, great for stopping
bullets, acted like a thermal blanket, leaving me soaked in sweat
and panting for breath. I shit you not, it was like a fucking sauna.

It didn't worry me that we might be landing straight into
the middle of a Taliban ambush. We'd been warned that the
landing zone might be hot. Casualties were expected, the risks
were high. Fine. Just get me on the ground and off the fucking
chopper.

Strapped to my chest was my SIG 9mm pistol and a load of explosive ordnance disposal (EOD) kit. Ammo pouches on my hips held at least six mags of thirty rounds – in Afghan everyone had to be ready to fight. In one hand I held my rifle – the 5.56mm SA80 – a weapon with a bad reputation, but by 2009 effectively it had been rebuilt and was pretty decent. In the other hand was my day-sack, containing everything I needed to defuse IEDs.

The Chinook had been stripped of all its seats so more soldiers could be crammed in. Forty of us were squeezed inside an aircraft designed to carry half that number. That's forty fully equipped troops carrying rucksacks and weapons, all sitting or squatting, unable to move. I would have happily paid a grand for a few more inches of legroom.

The engines screamed with the demands of flying at low level, hugging valleys, using the natural cover of the barren Helmand desert. I closed my eyes hoping to doze but something began pushing against my leg. 'Jesus, give it a rest,' I groaned. I reached forward ready to lash out, expecting an arm or leg but instead grabbed a handful of fur.

It was the explosive search dog sniffing at my kit. The dog's senses had gone crazy – my day-sack was full of explosives. I gently stroked its fur and felt his panting breath on my hand. It must have been suffering far more than me but the dog lay quietly without complaint. Thoughts of my own dog, a hyperactive young cocker spaniel began to fill my mind. I called him Sabot, after a piece of ammunition – what do you expect from an EOD soldier? I was gently transported to happier times, playing fetch, going for long wintry walks, Sabot at my side.

'Five minutes,' the RAF loadmaster signalled.

The Chinook had been airborne for about fifty minutes

and the smell of aviation fuel was starting to make everyone feel nauseous. An acrid stench of fresh vomit began to waft through the chopper and I started to gag; there are only a few things in this world that make me want to throw up and that smell is one of them.

A young soldier, still a teenager, was retching violently. Tears were streaming down his face as he struggled for breath. We were all scared — none of us knew what the future held.

His section commander leaned over — anger in his eyes — mouthing the words: 'Get a fucking grip.'

'One minute,' the loadmaster shouted holding up a solitary finger for those who couldn't hear.

I tried to stand but my legs, numbed into paralysis by sitting cross-legged, buckled and I collapsed in a heap. A hand reached down from above helping me to my feet.

'Cheers, pal,' I said but my words were lost beneath the deafening roar of the engines.

The helo had barely touched down before the loadie started screaming for everyone to get off. A stationary chopper in Taliban territory was a sitting duck. I charged into the dark void, soldiers around me stumbled and fell. Chaos.

I ran clear and fell on my belt buckle. The ground was unexpectedly wet with dew and smelt clean and fresh — not what I was expecting. I looked up to scan the ground ahead and felt my helmet hanging half off my head as though I was a recruit in the first week of training. A basic error. I'd spent the last two days squaring my kit away for the operation and I'd forgotten about my helmet. Hours had been spent getting my kit sorted, making sure everything was where it should have been. Personalising my body armour to make sure it fitted comfortably, giving me easy access to my tools and pistol. It was amazing how many hours could be whiled away ensuring that everything worked and was comfortable. A little bit of OCD went a long way in Afghan.

In Helmand your kit was your life-support system. Body armour, pistol, helmet, field dressing, tourniquet (in case you lose a leg or two), morphine, to dull the pain of a traumatic amputation, wire snippers, smoke grenades, and the all-important paintbrush, used for clearing the sand away from the IEDs. I kept my 9mm SIG pistol within easy reach – it was my close protection weapon. But if I had to use it in anger then something had gone seriously wrong.

I also had another 50 kilograms of kit that I squeezed into my Bergen rucksack and that was meant to be 'light scales', meaning you took what you could carry, nothing more. I didn't have the luxury of a bomb disposal suit – a 50-kilogram Kevlar padded jacket and trousers combo with ballistic plate designed to allow the person inside to, within reason, survive a blast. I couldn't run in it and so the suit was about as tactically sound as a Day-Glo vest – no use in Afghan.

Fuck up over here and it's game over. What's left of me gets mopped up and flown home in a box and I become just another sorry stat on an ever-growing casualty list. A brief mention on the news, grieving parents, tears, friends talking of a brave soldier who gave his life for his country. A few minutes of useless fame before the next pissed-up celebrity steals the headlines.

Not the end I had in mind. This was my first mission in Afghan and I wanted to do well. I wanted to be the operator who can be relied upon – not some idiot that turned himself to red mist first time out. I'd come too far, worked too hard and sacrificed too much for it to all end on day one.

I was in charge of a Counter-IED team on Operation Herrick 10 – the code name for the war in Afghanistan.

The main headquarters was Camp Bastion, a vast tented city in the middle of Helmand that acted as a central hub for British and NATO forces. It grew in size every day; at any one time several thousand troops would arrive, be preparing to leave or waiting to go into battle. The place was almost self-sustaining, producing its own water and getting rid of its own waste. There was a hospital, complete with trauma team and Intensive Care Unit, dining halls churning out thousands of meals a day, gyms, coffee shops, a NAAFI with satellite TV and a Pizza Hut. It all helped to remind us there was life beyond the shit-filled ditches of Helmand. Bastion also had an airport, which had it been in England would have been almost as busy as Luton. There were even traffic police to ensure that troops stuck to the camp speed limit of 15mph. That was life inside the wire. But out in the badlands of Helmand life was a little different.

Inside our cavernous, white air-conditioned tent in Bastion talk was absent. The piss-taking, jokes and banter that filled idle minutes had been replaced by focused silence. It was kit-check time. Check, check and check again. The packing and reorganising was partly out of necessity and partly to keep our minds occupied, a way of wasting a few hours in between eating, trying to sleep and reading. Soldiers throughout the centuries have done the same, attempting to control their nervous anticipation as they waited to go into battle.

My No. 2 and second-in-command, Corporal Lewis Mackafee, was keen to get out. One thing he wanted was a firefight with the enemy. Secretly we all did. We all wanted to say that we'd been in contact but you needed to be careful what you wished for, especially in Afghan.

The Electronic Counter Measures (ECM) Operator, Lance Corporal Dave Thomas, was very bright, but quiet, and always on top of his kit, making sure it was clean and in good order. His equipment was top secret, or at least how it worked was. It was designed to jam radio frequencies so the Taliban couldn't target us with remote-controlled (RC) IEDs.

The search team, the other part of my unit, had trained together for over a year and had grown as close as brothers. The search commander was Corporal Alan Chapman, a gleaming soldier and a born leader. His team looked up to him, especially the younger lads who were barely out of their teens: Matt, Malley, Harry, Sam and Robbo, who were bright lads with a great attitude, the requirements for a High Threat Search Team. Most of their mates were probably at uni or back home in the pub cheering on their favourite football team.

Dust as fine and soft as talcum powder blanketed everything inside Bastion. Tents, vehicles, aircraft, the gym, even the toilets, nothing was spared. But you learned to deal with it. Someone once said the dust is mainly composed of centuries of human shit dried by the desert heat and turned to dust by the desert winds. Now the British Army were sucking it up, fighting a war that was never meant to happen against an enemy who had no concept of defeat. Some of the people we were fighting had been at war longer than most of us had been alive. The Taliban might be poorly educated, ill-equipped and outgunned but they were committed and loved nothing more than a good dust-up.

Brimstone 42 – the call sign of my Counter-IED team – were itching for action. I know that sounds like a cliché but it was the truth. We were squared away and swept up. Now we wanted to test ourselves, take on the Taliban and pull bombs out of the ground. We wanted to save lives and win our war. Like every soldier arriving in Helmand, my guys had been trained and tested to within an inch of their lives. In theory there was nothing more we could learn. Each one of us knew everything there was to know about our trade — the only thing we lacked was experience.

'If you remember one thing remember this: in Afghan what can go wrong will go wrong,' one of the instructors said to my team on the last day of Role Specific Training (RST) three days earlier. That simple statement played over and over in my head. It became my own personal mantra. In Afghan what can go wrong will go wrong, so plan accordingly.

Soldiers died there every day because they either messed up, became complacent or were just unlucky — two out of three were in their control. That was the reality and the quicker you learned that the better. The best you can hope for at the end of six months is to be alive — preferably with both arms, legs and your bollocks intact. Anything beyond that is a bonus.

The Chinook that had dropped us lifted into the night sky creating an instant brown-out as dust and crap was kicked up into a mini-whirlwind by the downdraught of its rotor blades. I buried my face in the damp desert and waited for a few seconds before clambering to my feet. As I lowered my night vision goggles (NVGs) night became day and it became apparent I was not alone. The night was lit up by the bright infrared beacons mounted on the side of the soldiers' helmets, which were used to help aircraft, helicopter gunships and ground troops to identify friendly forces. A scene of utter chaos began to unfold around me. Hundreds of soldiers were spread across the fields, seemingly without anyone in control. Chinooks were landing every few seconds disgorging an army of troops. It was day one of Operation Sarack — a battlegroup search-led operation into a Taliban-held area of Helmand.

Two large compounds – basically farms – had been identified as potential IED-making factories. The production of the bombs had become a cottage industry; hundreds, possibly thousands, were being made and they were having a devastating impact on the war. 'Improvised' meant they were constructed from almost any materials – the Taliban could make a bomb out of two pieces of wood, hacksaw blades, some wire, a Christmas tree light and about 10kg of home-made explosives, the main charge. A 20kg main charge will blow you to pieces, anything bigger and a mop will be needed to deal with what's left.

The plan was to swamp and secure the area with troops, seal off the compounds, clear any Afghans, either willingly or otherwise, and then conduct a detailed search. Anything that looked like an IED would be handed over to my Brimstone team to deal with.

Senior officers will spend days, sometimes weeks, planning military operations. Orders sessions can last several hours as the information distils down from the top brass to the soldiers on the ground. It is a massively time-consuming process where every eventuality is planned for. But as every soldier knows no plan survives contact with the enemy.

Almost immediately, the mission, at least my team's part in it, began to unravel. Initially two Brimstone teams were supposed to deploy on the operation but twenty minutes into the briefing that was cut to one. Then, just as we were about to board the helicopters, I was told that our objective had now changed. Again not a massive issue as the fundamentals of the operation remained: get to the objective and clear it – simple.

All Counter-IED teams carry the prefix 'Brimstone' as part of their radio call sign and my team consisted of eleven soldiers: a four-man bomb disposal team – that's me, my No.2, an Electronic Counter Measures (ECM) Operator and my infantry escort to watch my back while I was dealing with the bomb. I was also supported by a Royal Engineer Search Advisor (RESA) and a Royal Engineer Search Team (REST), which consisted of six very bright and ridiculously brave soldiers. They found the bombs for me to deal with. Brimstone 42 was part of the Counter-IED Task Force, a special unit created to tackle the increased number of IEDs.

The last-minute objective change meant my team were split across two helos, so they were God knows where on the battlefield when we hit the landing zone. After a few minutes of scouring the landing zone I spotted my No.2, Lewis, heading towards me. Following behind were Dave, the ECM Operator and my infantry escort. It was good to see them. I could deal with changes to the plan but if we had been split up we would have been no use to anyone.

I dropped to one knee in the middle of a field as the team came together. 'All right, lads? Everyone OK?' I whispered. They nodded but no one spoke. 'We're moving off to the north, that way. The sun is coming up on our right to the east. We've got about a K [kilometre] of tabbing to the objective.'

If the fighting had kicked off at that moment we'd have been in serious trouble. The ground was boggy. Mud clung to my boots. Trying to run, weighed down by kit, would have been impossible. No one had mentioned that in the briefings. The fetid smell of human shit hung heavily in the air, an indication that habitation was close by, and the night was sticky and warm. I was drenched with sweat and beginning to dehydrate. Above were bats feasting on mosquitoes dive-bombing the line of troops stretched out into the darkness. I looked up at the night sky. There was no light pollution and

I gazed in awe at the vastness and clarity of the Milky Way, twinkling light years away above me. I was oddly comforted in the knowledge that it was the same sky I could see from my home in England and I found myself smiling at its beauty.

As we moved off again one of the infantry corporals began gobbing off about someone forgetting to tape up an infrared beacon to reduce its brightness. Only a tiny pinhole was needed otherwise the infrared light effectively renders night vision goggles useless by blurring them out.

'Fucking atts and detts . . . the wankers have forgotten to square away their IR beacons – amateurs. Probably never been out on the ground before.' 'Atts' and 'detts' were attachments and detachments – the Brimstone team. He had said it loud enough for everyone to hear even though we were supposedly on a tactical approach to the objective. I had a quick look about and saw that the offending beacon was attached to one of his lads and not wanting to look like a twat for not being on top of his men the idiot blamed my guys.

'Oi, dickhead – wind your neck in,' I said an inch or so away from his face. My words stopped him dead in his tracks. Not knowing whether to shit or piss he muttered an apology.

In single file, walking slowly and in silence, we made our way through the wheat fields, stopping every now and then for no visible reason. Somewhere up ahead a lone soldier cleared a path with a metal detector, moving slowly and methodically searching for IEDs. Our lives were in his hands.

The column ground to a halt. I again dropped onto a knee, waiting for the rest of the team to emerge from the predawn gloom. One by one they appeared and formed a semicircle around me.

'I never knew a K could be so knackering,' Sam whispered.

A ripple of soft laughter fluttered through the team – spirits were high.

I gulped down water and wiped the sweat from my eyes. Ahead the infantry were moving in to secure the target – a large compound with mud walls designed to keep intruders out and protect those inside. In all likelihood the compound was around when the British first invaded Afghanistan in the early nineteenth century.

As we chatted quietly an infantry sergeant emerged from the darkness. A large, confident grin was spread across his dirty face.

'Right, lads, make yourselves comfortable. You're going be here for at least an hour. No smoking or brews but you can get something to eat,' he said before disappearing back into the night.

I got as comfortable as I could using my day-sack as a back-rest to lean on and tried to relax. I noticed a young soldier shivering in the dark. 'You all right, mate?'

'Just cold, Staff,' he answered, teeth chattering. I reached into my Bergen and pulled out an old poncho liner.

'Wrap yourself in that. We're going to be here for a while. And take on some water – you'll be all right.'

I dropped my night vision goggles back down and noticed that some of the team had nodded off. An hour or so later, around 0430 hrs, a message filtered its way down to my team that we had to be ready to move by 0445 hrs.

The young soldier who had been shivering an hour or so earlier neatly folded my poncho liner and handed it back to me, smiling. 'Thanks but you didn't need to fold it,' I added before stuffing it back into my pack.

Everyone struggled to stand beneath the weight of their kit with legs stiff from the cold. One by one, the soldiers began to follow the man in front in a long single file. The route was marked by guides from a reconnaissance unit ensuring that we were heading in the right direction.

Through the gloom, I spotted our first objective, the compound with typical fifteen-foot-high and two-foot-thick walls. Groups of soldiers began breaking away taking up defensive positions around the outside wall. I headed for a corner of the compound where an orchard offered a bit of cover if a contact kicked off. Gradually, Brimstone 42 arrived, dropped their kit, took up fire positions and waited for the next set of orders. We had now entered the realms of a classic military operation – hurry up and wait.

The first sign of dawn over in the east was greeted by a chorus of birdsong. Still cold and leaning against the fifteen-foot compound wall, I watched as the sun crept into the dark, hoping that it would reach us by the time we had to move again. A little bit of heat would have done wonders for morale. As light began to flood into the valley, a mist appeared and hung like a white veil across the hand-groomed fields surrounding us. The Islamic call to prayer echoed across the land, hungry dogs barked and in the distance, and several fields away, men wearing turbans and wrapped in blankets began to emerge from their homes. They paid us little attention as they squatted down to shit in the same irrigation ditches many of us had just walked through.

Helmand is located in southern Afghanistan and has a border with Pakistan. It is largely desert apart from the area either side of the Helmand river, a lifeline running through the country like a major artery, irrigating the land and turning parts of the desert into a lush fertile plain. This area was known as the Green Zone and where the majority of the population resided. It was also the region the Taliban wanted to control.

I scoured the landscape through my weapon-sight, marvelling at the pre-industrial beauty of rural Helmand. Life had changed little for hundreds of years. Invaders had come and gone but the Afghans seemed to have an almost superhuman capability to endure.

Just as I was becoming lost in my own thoughts the clipped tones of a public schoolboy brought me back to reality.

'Where's ATO?' demanded a young second lieutenant who looked as though he had literally just left Sandhurst military academy. He was referring to me — Staff Sergeant Kim Hughes. I'm an Ammunition Technician but in Afghan everyone was called Ammunition Technical Officers (ATOs) — the bomb disposal specialists.

'I'm the ATO, sir,' I responded, expecting a quick brief on the latest developments.

'You're at the wrong objective,' he said with a tinge of blame as though the mistake was mine. He was probably only on his first operational tour but appeared full of confidence, which could be both good and bad.

'What? No, this is our objective,' I replied testily. 'We were supposed to go to the other compound but the plan was changed yesterday. This is our objective. This is the bomb factory and we're here to clear it.'

But as the words came out of my mouth a half smile crept across his face. 'Shit happens. Things change and so has your objective. An IED has been found at the other compound and that's where you should have been sent to.'

'Are you taking the piss, sir?'

'No, Staff, I'm not. You are needed over there,' he added, pointing in the direction of another compound, around seven hundred metres away.

'So how are we going to get there, sir?'

'Tab,' he responded, as he walked away.

It was now daylight, the Taliban were awake, had finished morning prayers and were ready to fight. Now my team had to walk across open ground for seven hundred metres with no cover because someone hadn't got their act together.

'Officers couldn't organise . . .' the sentence drifted away unfinished. The lads chuckled to one another as I walked over to the search team to break the good news.

Dave interrupted: 'Staff, just got information on the radio. They've got definite confirmation of an IED at the other objective.'

'Roger, tell them we'll be there in the next twenty mins.' The plan was unravelling and fast.

The Taliban would have clocked us as soon as the Chinook landed. My mind began to race. They were probably already in their ambush positions or moving towards them. There was no choice but to cut straight across the poppy field. The crops were about knee high so a bit of cover for us if there was a contact but also cover for them.

I called everyone together beneath the shade of a fruit tree. The guys were sitting and kneeling and listened attentively as I charged through a quick set of battle orders. Sapper Sam Jack, one of the younger members of the search team, was nodding as I spoke. He soaked up every bit of info. An excellent soldier, bright and super-fit with a huge amount of common sense. Exactly the sort of bloke you want in your team. He already had that sense of authority, which even those more senior respect. I knew back in training that he was going to be a vital member of the team. He was the first to volunteer for the more difficult tasks and never complained. One of those guys that binds teams together.

'We've got to get ourselves over to that compound,' I

explained, first pointing at the map and then at the building around seven hundred metres away. 'We're going to be exposed moving across the field and any attack is likely to come from that tree line. I want REST to lead, RESA and I will follow, the remainder behind me. If we get attacked go firm and return fire. No unnecessary stops. The less time we are in the open the better. Ready to move in five.'

Sapper Michael Malley, another top soldier, was testing his mine detector — he was point man, probably the most dangerous job in Helmand. He either finds bombs or steps on them. Sam had volunteered to follow directly behind Malley.

The sun was now in the sky and I could feel the heat burning my neck as I squinted through the diamond-white light to the fields beyond. The front man set off at a speedy pace and in a matter of minutes we were breathing heavily and dripping with sweat. Somewhere in the distance the crackle of automatic gunfire split the early morning silence. No rounds were coming our way so we cracked on.

Several bangs followed. 'RPGs,' I said to myself. In the distance I could see farmers moving into their fields — or were they Taliban? I powered on, becoming increasingly incensed that my team was now completely exposed. By the time we reached the target I wasn't in the mood for any more mistakes. Unlike the first objective, the compound was located within a small hamlet of four farms, each surrounded by lush green fields growing a mixture of opium poppy and marijuana, drugs used to fund the Taliban's fight against NATO.

The area around the compound had been secured and tired-looking soldiers were monitoring tracks and potential Taliban firing points. The team gathered by a small stone wall and I told them to have a brew and get some scoff when I noticed Sgt Lee Ward, my RESA, was already chatting to an officer. Lee was a seasoned pro and as the Search Advisor was a key member of the team. But on this occasion he was overstepping the mark. I was the boss. I was the guy who made the decisions. The fact that we had been told there was an IED here changed the nature of the task. It was no longer a search-led operation and Lee should have understood that. Major mistakes start as minor mistakes. If everyone does their jobs properly you eliminate the risk of it all going horribly wrong. I was now really pissed off. We'd been messed around for the past twelve hours and now an officer was chatting to my RESA when there was an IED to be dealt with. My temper got the better of me.

'Right, what's going on?' I said.

The officer, a ginger-haired lieutenant who was barely out of his teens, looked at me with a 'You can't talk to me like that' look on his face.

'Right, sir, I've been told there is an IED here. Why haven't you spoken to me about this? Why are you speaking to the RESA?'

The officer looked taken back and slightly hurt, then said: 'What are you talking about, Staff? There's no IED here.'

I exploded. 'Then what are we doing here? Not only have we been messed about from the get-go, we've been forced to tab across open country to get to this location because you said there was an IED and now you're saying there isn't. So what is it?'

'There's no IED, we just want the compound searched in case there is an IED. Obviously a breakdown in communication your end.' I looked at him incredulously.

'Fine,' I said, shaking my head. 'I'm going to be sitting over there with my team.' I turned to Lee and added: 'Crack on with your search. I'm here if you need me.' Lee nodded, not saying anything.

My team looked at me waiting for a response. I took my helmet off, sat down and took on some water. They were waiting for my reaction. I could see them trying not to laugh. I closed my eyes and folded my arms across my body armour and yawned loudly. 'Wake me if anything happens,' I said to no one in particular.

Cpl Alan 'Chappy' Chapman, the REST Commander, began to organise the team and gave them a quick briefing on how he wanted the search to progress. Chappy was a born leader and a tough no-nonsense soldier who was held in great respect by his team. Although he was only in his early twenties he had the wisdom of a seasoned veteran. While they busied themselves, I slipped into a deep sleep.

2

Man Down

Afghan compounds vary in size considerably but most follow a similar pattern. They are usually surrounded by high mud walls that have been baked concrete-hard by the sun. In some cases the walls are two or three feet thick and are almost impenetrable. Within the walls are a number of buildings, stables and stores along with the main dwelling.

As I dozed, the search team entered the compound and began their hunt, looking for anything resembling bomb-making equipment: wires, home-made explosives or ammonium nitrate-based fertiliser – which can be turned into high explosive with a little bit of know-how – improvised detonators, pressure plates and yellow palm oil containers which the Taliban used to hold the main explosive charge. The scene inside the compound was chaotic and the buildings may well have been abandoned just prior to the soldiers' arrival. Sam, Malley and Harry began searching through some of the smaller buildings while Chappy stood back and controlled the operation.

Sam headed into one of the stables, scanned the area with his metal detector, searched into the corners with his torch and reappeared. 'Nothing in there.'

'Roger,' Chappy responded.

Harry was the next to reappear. 'That one's empty too,' he said referring to a small windowless building behind him. 'It just stank of shit.'

As the rest of the team broke into laughter, Malley came tearing out of another building. 'Shit!' he shouted so loudly that all heads turned towards him. Close behind was a massive, snarling dog, teeth bared and foaming at the mouth. Afghan dogs had a reputation for being aggressive and often infected with rabies. Harry, who was probably the team's best shot, brought his rifle up into the aim and fired a single shot at the dog as it leapt at Malley. The bullet struck the animal in the chest passing through the dog's lungs and heart. It was an excellent kill shot and the dog was dead before it hit the floor. But a 5.56mm high-velocity round carries a lot of kinetic energy and the bullet continued on its trajectory first hitting the ground, ricocheting upwards where it struck the compound wall before tumbling and spinning towards Sam. The bullet fragment hit Sam's face with a sickening thwack, passed through Sam's right eye socket before puncturing the front of his brain. He collapsed like a puppet with the strings cut.

Initially all eyes were focused on the poleaxed dog, then Chappy saw Sam lying on the floor with blood pumping from his face.

'Man down!' Chappy shouted. 'Man down.'

I was woken first by the shot and then Chappy's voice, full of panic and fear. 'Man down', two words no soldier wants to hear. It's never said lightly. It means there's a casualty and it's serious.

I grabbed my rifle and instantly brought it to my shoulder, fumbling for the safety catch with my index finger. I quickly scanned the area to my front in the hope I might see the enemy and return fire, but nothing.

Chappy screamed again, 'Medic — where's the fucking medic?!'

The next few seconds were a bit of a blur as Lewis and I raced into the compound. The team were over in the far corner, some standing, others kneeling. Other soldiers were looking on, their faces white with fear. Time froze and everything went into slow motion. People's mouths were moving but I couldn't hear their words. I was trying to take everything in, trying to formulate some kind of threat assessment, trying to get the answers before even asking the questions.

Then I saw Sam. He was lying on the ground, his feet twitching violently. Chappy, kneeling next to him, looked up at me and mouthed the words: 'He's fucked.' It felt like I was in some sort of surreal dream.

Chappy quickly explained what happened but even then I couldn't really believe what I was hearing. It was a one in a million chance. If he had moved a fraction of a second earlier or later the bullet would have missed him. But this was not to be his day. It was bad luck in all its horrific effect.

Harry was slumped against a wall, his rifle between his legs with tears rolling down his face. He was as white as a ghost and shaking. His eyes were fixed on a congealed blood trail slowly being absorbed into the floor.

Sam let out a terrible, agonised moan, like a fatally injured animal. His right eye was closed and swollen. Blood was running down the side of his face and had pooled into a small, deep-red puddle by his ear. My stomach turned as I knelt beside him. Chappy was holding his hand: 'You're gonna be fine, Sam, nothing to worry about.'

Sam tried to lift his hand to his face, but was gently stopped by Chappy. 'Don't touch it, you're going to be OK.' I was raging, wanting to scream, what a waste. It's one thing to get injured by the enemy, that's part of the deal and perhaps expected. But this was something else.

Sam was in a very bad way. His breathing was laboured and his body was convulsing violently. A medic arrived and immediately went to work, ordering the lads to back off and give him some space. He checked Sam's vital signs, his breathing and heart rate. He gently opened Sam's eye to get a clearer look at the wound. He winced as though he could feel Sam's pain. I stood up and walked towards Lewis Mackafee, who looked shell-shocked.

'Lewis, give me the satphone. I need to speak to the Ops Room. And then go sit with Harry.'

I walked about the compound trying to get a satellite lock on my phone. Behind me I could hear the signaller calling in the nine-liner, basically a casualty reporting system that enables the Mobile Emergency Response Team (MERT) to be deployed.

Back in Bastion, one of the watch-keepers answered.

'This is Staff Sergeant Hughes, Brimstone 42, get me the SAT [Senior Ammunition Technician] now.' The SAT, WO1 Jim Hutchison, was the in-theatre expert when it came to anything Counter-IED. He was also a close mate and more importantly my boss. Jim had been a bomb disposal operator for almost twenty years and had been involved in just about every conflict since the Falklands War. He always offered a cool head in a crisis and what he didn't know about bomb disposal wasn't worth knowing.

Jim came on the phone. 'All right, pal, how's it going, the guys OK—?'

I cut him off, 'Sapper Sam Jack has been shot. He's taken a round to the face. It's bad.'

'Kim, wait,' he said before turning to the entire Ops Room staff: 'Shut up!' he shouted. 'Anyone who doesn't need to be here, get out.'

'Kim, I'm back. Tell me everything.' We talked for the next ten minutes as I gave him a detailed account of what had happened. As I listened to myself it seemed unbelievable.

'You need to get over to the hospital when Sam comes in because, to be brutally honest, I don't think he's going to make it. I'm also going to throw Sapper Harry Potter on the aircraft. He's in shock and won't be any good on this op now. It was a one in a million accident. It wasn't his fault but he's taken it badly.'

'Roger, Kim. Stay safe.'

As I put the phone down I looked over to see the guys carefully putting Sam, who was drifting in and out of consciousness, on a stretcher.

'Sam, the chopper's inbound,' Chappy said reassuringly, as he frantically scanned the horizon.

'You're such a drama queen, Sam,' I said trying to lighten the mood. 'All this fuss. There are gonna be lots of hot nurses feeding you grapes and giving you bed baths.'

'Lewis, get Harry ready, get his weapon unloaded. Malley, do the same with Sam's shooter . . .'

Then I heard the distinctive sound of a chopper approaching; never before had I been so happy to hear it.

I pointed at one of the soldiers who had secured the compound earlier. 'You, go and mark the HLS with smoke.'

A little while later a green cloud of smoke was beginning to form. The helicopter was a US Black Hawk, call sign 'PEDRO' and manned by US para-rescue special forces who would go anywhere at any time to save the lives of injured soldiers. Hovering high above was another Black Hawk, scanning the ground looking for Taliban.

The helicopter landed nose on to the smoke grenade and the immediate area went into brown-out from the dust being kicked up by the rotors. Over my shoulder, I could see three of the team lying across Sam, protecting him from the dust cloud.

The medic gave the thumbs-up to approach and six of us carried Sam to the chopper, while Harry followed on close behind. The Black Hawk's side door slid open and Sam was gently eased into the cabin where the medics immediately began their work. A few seconds later the chopper was airborne and Sam was gone. I watched as the helo disappeared into the wide blue sky before walking back to the compound, head bowed and silently praying that Sam would survive.

The entire team was effectively in shock but as tragic as the incident was there was still a job to do. I pulled Lee and Chappy over to a quiet corner of the compound and told the rest of the lads to get a brew on.

'Sam is in the best place he can be,' I said, and they both agreed. 'This is important. Can we still function operationally? We're two searchers down?'

'We're good,' Chappy answered. Lee nodded.

'Good. Then let's get back to work,' I replied.

The team began to search the compound systematically, room by room. The searchers were focused but I knew they were hurting.

'Fuck,' Malley said loudly to himself. A used syringe needle had stuck into his glove but fortunately had not punctured his skin. 'There're dirty needles everywhere,' he told the rest of the team.

Needle stick injuries were extremely serious. AIDS and hepatitis were major problems in Afghan and anyone even suspected of being injured was on the first available chopper back to Bastion, where medics pumped you full of drugs.

An hour later the search was complete and there was no evidence to suggest that the compound had ever been used as a bomb factory. Our first operation and we were the victims of bad intelligence. We all felt that Sam had been injured for nothing and the sense of waste was almost overpowering. I tried to tell the lads that we'd done a decent, professional job but they weren't stupid. No one said anything but we all knew our first operation seemed to have been cursed. Days of planning, kit prep, equipment checks, briefings, all for an hour's work with nothing to show for it apart from a seriously injured colleague.

I sat down leaning against one of the compound walls. I opened up my ration pack, got my Jetboil going and began making a brew. I looked around at the guys and they were all lost in their own silent thoughts. The search team had lost a brother on their very first mission.

I decided to try the Ops Room on the satphone for an update on Sam. A little good news at this point was massively needed. The phone connected and Jim answered almost instantly. I immediately sensed the Ops Room was on edge as well.

'How you guys holding up?' said Jim. His familiar voice was welcoming.

'As good as can be expected. Any news on Sam?'

'He's in theatre. He's critical but still with us. Providing he makes it he'll be flown back to the UK in the next twenty-four hours. His war's over. Do you need anything?'

'No, just a lift out of here. We've completed our search – there's no point in us being here now.'

Jim then handed the phone to Major Eldon Millar, the Counter-IED Task Force officer commanding, the guy in charge.

'Kim, how are you?'

He was one of the best officers I knew.

'All right, boss. The guys are strong but concerned about Sam.'

'Sam's in good hands. We are trying to get you off the ground. Hopefully we'll get you back in today.'

The team's welfare was now my top priority. We were two men down and therefore not an effective asset for the battlegroup. The guys would have risen to any challenge but their minds were elsewhere and so was mine. It wasn't as if we were needed on the ground. I wanted to get the guys back to Bastion so decided to speak directly to the infantry company commander. As I walked outside I noticed the younger soldiers looking at me.

I looked down and saw that my combat trousers had been stained by Sam's blood. His blood was also on my hands and my body armour. I hadn't had time to notice.

I eventually found the OC chatting with a couple of other officers. They were laughing and smoking cigarettes.

'Sir, can I have a word?' All their eyes were drawn immediately to my trousers.

'Staff, any news on your man?' the OC asked.

'He's in theatre undergoing surgery,' I replied. 'Sir, as you're aware, an IEDD team is a mission-critical asset and a rare commodity in Afghan. Units all over Helmand are crying out for us. We are achieving nothing here. I need to get my team off the ground back to Bastion and then on to another mission.'

The OC was sympathetic but explained that it was unlikely

'the powers that be' were going to send a helicopter just to take my team back there. I knew he was right but I wasn't keen on the idea of sitting in a compound for the next forty-eight hours wondering how Sam was. Thoughts turned into doubt, doubt into blame, followed by short tempers and arguments.

Another few hours passed, the guys were threaders. The odd bit of banter was bandied about but no one was in the mood. I closed my eyes, trying to focus on something else, trying to get the vision of Sam out of my mind. I thought of my son. What was he doing? Was he thinking about me as I was him? My thoughts then turned to my crumbling marriage and all the shit I had to look forward to at the end of the tour. I tried my best to think about the good things in life, my mates, my family. What about Sam's family? There would have been that knock on the door then the horrible realisation that nothing will ever be the same again.

'Staff . . . Kim . . .' I opened my eyes. The OC and Chappy were standing over me.

'What's going on?' I asked hesitantly.

'You've got an aircraft inbound. Be ready to move in five minutes,' the OC said.

'Chappy, get the boys ready,' I said but the team were ready to move out. Chappy offered his hand to help me to my feet.

It turned out that a Chinook was passing near to our location and had been offered to give us a lift back to Bastion.

'Guys, stack up on that wall,' I said as the sound of the chopper grew closer. I quickly walked over to the OC and offered my hand in thanks. 'Sir, thanks for your help. Stay safe.'

'You too, Staff. I hope your man's OK. No doubt we'll meet again soon.'

The Chinook touched down in the exact same spot as the

Black Hawk that evacuated Sam. The guys filtered out of the compound and headed towards the aircraft's tailgate.

I counted everyone onto the aircraft before giving the thumbs-up to the loadmaster. Seconds later we were airborne. The relief was almost overwhelming and I suddenly felt exhausted. The helo climbed steeply into a darkening sky. I leaned back and closed my eyes but sleep wouldn't come. The forty-minute flight back to Bastion seemed to take forever, my stomach turning at the thought of what was waiting for us.

As the Chinook banked and prepared to land, I could see the vast base illuminated in the dark, like a small English town. I searched for the hospital, where Sam was fighting for his life, wondering whether he was dead or alive.

The Chinook landed and the team virtually ran to the Army lorry taking us back to the EOD Task Force Ops Room. The drive back was only a few minutes and as we arrived I stood up and blocked the rear of the vehicle.

'Just wait, fellas. We don't yet know how Sam is. We all want answers, but it's not going to help us all piling into the Ops Room. Lee, Chappy, with me, the rest of you, weapons away first and meet us outside the Ops Room. No arguments. Get it done.'

I handed my rifle and pistol to Lewis and headed to the Ops Room.

The three of us, covered in dirt and blood and unshaven, were not in the mood for any sly comments. The room fell silent as we entered. Jim raced towards me and hugged me like a long-lost brother.

'Shit day,' I whispered to him.

'I know,' he replied.

'How is he?'

'Not good,' Jim responded. 'Still not out of the woods but stable.'

Major Eldon Millar, the Officer Commanding of the EOD Task Force, then appeared from the rear of the Ops Room. His usual calm, relaxed demeanour was absent as he took my hand, shaking it hard.

'Thank you, Kim,' he said. It felt weird. I'd done nothing.

'Boss, it was the boys who were there for Sam. They did him proud, they did you proud.'

The OC went outside and addressed the team: 'Men, Sapper Jack is stable. He's out of surgery and in Intensive Care. He will fly back to the UK tonight where he will be looked after. His family have been informed and they will meet him at Birmingham in the morning. You've had a hard day and have come out the other side. Things have gone bad but you have done well. Our thoughts are with Sam – he is in the best place he can be. Get some well-deserved rest.'

'Sir, how's Harry?' Malley asked.

'In shock, but OK. He now needs his friends around him. This was a terrible accident and no one is to blame. He's blaming himself, and he needs you to be there.'

The OC walked back into the Ops Room and the lads slowly made their way back to the team tent. Jim and I sat for an hour or so chatting about the day's events before I returned to the tent.

Everyone handled what happened to Sam in their own way but I learned a long time ago not to dwell on events over which you have no control. My coping mechanism was not to think about the 'what ifs'. I knew that I could be killed or seriously injured every time I went beyond the wire but I chose not to think about it. Sam's wound was horrendous but I locked the image away. I didn't need a shoulder to cry on or someone to talk through my innermost fears. I had bad dreams while I was in Afghan, dreams in which I lost both legs or had been killed, but I never spent much time thinking or worrying about them. That was my way of dealing with death and the fear of being killed. It didn't mean that I was never scared. I was but it meant that I didn't become preoccupied with my own mortality.

Later that evening Harry rejoined us after the medics had given him the all-clear. He still felt terrible but accepted that it wasn't his fault that Sam had been wounded. Within an hour of his arrival the piss-taking had started at Harry's expense – we were moving on.

3

Leaving

Back on 6 April 2009 my team arrived at RAF Brize Norton, the vast base in the Oxfordshire countryside that served as the main point of departure for Afghanistan, twenty-four hours before our flight was due to depart. Over 9,000 soldiers were flying out as part of a 'relief in place' – commonly known as RIP – to begin their tour. While we were flying out an equal number – the survivors of the previous Operation Herrick – were flying home. The logistics were unbelievably complex and the entire operation takes place over a four- to six-week period.

That last night was spent in the awful Gateway House Hotel, a monument to bad 1960s architecture. The 'hotel' was based inside the camp and was used to house troops preparing to fly off to combat zones. As a SNCO, I was given a single room but it was nothing to shout home about and only served to underline my anonymity in the vast operation. The hotel room had a single window that couldn't be opened and contained cheap, stained furniture. It was as if the room had been designed to make the whole experience of flying off to war even more miserable.

Around a hundred of us were woken at about 4 a.m. I showered and shaved and then made my way to the canteen for a cooked breakfast before boarding a coach to the departure terminal. There was a dreadful sense of finality about everything. Everyone, irrespective of rank, was caught between the dread of departure and the desire to get on with the job – but that didn't make leaving any easier. The departure lounge was like something out of the 1970s where customer care was the lowest priority. The room contained a couple of gaming machines, a corner where you could play on an Xbox and a kiosk selling weak tea and Haribo sweets and that was about it. At one end was a large window offering a view out onto the runway and our transport, an obsolete RAF TriStar, illuminated by spotlights and surrounded by fuel trucks and loading vehicles.

Brize Norton is a miserable place to start a journey into a war zone. It is bleak, anonymous and impersonal and on the day we departed it was dark and pissing with rain. Hundreds of soldiers milled around the depressing fluorescent-lit departure hall and I couldn't help but wonder who among them wouldn't make it home. The young spotty-faced soldier straight out of training, his vocal bravado masking his fear? Or the veteran sergeant, who'd already chalked up a couple of tours in Iraq and Afghan? Or the young officer straight out of training and wondering whether a career in the Army after university was such a clever career choice after all? Or me – would I survive? After all, in the end it was all about luck.

No one ever goes to war thinking they are going to get killed. Every soldier assumes it's going to be the other bloke who gets shot or steps on a bomb and makes the final journey home in a body bag. I suppose that's always been the case, from the Battle of Agincourt to the Somme. That's a good thing. The belief that it's your mate not you who will be killed builds teamwork. If soldiers thought they were going to be killed, they'd only be interested in their own safety. We'd constantly be looking out for ourselves and not each other. The team would break down, you'd stop watching each other's backs and of course the concept of self-sacrifice, laying down your life to protect your mates, goes out of the window. So you check your own kit and each other's. You make sure the guy watching your back is switched on and motivated and you ensure that you stay alert when you're watching his. Despite convincing ourselves that we weren't going to get killed, we also knew that not all of us were going to make it home in good shape.

They had said their tearful goodbyes, given their final hugs and promised their love ones they'd stay alive. I slumped into a row of moulded plastic chairs and surveyed the room and then it struck me – half of the soldiers surrounding me were kids that HMG was sending to fight a dirty war in the world's biggest shithole.

Some of them were so young – I mean really young. Teenagers, aged eighteen and one day. Army rules state that you have to be over eighteen to die for your country. It was a hangover from the days of the Troubles in Northern Ireland. In 1971 a seventeen-year-old off-duty soldier was murdered in a brutal triple killing. The incident led to the raising of the age limit for soldiers serving in Northern Ireland to eighteen and that subsequently became the benchmark for all operations. In 1982 several Paras just under eighteen years old were allowed to travel to the South Atlantic and took part in the Falklands War but that was against the official policy.

During the war in Afghanistan, the Army needed every soldier it could get. Lads would join up at sixteen and a half, complete their recruit training, join a battalion, undertake their pre-operational deployment training, but were still under the age of eighteen by the time their unit deployed. So they were left behind waiting, ticking off the days, until they reached eighteen – the very next day they would be sent to war.

Some of those at Brize on that miserable day were barely out of puberty – now they were about to join a war against a ruthless and brutal enemy. Jesus, how must their mothers have felt. You could see the fear in their eyes, what they were thinking. Back home their mates were on the piss, shagging their girlfriends and here they were on their first trip out of the UK to a hellhole and many wouldn't be coming back.

Operation Herrick 10 ran from April through to October 2009. Each Operation Herrick lasted six months so there were two a year every year from 2004 to 2014. But Operation Herrick 10 was a bitch. The casualty figures for 2009 show that ninety-one troops were killed in action and over five hundred were wounded. It became clear during the pre-deployment training that it was going to be a tough tour. No one wanted to talk about casualties but we could work it out ourselves. In 2008 the stats showed that 47 soldiers and Royal Marines had been killed fighting the Taliban, while 235 had been wounded. So working on those stats you had a 3 per cent chance of being killed or wounded in battle – as I said earlier that meant it was going to happen to the next guy.

But it wouldn't be endless days of patrolling and firefights interspersed with mind-numbing boredom for everyone. Many of those who were going out to Afghan would never leave the safety of Bastion – only for R & R and their eventual flight home. They were as safe as houses. The main threat for those lucky arseholes was diarrhoea and sunstroke. You see, everyone had a different war in Afghan.

Not surprisingly the flight was delayed by several hours – a bolt connecting the engine to the wing had rusted away; at least that was the rumour doing the rounds – and it meant another couple of hours sitting on our arses.

Eventually we boarded, by rank order, which meant that I had a half-decent seat – the junior soldiers got what was left. I stuffed my body armour and helmet, which I'd need to wear on the last leg of the flight into Bastion, under my seat and tried to relax. Flight attendants dressed in flying suits handed out boxed packed lunches of cellophane-wrapped white bread sandwiches and biscuits with dubious sell-by dates along with cans of a cheap fizzy drink – no expense spared for the boys going off to war.

The first leg took us to Cyprus, where the TriStar refuelled and took on some more passengers and from there we flew into some desert air base. The last leg was by Hercules directly into Bastion. The journey had taken close to eighteen hours and during the final stretch, the last hour into Bastion, we sweated our balls off wearing all our kit plus body armour and helmets. The aircraft stank of aviation fuel, bad breath and farts. Had the journey from Brize to Bastion been designed to be longer or more uncomfortable, the RAF could not have done a better job.

The Herc landed with a thump. Its huge rear door slowly opened and seemed to suck in the hot, dusty desert air. Straight away I could smell it – that Afghan smell, a mixture of dirt and shit left to ripen in the sun, and it never left me, not for the whole six months.

It was 2 a.m. local time but the base was as busy as a city in rush hour. Apache gunships were coming and going and several aircraft seemed to be landing all at the same time. The sky was inky-black but the base was illuminated by hundreds of bright floodlights. We saw other troops at the end of their tour waiting to board our aircraft to take them back home. They looked thin and haggard, and older than their years. They stared at us, faces revealing a mixture of contempt and pity but they said nothing. They were either too tired or simply couldn't be arsed.

A fleet of buses decked out Asian-style took us to a holding area where we were reunited with our kit. I was punch-drunk with fatigue and my patience was wearing thin. Eventually we were driven to our new home, a large white, dust-filled tent with broken air conditioning, several stained cot-beds and a few dirty pillows. My team were silent, lost in their own thoughts – home never felt so far away. We had arrived.

4

How Did I Get Here?

It was almost inevitable that I ended up serving in the Army. My brother was a soldier and so was my dad and I had acquired all of the necessary qualifications: an unhappy home life, lack of job prospects, academically weak and a love of guns and explosions.

My childhood was pretty miserable probably because my parents split up when I was five and my mum remarried another soldier, a violent Scottish tosser who took a great deal of pleasure meting out his aggression on me and my mum. Looking back I think he couldn't handle the fact that although he may have been something in the Army, in Civvy Street he was a nobody. After he left the Army we moved out of our service house and into a 1960s council estate in Telford called Woodside. If you lived in Woodside you had somehow failed, or that's how it seemed to me.

I think he resented having to provide for a wife and three children, who weren't his own. He seemed to take a sadistic delight in physically abusing me. Like most kids I was a bit of a handful and if I was too naughty I got sent to my room where I would have to sit and wait for the inevitable beating. His heavy footsteps as he climbed the stairs would fill me with dread. He would enter my bedroom and say nothing, not a word, and then he'd lash out with a slap across the face. I'd fall to the floor too scared to get back up and wait for him to leave the room. Later, when the dust had settled and he'd gone to the pub, I'd come downstairs and get a cuddle from my mum. I adored her but I think she was probably scared of him as well.

School should have provided some sort of refuge but it didn't. I had somehow bluffed my way into the newly built Thomas Telford School, a technical college, full of really bright kids. The school required all potential applicants to undertake an interview, sit a few tests and talk about a particular book they liked. But I could barely read and the only book I ever owned was one about Sherlock Holmes. It was full of pictures of his tales and although I didn't read any of the stories I was able to give a pretty decent account of the book based on what I had gathered from the pictures. Astonishingly, I passed the interview and got a place. My mum was over the moon but at the back of my mind I was terrified.

On the day school was due to start it began to dawn on me that I was going to be at the bottom of the class. The walk to school on that wet and windy September morning was one of the hardest of my life. I don't think I ever felt so lonely and vulnerable.

By the time I arrived in my classroom, I was a wreck. My teacher was straight out of central casting. She looked ferocious, wore thick-rimmed glasses and had little time for the less able members of her new class. She went around the room asking each boy or girl to introduce themselves. Then she came to me. I truly wanted the ground to open and swallow me up. 'Kim, Kim Hughes,' I stuttered. Rather than take pity on my obvious discomfort she told me to stand in front of the class and read a passage from a book. I slowly walked to the front of the classroom like someone facing a firing squad. Disaster loomed. The words on the page in front of me seemed meaningless and there were several I had never seen before. I started reading but immediately stumbled. The sniggering grew louder and the teacher walked across the room and stood behind me. Beads of sweat began to trickle down the side of my face. Every ten words or so I stumbled and ground to a halt, forcing the teacher to intervene and pronounce the word for me.

I could have only been standing there for a few minutes but in that short time the damage was done. I sat down and wanted to cry. A boy leaned over. 'What's wrong with you? Can't you read?' I looked at him pleadingly. 'I haven't got my glasses with me.' From that moment on I was the thick kid with the girl's name.

By the afternoon my humiliation was complete when all the kids in my class were told to queue for lunch and to have their money ready.

'I've got my lunch in my bag,' I said. The teacher looked at me quizzically. 'I've got a packed lunch.'

My mum didn't have much money and it was cheaper for her to make me sandwiches than to give me the £1.00 for a school lunch. The fact that I couldn't afford school dinners was just more ammunition for the kids in my class.

The bullying began on day one and continued for almost five years. Every now and again I'd go toe-to-toe with some arsehole who'd pushed the piss-taking just that bit too far. But as we got older the jibes became more sarcastic, more witty, more hurtful and I wanted out. By the age of sixteen, I was spotty, a bit overweight, bored and had begun knocking around with a real bunch of losers who drank or smoked weed.

The Hughes family did not come from academic stock. As far as I'm aware we didn't have a single A level to our name and neither I, nor my brother and sister were going to break the mould. And Telford in the 1990s was about as grim as life could be. Unemployment was high and job prospects were very low.

My one escape from my violent stepfather, the school bullies and the drudgery of Telford was the Army Cadets. I loved every minute of it and looked forward to the training, shooting, the weekend camps and even the drill. No one cared whether I could read or write, or that I was overweight or even that my first name was Kim. When I put the uniform on I became a different person, I was a soldier, at least in my head I was. Cadets was my escape from my shitty home life, it was the one place where I could be myself.

My other passion was fireworks and one of my favourite times of the year was 5 November. I would spend money I had spent months saving buying as many different types of firework as I could afford. I would spend hours locked away in my bedroom, taking them apart to see how and why they went bang and what made all the different colours. I wanted to know why rockets exploded and why Roman candles fired balls of fire into the air. I once blew up my stepfather's prized garden birdhouse after I emptied the contents of a couple of fireworks into a plastic cup, made a fuse and placed it inside. The explosion was far more violent than I had expected and I spent the rest of the day hammering the birdhouse back together.

That was my life and I had no real burning desire to join the Army until I was in my final school year when one of the teachers asked how many children wanted to go on a school trip to France. Everyone's hand, except mine, shot up. My mum didn't have the money to pay for it and there was no way my stepfather was going to pay.

The teacher moved around the class asking each pupil if they would be coming on the French trip.

'Kim,' the teacher said expecting me to say that I would be coming.

'I won't be coming,' I replied.

'Why not?'

'Because I'm going to join the Army.'

Laughter broke out across the classroom as if none of the other kids believed me but I didn't care. Right at that moment I had decided that school had taken me as far as it could and another life, full of excitement and travel, or so I thought, was on offer.

That summer I sat my last exam, which I knew I had failed, got up out of my chair and left school for the last time. No longer would I have to suffer the daily humiliation of being the thickest in the class. No longer would I walk into that friend-less classroom smelling of stale, watered-down disinfectant. I walked through the main gates out onto the road, turned and looked at my old school for one last time. Its modern facade was already beginning to show the early signs of neglect, rub-bish spun in a windy circle on the playground while the final bell of the day rang through the school. This was meant to be the place that prepared me for life but instead I spent five years feeling useless and undervalued. I felt a surge of anger rise up through my body. 'Fuck you!' I shouted for as loud and as long as my body could muster.

In the sky the sun was shining brightly and for the first time in my life I felt truly free.

The following morning I dragged my mum to the local Army recruitment office in Shrewsbury. I was sixteen and needed my parents' consent to join up. The West Midlands was a fertile recruiting ground for the Army; prospects for the town's population of disaffected, feckless youngsters, like me, were diminishing. The Army's unofficial recruiting motto was 'Join up and see the world', but it could equally have been 'We'll take anyone'.

A former shop on the town high street was the recruitment office; posters of young men driving tanks and throwing themselves around assault courses were displayed, along with pictures of soldiers scuba diving and sailing in glamorous locations. As I entered the office, a balding sergeant in his brown No.2 dress uniform appeared from behind a counter, wiping the remnants of a late breakfast, or early lunch, from his mouth.

He was sweaty and red-faced, severely overweight and with no discernible neck. His fat, sausage-like fingers were nicotine-stained and his uniform was straining across his expansive girth. He introduced himself as sergeant something or other. 'What can I do for you, son?'

But before I could answer my mum said: 'He'd like to join the Army.'

'Oh, and why's that?'

'I want to learn a trade, travel, do something useful with my life,' I fired back wanting to show that I knew my own mind.

'Good – you can't do better than join the Army. Look at me, twenty-two years' service, leaving on a cushy number with a nice pension.'

He said he had seen the world and loved every minute of his service life. His uniform bore a single medal ribbon indicating that his operational service had been restricted to Northern Ireland.

'Any thoughts as to which outfit? You'll want to be in a corps if you want a trade? Got any GCSEs?'

I shook my head. As far as I was concerned the Army was the Army. It was my ticket out of Telford. I knew nothing about regiments or corps.

'The Royal Logistic Corps needs people like you. Can you drive?'

I shook my head again.

'No matter, they'll teach you. You'll learn a trade, get your car and HGV licence for free. Every unit in the Army needs drivers. It will be a brilliant career and when you leave you can walk into a well-paid job as a lorry driver.'

I needed no more convincing.

A few more interviews were followed by a couple of familiarisation visits and by mid-1996 I was recruit 25053515 with Masters Troop, part of the Army Training Regiment at Pirbright Barracks in Surrey.

Recruit training was everything I'd hoped for – the drill, fitness training, skill at arms. Our corporal instructors taught us how to wash, shave, clean our boots, iron our clothes and for the first time in my life I found something at which I seemed to excel. I felt as though I was growing in stature every day.

But about three weeks into the course I started to feel homesick. I'd often wander the corridors of our barrack block at night, while everyone else was asleep, sometimes fighting back the tears and hoping that the homesickness would go away but instead it got worse with each passing day. I felt lost, alone and trapped. I wasn't bullied; the NCO instructors weren't exactly friendly but neither were they unpleasant. The problem was with me.

In week three of basic training, one of the other recruits mentioned something called PVR – Premature Voluntary Release. It's like a Monopoly get-out-of-jail card for recruits – play it and the Army have to let you go. Before I knew it I was back home with my mum.

Mum gave me a massive hug as I walked in through the front door. My stepfather just looked at me with utter disdain and said nothing. I expected no sympathy from him and received none. I was happy to be home but my future in Telford, the arsehole of the world as far as I was concerned, looked bleak. Over the next six months, I drifted from job to job, working as a manual labourer on building sites for a while before ending up with an apprenticeship at a robotics factory but I was soon bored. More bored than I could have possibly imagined.

Then, one morning I woke up and I decided right then to rejoin.

The following day I was back in the same recruitment office – a different sergeant, who viewed me with deep suspicion even though it was 1997 and the Army was supposedly struggling for recruits.

'Why should we take you back?' the recruiting sergeant said when I asked to rejoin. 'We gave you one chance and you threw it back in our faces. We can't afford passengers, we need people with commitment. If you can't hack a few weeks in recruit training how are you going to hack it on the front line when you go to war?'

He was being overdramatic but he was right of course. I managed to convince him and others along the way during the application process and within a few months I was back in the Army. This time I was prepared and up for it.

Back at Pirbright I had a bit of a head start on the other recruits and found the first fourteen weeks of basic training easier than most. I was ahead with drill, the weapon training and the discipline – second time around I really embraced the whole challenge and the time flew by.

The Army is an easy target for critics who claim it takes uneducated men and women who can't do anything else and turns them into killers. There's probably some element of truth in that but what the Army also does is offer everybody an equal chance. It doesn't care where you come from, whether you have an accent or what sort of home life you've had. It doesn't discriminate or prejudge. The Army will offer you a career, teach you a trade, help you get qualifications but it expects a lot back in return. Ultimately, the Army expects you to fight and if necessary die for your country and every single one of us who made it to our pass-out parade knew and accepted the terms and conditions. For many of us, becoming a professional soldier was the only thing we had ever really achieved and for the first time in my life I think my mum was truly proud of me.

Following the pass-out parade, I had a bit of leave and was posted to Princess Royal Barracks in Surrey, the infamous holding unit for members of the Royal Logistic Corps. Deepcut was effectively a transit camp where soldiers still in training were posted for a few weeks or months while they waited for a vacancy on a course. Deepcut was a miserable place and very badly managed at that time. There was no sense of esprit de corps and a heavy air of depression and disorganisation hung over the place. I spent several weeks at the barracks before completing the next phase of my training – driving courses.

For someone heading into the RLC, I showed no real flair as a driver. I failed my car test three times and my HGV another three times – in fact I failed on so many occasions that I was kicked off the course and had to do a resit from the beginning. After finally completing my basic licences I was sent to the Defence School of Transport in Leconfield, Yorkshire, for my conversion training to military vehicles, where you can learn to drive just about any vehicle in the Army, before I was posted to 13 Transport Squadron, part of 8 Transport Regiment, located at Marne Barracks, near Catterick in Yorkshire.

After a couple of years driving around the training areas of the UK I began training for an operational tour in Northern Ireland. I didn't know it at the time but the next six months would become some of the most important in my life.

While most of my mates were despatched on driving courses to support the various units going across the water, I was told I would be supporting a Bomb Disposal Unit and I had to learn how to drive a Tactica, a vehicle used by the Explosive Ordnance Disposal (EOD) teams. At the time I thought I had been given a raw deal because I was going to be on my own stationed in a patrol base called Girdwood in north-west Belfast – the heart of the Provisional IRA.

Back in the 1990s Belfast was a city with a personality disorder. One half was relatively normal, just like any other city in the UK, with a thriving centre, chic, expensive restaurants, designer shops and trendy bars and clubs. But cross over into the west and you entered a different world. West Belfast was a Catholic stronghold where the IRA ruled with an iron fist. The Troubles might be over but the murders, punishment shootings and bomb attacks hadn't stopped. Armed British soldiers still patrolled the streets and were largely regarded by the Catholic community as the enemy.

With my training completed I was attached to an Army bomb disposal team with the call sign 'Bobcat', which consisted of the ATO, his No.2, an Electronic Counter Measures (ECM) Operator, two drivers and four infantry escorts who accompanied us wherever we went in a Snatch Armoured Land Rover. My job was to drive the No.2's vehicle, which contained all of his equipment and various EOD robots, called wheelbarrows.

Initially, in the early days of the tour, I would deploy to an operation without much idea of what was going on. I simply saw my job as driving the vehicle. A usual shout would consist of someone reporting a suspicious vehicle or package to the police, who would task us, Bobcat, to deal with it. I'd drive one of the vehicles to the scene at which point the ATO and the No.2 would take control of the situation. While the bomb disposal team set about their task I would look on in fascination and felt slightly disappointed that I couldn't be more involved.

About two weeks into the tour, Bobcat was deployed near the Divis Flats, a grotty West Belfast council estate, dominated by a tower block and 1960s housing. The estate had become synonymous with the Troubles and was about as pro-IRA and as anti-British as you could get and had been a graveyard for soldiers since 1969, when the Troubles began. A possible pipe bomb had been reported and, given the location, was treated with a little bit more caution. As I sat in the driver's seat watching a crowd gathering on the other side of the police cordon, the ATO – Staff Sergeant Andy Gee – emerged from the back of his vehicle dressed in his full bomb disposal suit and headed towards the suspect device.

'What's he doing?' I asked the No.2 as I climbed from the vehicle.

'He's going to have a look at the bomb. The bomb suit

should protect him if something goes wrong, providing he isn't too close.'

Andy returned about half an hour later, took off his helmet and as far as I was concerned had become the hero of the hour. Everyone appeared to be hanging on his every word, he was the centre of attention and looked unbelievably cool.

For the first time in my Army career I had encountered something I found truly fascinating. Up until that point life had been OK. I had learned how to drive, been on a few foreign exercises but I felt as though I was drifting aimlessly with the tide. But bomb disposal was different. It was as if a series of light bulbs had gone off in my head. I could be a soldier and play around with explosives.

As the tour progressed I began to ask Andy more questions about what he was doing and why he was doing it. He was very encouraging and keen to promote the trade and then one day turned to me and said: 'Why don't you give it a go? Transfer and become an Ammunition Technician. It's the best job in the world. Why be a driver when you can go into bomb disposal? It's a difficult trade to get into, there's a lot of competition but if you want it, go for it. What have you got to lose?'

Night after night I would go back to my room in Girdwood, lie on my bed and think about what Andy had said. I watched my mates going out on various driving details doing some right shit jobs and when they weren't driving they would be put on some meaningless task, guarding the gate, often at night and being treated as a general dogsbody. I wanted more out of the Army than that. But the self-doubt and lack of self-belief that had dogged my school years soon returned and I thought I'd never be selected. But as the weeks went by it began to dawn on me that I wanted to change direction and go into bomb disposal.

About halfway through the Northern Ireland tour I was
sent on my Military Proficiency Course, a sort of assessment that every soldier needed to pass to get promoted to
lance corporal. The course took place in Palace Barracks,
a red-brick Victorian Army base just outside Belfast, where
we were taught the basic skills required to be a junior noncommissioned officer (JNCO). I was one of about thirty
soldiers, all drawn from units across Northern Ireland and
presided over by senior NCOs, called directing staff, known
to us as the 'DS', who would judge us on our suitability as
JNCOs. Most of the guys wanted to do well and pass because
it meant more money and was the first step on the promotion
ladder. As well as learning drill commands and being lectured
on how the Army functions at the NCO level, we were also
required to give a ten-minute lesson on something interesting.
I was a bit stumped so decided to go and see the guys at the
bomb disposal unit inside Palace Barracks and asked the ATO
if he could help.

'Why don't you show them how to make a demolition
charge and how to blow something up like a hand grenade?'
he said. 'It's pretty easy. I'll show you, then go off and practise
it and then show me and you'll be set.'

'OK, thanks.' I couldn't believe it. Even at that stage I knew
it was a great idea. He showed me how to prepare the explosives, the det-cord, the detonator and the electronic initiator
that makes it all go bang. I borrowed a load of inert items from
the EOD team and practised relentlessly until it was time for
each of us to give our lesson.

One guy gave a lesson on how to polish boots, another
on how to make a cup of tea and someone even gave one on
how to tie a tie. It was supposed to be an assessment of your
ability to plan and execute a lesson – the subject matter was

secondary. Then I gave my talk and the DS loved it and I was awarded top student on the course. It was a seminal moment in my Army career. At first I couldn't believe that I could be the best at anything but then I thought, 'Why not?' It was at that moment I realised I was no longer the fat kid with the girl's name. The Army had changed me as a person or at least allowed me to grow in a way that Civvy Street never would. I now had an opportunity to do something different and I was determined to seize it with both hands. I returned to Girdwood that afternoon keen to transfer trade and become an Ammunition Technician. On my first day back I sought out a good mate, Lance Corporal Trevor Woods, a really chilled-out guy, and told him that I was thinking of transferring.

'Listen, mate, if you wanna transfer then go for it, if not don't. But people will take the piss, they will say that you couldn't hack being a driver and they'll call you a deserter, all that shite. The seniors will try and stop you, so if you go for it be prepared for that.'

As always Trev's advice was sound.

The tour ended and we faded away on leave to different parts of the UK. I counted down the days until I could return to Catterick and on the first morning back I requested permission to transfer to become an Ammunition Technician. For the most part everyone was pretty enthusiastic and the only real hurdle was the seemingly endless amount of paperwork that needed to be completed.

The Royal Logistic Corps accepted my request. I was to undertake training as an Ammunition Technician – providing I passed the selection process.

5

Bomb School

Before anyone was going to let me near a bomb the Army needed to ensure that I had the mental capability to deal with the pressures of bomb disposal and that meant a visit to a psychologist. The psychometric evaluation took place in early February 2000 in a small classroom at Princess Royal Barracks, Deepcut, where I spent a day and a half answering questions about my childhood, family life and what made me happy or sad.

After the questionnaires, several on-screen computer tests followed that required me to identify shapes, patterns and sequences. Once the tests were over I was ushered into a small room where a smiling female psychiatrist in her late twenties was sitting behind a desk waiting to grill me. Spread across her desk were my completed questionnaires with red circles and arrows pointing to my answers.

'Do you have any concerns you'd like to share?' she said smiling.

'Like what exactly?' I responded, shifting in my chair and trying not to sound rude.

'Any family issues? What was your relationship like with your stepfather?'

I wanted to say that he was a child-beater but instead I offered: 'Not bad, I suppose. We have had our differences but it's pretty good really.'

And so the next few hours passed, she probing, me defending but trying to appear as helpful and as open as possible.

I must have succeeded because a few days later I received my joining instructions and by the end of the month I was starting the first day of the week-long Ammunition Technician selection course at Marlborough Barracks in Kineton, Warwickshire. As well as being a training centre, the Kineton base also serves as an ammunition depot, one of the largest in Europe, where everything from .22 rounds to guided missiles are stored.

The training centre was split into two separate elements, bottom school and top school. Bottom school teaches potential Ammunition Technicians (ATs) and Ammunition Technical Officers (ATOs) their trade skills. The difference between the two is ATs are soldiers and ATOs are Commissioned Officers. They are both experts in explosives, bomb disposal and ammunition storage, an unglamorous but vitally important job.

The top school, also known as the Felix Centre, is where bomb disposal is taught. All elements of bomb disposal, from basic Improvised Explosive Device Disposal (IEDD) to the High Threat course, which has to be passed if an AT or ATO wants to serve in Afghanistan, are taught at Kineton. Confusingly, while on operational deployment we are all known as ATOs. Kineton has a training area that can accommodate just about every scenario a bomb disposal operator might encounter. There is a small purpose-built town containing houses, a farm, a hotel and train station, garage forecourt and petrol station, allowing bomb disposal students to be tested in very realistic situations.

There were thirty students on my AT selection, all nervous and eager to impress, knowing that every move we made, our attitude and ability to deal with whatever was thrown at us, were under constant scrutiny. The assessments included tests in maths, mechanical reasoning and problem solving.

Almost as soon as the tests began, I felt my confidence begin to ebb away. That nauseating feeling of being the thick kid in class suddenly returned and I became convinced that I would fail. After a day in the classroom we were given homework on weapons and explosives. I studied late into the evening and was confronted by a near impossible test the following morning.

At the end of the week we assembled in the main lecture theatre and waited for the results. I was convinced that I had failed and was annoyed with myself for believing that I could amount to anything more than an Army driver.

Those who had failed, or were deemed not to have the skills needed to succeed in the AT trade, had their names read out and were asked to leave. By the end of that morning only ten out of the original thirty students were left, and I was one of them. I felt like I had won the lottery and the sense of relief in not having to return to my old unit as a failure was almost overpowering.

The actual Ammo Techs course began in May 2000 and any thoughts that I had completed the difficult part by passing the selection phase were soon forgotten. Over the next six months I learned about every piece of ammunition used by the British Army in far greater depth than I thought was possible. It was science on steroids. I had convinced myself that the course was going to be all about bomb disposal but I couldn't have been more wrong and before long I started wondering whether I had made the right career choice. It wasn't just that the lessons were unbelievably difficult, I was bored.

Around halfway through the course I got called in to see the commanding officer. I assumed that I had fucked up in some way and was in for a major bollocking, or worse the instructors realised that I couldn't cut it and were going to bin me. I left the classroom with my mates looking at me no doubt wondering the same. I walked to the CO's office with an overpowering sense of dread but he was all smiles and told me that I had been promoted to lance corporal. I breathed a sigh of relief, shook his hand and walked back to the classroom feeling ten feet tall. Despite being promoted, I was still struggling badly and panic began to set in. The prospect of failure and returning to the RLC as a driver was the nightmare scenario but at that stage I honestly thought I had more chance of flying to the moon than becoming an Ammo Tech. Theory lessons seemed to get longer and the exams harder. We'd study a subject to death, such as the characteristics of artillery shells, learning absolutely everything there was to know about them and then a test would follow before we moved on to the next phase. Every night I would go to bed thinking the next day I would be found out and binned. But it didn't happen and I got to the finals week – the most important phase of the course.

Through a mixture of bluff, hard work and a lot, and I mean a lot, of help from my fellow students, I passed. I was an Ammo Tech. I was on an enormous high for about three hours until we received our postings. An instructor read out a name, then the unit and place where we were being posted.

'Lance Corporal Hughes – Fallingbostel – congratulations,' said my instructor without a hint of irony.

'Fallingbostel – cool. Where's that?'

'Germany,' he responded with a smile.

'You have got to be taking the piss,' I said not so silently to myself.

My heart sank and I felt totally crushed. My thoughts immediately turned to my girlfriend and whether our relationship would last. We'd been seeing each other for a couple of years, travelling across the UK to visit each other, but Germany was another country.

Once the bad news had sunk in I phoned my new troop warrant officer to introduce myself and tell him that I would be joining his troop after some leave.

'Hello, sir, I'm Lance Corporal Hughes. I've just qualified as an Ammo Tech and I'll be joining your troop.'

'Yep, nice one. Looking forward to meeting you. Any questions at this stage?'

'Yes, sir. Can you give me an idea of how much bomb disposal we'll be doing?'

My question was greeted with raucous laughter.

'Well, is that a lot or what, sir?' I added, slightly irritated.

'No, mate, we hardly do any. In fact, correction, you'll be doing nothing. The Germans take care of everything outside the wire and nothing ever happens inside,' he added as if I should be pleased by this.

I was devastated. I'd spent seven months training my arse off for a job I wasn't going to do.

Despite my disappointment, Germany wasn't that bad. Although the Cold War was over, there was still a lot of ammunition that needed looking after and I managed to do a lot of really useful EOD training. The days passed quickly and a year or so later I returned to the UK in 2001 to complete my No. 2's course.

By the time the course ended, Al-Qaeda had destroyed the World Trade Center in New York and British and American forces were on the ground in Afghanistan. The world was changing and although a war was beginning in Afghanistan I was sent to Bosnia where another lengthy conflict was coming to an end. I was based in a place called Šipovo and the tour largely consisted of six months of parties, women and booze. Every now and then I'd get a call to blow up the odd unexploded shell but the real eye-opener for me was how the rest of the Army viewed those lucky enough to work in EOD.

I was now in the cool gang, doing a job 99 per cent of people would walk away from. Everyone wanted to be our friends. We were the ones throwing fancy-dress parties when everyone else was bored shitless. For the first time in my life I felt part of something and my confidence soared. It was and remains one of the best periods of my Army life.

But like all good things it came to an end and six months later I returned to Fallingbostel, back to the drudgery of Germany post-Cold War where nothing happened. It was a great posting if you wanted to hone your adventure training skills or become fluent in German – but for an aspiring bomb disposal expert, Germany wasn't the place to be. The terrorist threat was zero. Most of my time was spent conducting ammunition accident investigations on Honer ranges, a vast area of land where every type of weapon system from artillery to tanks to missiles were fired. Mix soldiers, ammunition and a weapon system together and somewhere along the line there will be a problem and it was the job of the ATs to establish what went wrong.

I was getting all the ticks in all the right boxes. I saw myself as a career soldier, fully committed to the Army but I never lost sight of my desire to become a High Threat operator. I completed another tour in Northern Ireland and got married to my long-term girlfriend. Life looked good even though war was coming and Iraq was the target.

The build-up to the war in Iraq started to take on a momentum of its own in early 2002. There were no official orders as such, just a sense that the Army was preparing for something big. Units began carrying out their own contingency plans and training so when eventually the orders to prepare for war came through no one was going to be left cold. As D-Day for the invasion approached, it became clear that I wouldn't be involved – at least not in the early part of the war. Like many others, I was pretty pissed off, mainly because most of us wrongly thought the war would be over in a year or two at the very most.

While the rest of the country seemed to be against the possibility of war – I was aware of the controversy, the mass protests in London and the resignations by government ministers – the feeling in the Army couldn't have been more different. Firstly, soldiers obey orders, that's the job. Very few, if any of us, were willing to question the chain of command. We're trained not to and besides if anyone was unwilling to go to war at the behest of the government then they were in the wrong job. Soldiers do not endlessly sit around wringing their hands wondering whether they are doing the right thing, that's not the culture. You suck it up and get on with it.

No one I came across was overly gung-ho, it was just that as a soldier you want to experience combat – after all, that's the job. The real fear was whether Saddam Hussein would be prepared to use his arsenal of weapons of mass destruction (WMDs) against invading troops. Intelligence reports suggested that he had tons of chemical and biological agents, which if used would result in potentially thousands of British and American deaths.

While the preparations for war gathered pace, I was on another course at Kineton cursing my luck and realising that with every day that passed my chances of being deployed to Iraq were diminishing. I tried desperately to get sent back to my unit so I had a chance of going but I was told to wind my neck in and get on with the course. It was like watching a ship with all your mates on board sailing off for some distant adventure while you were left behind.

George W. Bush unleashed 'shock and awe' on Iraq on 20 March 2003 and, like thousands of other soldiers in the UK or Germany who'd been left behind, I hoped the war wasn't going to be over too quickly. The last time the West invaded Iraq in 1991, the war was over in ninety hours. But Operation Telic, the code name for Britain's involvement in Iraq, was going to be different. The fighting was fiercer and there were more casualties.

Although I wasn't sent off to war, I was sent on the Joint Service IEDD course that was run at the top school in Kineton. As a consolation it wasn't too bad given that I was now on the path to becoming a proper bomb disposal expert. The course was six weeks long and the highlight was getting into the bomb disposal suit for the first time. I was like a kid at Christmas. It was a big moment but the excitement lasted for about three seconds. Then I was hit by a smell, which can best be described as 'sweaty arse-crack'. The smell was nauseating, almost overpowering, and I was left wondering how I was meant to work in a suit that made me gag.

It was one of those situations in life that was completely unexpected. For the past three years I had dreamed about the moment when I would eventually put on a bomb suit and when

I did it stank. The training suits were issued from the stores at the Felix Centre and so there was no great desire for anyone to look after them. Dozens of people had sweated, bled and probably pissed in them, at least that's how they smelt. The solution was to pour half a bottle of Febreze inside the suit.

I was a corporal at the time but had been given the rank of acting sergeant for the duration of the course and I later found out that having a junior rank and a perceived lack of experience I was expected to fail. The Iraq War served as a backdrop to the course and most of the students were glued to the television every night getting updates on the progression of US and British troops. Although success seemed to come relatively easily there was a sense that we were witnessing the beginning of a lengthy conflict.

Towards the end of the course I was called in to what was then the Joint Service Team's office.

'Sergeant Hughes – you are the fly in the ointment,' the team leader said looking perturbed.

'Sorry, sir?' I responded, confused and wondering whether I was about to be binned right at the end of the course.

'The course is primarily for students with the substantive rank of sergeant. You're a corporal and frankly you were expected to fail, but you passed, and you passed well. So well done. You have given us something to think about.'

I was buzzing. Back then it was almost unheard of to be singled out and praised while you were on the course. It remains one of the proudest moments of my career. I felt as if I had achieved something massive. If you're someone used to success I suppose you take things like passing courses in your stride. But I wasn't. Success in my life up until that point had been mostly absent. It was as if the Army was coming good on its promise to turn you into something you couldn't possibly have imagined. I realised that despite failing at school, I had hidden depths of determination and resilience that the Army was drawing to the surface.

But the sense of satisfaction was short-lived. Although now qualified as an EOD Operator, I was heading back to Germany with almost no chance of putting my newly learned skills into practice.

Over the next couple of years I managed to get back to the UK to cover for the bomb disposal teams while some of the EOD Operators went on leave or different courses. The work was mainly conventional munitions disposal – the sort of thing where someone discovers that the grenade paperweight that has been sitting in grandfather's office since the Second World War is actually live.

By 2004, I was once again serving in Germany, this time in Bielefeld, with 921 EOD Squadron, part of 11 EOD Regiment, which is part of the Royal Logistic Corps. I was now a troop sergeant and my eagerness to go to war hadn't diminished. By that stage so many soldiers had served in Iraq that I felt as though I was in the minority. I felt like a war dodger. I had volunteered numerous times but had always been knocked back by my HQ for different reasons, such as covering for people on courses. The endless refusals to send me were incredibly disappointing and I often wondered whether I was cursed.

My luck changed a few months later when another trawl for volunteers to go out to Iraq was issued. I applied and was accepted. It was as if a massive burden had been taken off my shoulders. I was going to war, I'd return home with a medal, no longer would I feel inadequate. The only downside for me was that even though I was trained in bomb disposal I would be deployed only as a member of the Ammunition Inspectorate, ensuring that the hundreds of tons of ammunition sitting in

Iraq were being properly looked after. While I was delighted, my wife wasn't very pleased. It was the year that she had planned to start a family, but despite her disappointment she was very supportive.

A month's pre-deployment training followed, which was the same training I received when I went to Bosnia but with different pictures. I gave my wife a hug, promised to write and call and arrived in Iraq in November 2004. My home for the next six months was the Shaibah Air Base, once the main military air base in southern Iraq, a vast complex surrounded by barbed wire, watchtowers and cut in two by a huge, concrete runway. It was home to various logistic units, the British Army's main headquarters and quite a few civilian contractors. Although the threat from insurgent rocket and mortar attacks was high, it was pretty quiet during the six months I was based there. I shared a room about the size of an ISO container – effectively a reinforced Portakabin – with another SNCO from the HQ. It was cosy, air-conditioned and we did our best to make it comfortable and to give each other a bit of privacy.

As wars go, being based at Shaibah wasn't too bad. The facilities were decent, food was good but best of all we had a bar with supposedly a 'two can rule' – which meant you were allowed two cans of beer a night. It was a rule that was often broken and the reality was that I was drunk quite a lot. Although I wasn't involved in any bomb disposal, working for the Ammunition Inspectorate was interesting. I visited various different units right across southern Iraq, to inspect their ammunition storage facilities to ensure they followed MOD regulations. If there were ever any ammunition accidents, such as negligent discharges or breech explosions, I would carry out an investigation to determine who, if anyone, was at fault. If the problem was with the ammunition then

I'd impose a theatre-wide ban on that type of ammunition. I might have been a REMF – rear echelon motherfucker (someone who never leaves the wire) – but at least I was in a war zone.

While life in Shaibah was pretty comfortable and quite a lot of fun, for those soldiers on the front line, in isolated bases often cut off for days on end, the war was very different. Bloody battles had become a daily occurrence. Convoys were being attacked and ambushed every day. Some of the main convoys from Basra Air Base into the city were dubbed 'Operation Certain Death' by the soldiers because the threat of attack and casualties was so high.

Not since the Korean War in 1950 had British troops been involved in such bitter fighting. Occasionally soldiers who'd been fighting for months on end would turn up at British headquarters looking haggard and exhausted, whereas most of the people behind the wire had to work out every day to stop putting on weight. It was sometimes hard to believe we were both fighting the same war.

The nature of the conflict was also changing. When I arrived in late November 2004, around 1,400 IED attacks were taking place in Iraq every month. Hundreds of tons of military grade explosive, which had been looted from Iraqi Army ammunition depots after the fall of Saddam, were being used in IEDs to kill coalition troops. In the early days of the insurgency, the bombs were deadly but relatively simple in design. But by 2005, the insurgents had developed a vast array of sophisticated IEDs. Some could be triggered by mobile phones, or remote control key fobs, others were designed only to destroy track vehicles. But the most deadly were composed of shaped charges able to penetrate most armoured vehicles. Production of those IEDs needed precision engineers and skilled armourers and many of those were supplied by Iran, who were happy to see thousands of British troops tied down in southern Iraq, an area which the Iranians believed fell within their zone of influence. Although no one knew it at the time, the use of IEDs in Iraq to kill British troops provided a taste of what was to come in Afghanistan.

I returned to the UK in April 2005, had a month's leave and as a reward for my service in Iraq was offered a place on the High Threat course, now known as the Advanced EOD Operators course. The course came with a reputation of a high failure rate and every EOD Operator attending was expected to be at the top of his or her game. Despite the course's reputation I was confident in my skills even though I was still relatively inexperienced. But within a week I knew I was well out of my depth. It was as if I had turned up for a very basic French course and everyone else was studying degree-level Mandarin Chinese. I couldn't even grasp the concept of a high threat environment. I muddled my way through to the assessment phase where my performance continued to go further downhill. I was failing almost all of the tasks but the instructors were very supportive and I was allowed to continue, not as a student under assessment but as an opportunity to watch, learn and gain some experience. It was a fantastically mature way of dealing with a student who would otherwise have failed.

During the six weeks I was at the Felix Centre, news began to drift in of the developing conflict in Afghanistan. A brigade-sized force based around 3 Para battlegroup had arrived in Helmand in April, established Camp Bastion, which back then was little more than a fence, a makeshift runway and a few tents, and began what it hoped was going to be several years of reconstruction and development.

Since the invasion of Afghanistan in 2001, the north, east and west of the country had gone through the same process with varying degrees of success. While the British and Americans had become distracted by the war in Iraq, other NATO countries had been hard at work in Afghanistan training the police and the army and trying to reconstruct parts of the country which had been devastated by thirty years of internal tribal warfare. Now it was the turn of Britain, Canada and the Netherlands to come good on an agreement made a few years earlier to commit several thousand combat troops to assist in the reconstruction of the south. When the agreement was signed the assumption was made that the Iraq War would be over or nearing its end. The reality was very different. Iraq was rapidly getting out of control and Britain and the United States had fallen into the fatal trap of fighting wars on two different fronts.

British troops arrived in Helmand prepared for a fight but hopeful they could continue with the mission of security and reconstruction. But the Taliban had other ideas. Following the collapse of the regime in 2001, a large number of Taliban headed south into Kandahar and Helmand and across the border into Pakistan and waited. By 2006 they had returned and a new war was about to start.

Despite failing the High Threat course I returned to the Felix Centre again in 2007 but this time as a B-team instructor at the IEDD wing, teaching the Joint Service IEDD course – the basic bomb disposal course. It was a top job, the one I really wanted, and a fantastic opportunity at an extremely busy and fast-moving period in the world of EOD. The conflict in Afghan had developed into a full-blown insurgency and IEDs, although rudimentary, were being used to attack British troops.

I was now a father, with a one-year-old son, whom I adored. Although professionally my career was going well, deep cracks had begun to form in my marriage. I had made that age-old squaddie mistake of confusing lust with love and marrying too young in the hope of keeping a relationship alive when it should have been left alone to die a natural death.

Rather than confront my personal issues, I buried myself in my work. As my time as an instructor came to an end, I was offered a place on the High Threat course for the second time and if I passed my reward would be a six-month tour in Afghanistan – the most dangerous country on earth. It was an opportunity I seized with both hands.

But joining the course wasn't that straightforward. I had to prove I had the skills to attend the course, which meant going to Northern Ireland to 321 EOD Squadron to complete what is known as Exercise 'Hard Prep' – effectively a selection process for the High Threat course. Successful completion demonstrated that an AT or ATO was ready for the course and I managed to pull it off. I finished as an instructor at the Felix Centre on the Friday and I was back as a student on the Monday on the High Threat course.

It felt very odd. I knew the set-up, the instructors, I even had my own tea mug in the brew area but I had to put all that behind me and focus on the next six weeks and make sure I acted and was treated like any other student. With my marriage rapidly imploding, I moved out of the family home and into a room in the Sergeants' Mess. It was a big decision and I wasn't sure whether it was the right one. But the course meant more to me than saving my marriage.

That first morning as a student I felt like an eleven-year-old again getting ready for my first day at school but those self-doubts that had dogged me all those years earlier had gone. I had developed into a more mature and confident individual. I arrived cleanly shaved in an immaculate uniform with razor-sharp creases. I had a new notebook, pen and more than just a few butterflies.

The course opened with a welcome brief in a classroom quickly followed by a theory exam to ensure that everyone was at the minimum standard required. The pass mark was 75 per cent and anyone who didn't achieve it would be on the next train home. Those who passed were split into three-man teams and each was assigned a bay outside the main teaching area on one side of a large parade square, known as the pan. The bays were small brick-built rooms, very similar to garages, each crammed with all the EOD equipment required for the next six weeks.

The first few days were an intense battering of everything to do with EOD. At just six weeks long there wasn't enough time to revise the basics of bomb disposal so anyone who wasn't up to speed immediately fell behind and risked being binned. Days started early and finished late and were filled with practical sessions and theory lessons while evenings were consumed with hours of revision.

Every now and again news would filter down of another IED attack in Afghanistan in which soldiers were killed or injured. Intelligence reports on the latest attacks were placed in a 'first look' folder, which we were encouraged to read and digest when time allowed.

Most of the theory lessons took place in a series of newly built classrooms. Maps of Afghanistan hung on the walls, each marked with dozens of red dots showing where IEDs had been found and cleared. The dots grew by the day, so much so that by the end of the course whole areas were covered in red. In the classrooms were examples of IEDs, which had been used by various international terrorist groups. Although they were all different in design, the basic model was the same – switch, detonator, main charge.

The meat of the course was spent dealing with the type of IEDs that troops were encountering in Afghanistan, such as pressure-plate IEDs – which are triggered by someone treading on the plate; remote-controlled – initiated by a mobile phone or other transmitting device; or command-pull – where the trigger is activated by someone pulling a length of string or wire. Instructors also produced scenarios involving booby-trapped bodies, or dead suicide bombers who were still wearing live vests, which the students were required to evaluate and defuse.

At the same time as the operators' course was being taught, the Counter-IED team No.2s and the ECM Operators were also taking part in their equivalent of the High Threat course. During the various tasks we would all come together and work as a team and the fact that we gelled immediately helped enormously. The course was unrelenting and the schedule punishing. A task in which someone performed well could easily be followed by another that was almost a failure. None of us ever felt comfortable, the pressure was intense and despite my initial feelings of confidence most of the students, me included, were dogged with self-doubt. As the course progressed the scenarios became more complex with the additional complication of a time factor. When one device was cleared, students were bounced onto another, and then another. There was no time to clear your head and reassess as the hours slipped by.

On my very last assessment, my best mate, Stu, was my DS and I was convinced I had messed up. The scenario was Afghanistan-based. A car had been abandoned and on inspection was found to contain 107mm rockets pointing at a patrol base. The vehicle had also been booby-trapped with a victim-operated device making the approach to the target quite difficult.

With any suspect IED, the first job the operator has to do is try to get as much intelligence about the device as possible from the local police or military who should provide some good intel on the 'pattern of life' in the area. The role of the main witness was played by Stu and he wasn't being helpful.

Almost from the beginning things started to go wrong. I also had problems with my robot, which kept breaking down and causing huge delays. My No.2 eventually got the robot working and tried to remove the rockets from the firing tubes but all we succeeded in doing was pointing them towards a village full of people. I had a three-hour window to complete the task and I was hugely behind schedule. I also had the added pressure of knowing that I had to complete the task successfully if I was going to pass the course. I had already failed one task and couldn't afford to fail another.

I thought it was all going horribly wrong right up to the point where I turned to Stu and said, 'Look, mate, I've fucked up. Why don't we stop wasting each other's time and just leave it.'

Thankfully Stu was having none of it and turned to me and said, 'Just shut up and get on with the task.'

Eventually I managed to defuse the device and clear the area. God knows how but I passed the final assessment and the course. I was so utterly amazed that I had now qualified as a High Threat Operator that I had to sit down on my own for five minutes and take it all in. I was now a member of a very exclusive club and it didn't seem real. Had I really come so far? The fat kid with the girl's name who could barely read or write was now a bomb disposal expert, qualified to work in the world's most dangerous war zones.

In a matter of days I would be sent to Afghanistan and expected to deal with every device the Taliban had in their armoury. Self-doubt began to creep in. The successful students were given the weekend off and on the Monday morning we met up again for a week-long Specific to Theatre Training (STT) package.

The course wasn't exactly 'Forget about everything you have just learned – this is the reality in Afghan' – but it was close. It was taught by two operators who had just come back from Afghanistan so they were able to give up-to-the-minute intelligence reports and talk us through the types of IEDs we were likely to come across. Their knowledge was gold dust.

'All of that kit in your EOD wagon – forget it,' one of the guys said as he threw a day-sack on the ground in front of us. 'If it doesn't fit in there you aren't using it. This course has taught you the "gold standard" of operating in a High Threat environment. I'm now going to teach you to operate in Afghanistan with nothing but the kit on your back.'

6

First Bomb

Every operator remembers their first bomb, just like you can remember your first proper kiss. It's a seminal moment, you've come of age. No matter what happens in the rest of your life you can call yourself a bomb disposal expert.

I've defused loads of IEDs but most are now blurred by the passing of time. One becomes difficult to distinguish from another. But not the first. I can remember every little detail, every second, the layout, the composition, the date, the time, the ground, the taste of sweat on my lips, even the smell that hung in the air. It's been seared into my consciousness, imprinted on my mind. And more than anything else I remember the relief, the overwhelming relief, that I didn't fuck it up.

My team got the shout less than twenty-four hours after Sam had been shot in that first fucked-up mission. Everyone was still feeling raw, especially Harry. But there was no time to dwell on what was just bad luck and everyone needed to snap out of it – our first bomb disposal mission was an opportunity to get back on the horse straight away.

Like every Counter-IED mission, the tasking came from the EOD Task Force Ops Room, the nerve centre of all bomb disposal missions in Helmand, which was housed inside a huge air-conditioned tent filled with computer monitors and radios. On the walls were the same maps as those in the Felix Centre back in the UK, where red dots showed where IEDs had been found or exploded. The place buzzed with a constant stream of data providing real-time information on contacts, IED blasts and casualties.

In overall command was a major, called the officer commanding EOD Task Force. His right-hand man was a warrant officer, known as the Senior Ammunition Technician or SAT, who was assisted by a small team from a variety of military disciplines, including the Royal Military Police and the Royal Signals. As well as monitoring insurgent activity around the province, Ops Room staff also had to make sure the five IEDD teams in Helmand were sent to the right place at the right time. Given that the province was roughly the size of Wales, balancing supply and demand was often an impossible challenge.

Our first bomb disposal mission came on 15 May 2009. It was a Friday but the days had already begun to merge together, one almost indistinguishable from the next. Danish soldiers, who were also fighting in Helmand, had found a device in their area and needed it cleared.

'You'll find out more when you get there' were the last words I heard as I sauntered out of the Ops Room and climbed onto the waiting 4-tonner. My team looked at me eagerly as the lorry bounced along the dusty Bastion track towards our rendezvous with a waiting Chinook, blades already turning.

'What we got?' Lewis asked.

'We have a bomb somewhere in Afghan. That's all I know. Usual briefing, you know the score.'

Ten minutes later we were airborne, flying north across the Helmand plain and into seemingly endless blue sky to a small Danish Army outpost called Patrol Base Armadillo. Leaving Bastion was like taking a journey back in time, especially when you were able to view the landscape from the safety of a helicopter. Helmand from above had an unusual majestic beauty almost in defiance of the simplicity of life in rural Afghanistan. Huge mountain ranges and steep valleys towered over villages and hamlets that had probably remained unchanged for centuries.

Our route shadowed the twisting Helmand river, which cut through the desert like a silver ribbon, creating a fertile floodplain, the Green Zone, where farmers tended immaculately groomed fields of wheat, melons and often opium poppy. The river, which never dried up, was fed by snow melt from the mountains hundreds of miles away in the Hindu Kush. It was the Green Zone's life-support system. Farmers worked every day apart from Fridays, managing their crops and caring for their livestock, while wives and daughters remained behind closed doors. Children cooling themselves off in the streams would dance and shout unheard words as the Chinook thundered above. As we flew past I wondered how many of those looking up at us were Taliban or at least their sympathisers.

One of the problems NATO soldiers faced was that the ordinary civilians were indistinguishable from the Taliban. They wore the same clothes, spoke the same language, lived in the same towns and villages and carried the same weapons. It was quite normal to see a farmer working his land with an AK47 slung across his back. Working out who among the population was an insurgent was horrendously difficult and often came down to the basic rule that if they were firing at you, they were the enemy. It had been drilled into us during our months of pre-deployment training back in the UK that the British Army was in Helmand to win hearts and minds. But whose hearts and whose minds? I often found myself asking, when most of the time you had no idea who the enemy were.

The Chinook banked and climbed and dived, never flying a straight course, never setting a pattern and hopefully never allowing the Taliban to get a bead on us. The flight served as a brief, but welcome, interlude between Bastion and the war – it was my Zen time, when I could sit and think but usually dozed. Afghanistan had been gifted with an abundance of natural beauty and, in more peaceful times, would probably have been a must-go place for those more adventurous Western tourists happy to spend a small fortune to spend a night or two in an isolated farm to experience a more simple, forgotten existence for a few days.

Armadillo was a standard strongpoint strategically positioned on a high, barren plateau above the Green Zone. It was the definition of the isolated outpost and was occupied by around twenty-five Danish troops. None of us had ever worked with the Danes before but they had acquired an awesome reputation as superb, friendly hosts and fearless warriors. From the relative safety of their base the Danes could track virtually all movement into and out of the surrounding area and could provide a friendly unit patrolling that portion of the Green Zone with real-time intelligence on any Taliban movement. Invading armies had used the exact same location to monitor unruly insurgents in the valley for two hundred years. The Russian Army before us and the soldiers of the British Empire a century before them had come to conquer the same area and all had failed. I couldn't help wondering whether we, the massed ranks of NATO's finest, would be any different.

The Taliban, who were masters of reading the land, recognised the strategic importance of the plateau and would crawl into the area during the hours of darkness to lay IEDs in the hope of killing a few of the returning troops the following day. Fortunately, the Danes were fully aware of the threat facing them and never took any short cuts – they would search carefully every location, new or old.

The patrol base was too small to have a landing zone inside, so the chopper landed outside the wire, on a relatively flat piece of unremarkable desert, a few hundred metres from the base. Within seconds of landing we had exited the aircraft and taken up a defensive position clear of the downdraught from the Chinook's rotors. On the crest of a hill nearby were two Danish Piranha armoured vehicles waiting to pick us up and take the team to the patrol base.

The Danes were pretty relaxed, lying on their vehicles sunbathing. One of the soldiers sat up as we approached and lifted his Ray-Bans, smiled and lay back down, while a tall bearded Dane approached us with his weapon slung over his shoulder.

'Hi, I've come to pick you up,' he said.

'All right, pal, I'm Kim, the ATO,' I said as I stuck out a hand.

'Hi and welcome to our patrol base. Jump on board and we'll take you to the Ops Room. Our ops guy will brief you on your bomb.'

The place was pretty basic and had once belonged to an Afghan farmer but was now one of hundreds of compounds being 'rented' for a small fortune by NATO. Its thick mud walls had been reinforced with Hesco, steel cages about two metres high and wide, filled with earth and stacked on one another. Inside were two single-storey dwellings, with domed roofs, reminiscent of biblical images of Jerusalem. The Ops Room was located in one building while the soldiers slept in another.

The other two corners were dominated by makeshift guard towers, allowing a 360-degree view of the surrounding countryside. A mortar pit with two tubes ready to rain down fire at a minute's notice were positioned in the middle of the compound. Soldiers washed using solar showers and there were a couple of 'desert roses', which were tubes buried in the ground at a 45-degree angle as a makeshift urinal, and the odd 'long drop' (deep hole with a toilet put on top) completed the sanitation.

Just as I was checking through my equipment prior to deploying I heard one of the lads say, in a very loud and disbelieving voice, 'Fuck me.' I turned to see all of the guys looking up at one of the armoured vehicles. Standing half out of the driver's hatch was a ridiculously hot chick.

It was almost as if she was demanding our attention. She removed her helmet and did that thing women do with their hair, slowly moving her head from side to side so that the long blonde hair unfurled down onto her shoulders. She looked like a supermodel, bang tidy and fit. I was left speechless and all I could do was laugh.

'Jesus Christ,' I said probably too loudly.

It was then that I noticed Lee, the RESA, had disappeared. 'Where's Lee?'

'In the Ops Room,' someone said. I was furious. On what planet did Lee think it would be OK to shoot off into the Ops Room without me?

By the time I got to the Ops Room Lee was already getting a full brief from the Danish commander.

'Hello, sir,' I interrupted. 'I'm the ATO. It's my job to clear this device for you.' I glared at Lee and instantly he knew I was pissed off.

'Do you mind starting your brief again?'

'Erm, yes of course,' the officer replied, slightly confused as to who was actually in charge. After the briefing we left the Ops Room and I pulled Lee to one side.

'What are you doing?' He looked shocked and as he was about to answer I cut in, 'We're a team – we go into these briefings together, not run off like some kind of arsehole thinking you'll have the upper hand if you get in there first. We've already seen how shit goes south in a heartbeat with Sam. The Danes have found the device, it's a clearance op, not a search. Got it?' I stormed off before he could respond.

By the time we arrived at the place of the IED find, the sun had reached its zenith and it was properly hot. I scanned the area for signs of enemy activity but there was no chance of being dicked, a term which was a slang hangover from the days of Northern Ireland – being dicked meant you were being watched by the enemy.

'Get the lads to clear us a working area over there,' I said to Lee, pointing fifteen metres to our front. 'After that they can chill, not much here for them to do.'

Lee nodded and headed towards his search team to issue instructions. I wanted the guys to remain switched on but as relaxed as possible.

'Dave, get ready. As soon as the search team have cleared an ICP [Incident Control Point] we're cracking on.'

I carried out a last quick kit check: paintbrush, trowel, snips, pistol. Checked and rechecked my metal detector and made sure my man bag contained everything needed for the task. Dave checked his ECM, fitting batteries and antennas, while Lewis made sure that his EOD weapons and firing cables were in good nick. Chappy gave us the nod that the area was clear and Dave and I began the approach to the target. I scanned the ground ahead looking for any obvious 'ground-sign' left behind after an IED is recently buried. I took the first step, then another. My mouth felt dry and my throat tight. My handgrip on the metal detector handle strengthened as I swung it from left to right, covering the ground to my front in an arc. The earth beneath my feet had been left parched by the early summer sun and made a crump, crump sound with each step, almost as if I was walking on snow.

I cleared an area for Dave, close enough so that his ECM would provide me with a security bubble in which to work but not so close he would be injured if the IED exploded. Dave was also my 'scribe', which meant that he took notes of my actions while I was on target so that if something went wrong and I was killed or seriously injured there would be a log of my actions.

The area around the target was virtually flat apart from a few almost imperceptible undulations, where a smattering of small, thorny, leafless plants had laid claim and were probably the only living things that could survive on such a barren, arid landscape.

I moved ever closer towards the device, consciously trying to remember everything I was taught during my training. No need to rush, nice and steady, the bomb wasn't going anywhere.

I paused for a few seconds and was surprised by the intensity of the silence. It was so quiet that even my own breathing had become a minor distraction and I suddenly felt calm and peaceful. My target was a red circle about forty metres dead ahead where the Danish soldiers had spray-painted the ground after discovering the suspect device.

After every few steps I marked my path with yellow spray-paint. By the time I reached the device two yellow parallel tracks about three feet wide, like two miniature railway tracks, stretched back all the way to the ICP.

I cleared another area close to the device, my working area, and carefully moved down onto my knees and then my stomach so that my face was just inches above the red circle. The earth smelt old and dusty and I began to probe gently with my fingers. It was me against the bomb – those were the odds and they were the best I was going to get. I took some comfort in the knowledge that if I did make a mistake I wouldn't be around to deal with the consequences.

'I can see the pressure plate, going for a closer look.'

'Roger, be careful,' Dave replied.

Reaching into my man bag, I retrieved my paintbrush and slowly, methodically, almost grain by grain, began to sweep away the sand, like an archaeologist uncovering a prehistoric fossil. A single bead of sweat ran on a track from my temple to my chin before dropping onto the sand. My lips were salty with the taste of dried sweat. It was going to be a long, hot day.

The pressure plate was oddly similar to those I'd trained with back in the UK, and I felt myself noticeably relax, almost as if I was back on the training area in Kineton. But this bomb was real and I was on my own. There were no instructors tapping me on the shoulder telling me to be a little less heavy-handed, suggesting I try 'this' instead of 'that'. I looked over my shoulder and through the watery heat haze I could see my team anxiously looking back, willing me to succeed.

The pressure plate was about a foot long and three inches wide and consisted of two pieces of wood, one on top of the other, separated by rubber spacers. On the inside of the two pieces of wood were two hacksaw blades positioned to touch when pressure was applied and the whole thing was wrapped in plastic, providing some rudimentary weather protection. It was a basic switch, the sort of thing an eleven-year-old might build in a science class. When pressure from a human foot forces the hacksaw blades to touch, the current flows, the detonator explodes followed immediately by the main charge buried underneath.

The NATO force gathered in Afghanistan was the most technologically sophisticated military coalition ever to be assembled in the history of mankind but it was being pushed towards defeat by basic schoolboy science and men who went into battle wearing flip-flops carrying 30-year-old Russian assault rifles.

I continued the excavation, sweeping the dust away and every so often letting Dave know what I was doing. I dug and probed with my fingers and flicked away more sand and then, just as I was beginning to question my actions, there it was just beneath the surface. A white piece of Iranian twinflex wire. I took a deep breath and silently congratulated myself. I was on the home straight.

'Dave, I've found a wire.'

'What does it look like?' he replied.

'It looks like a wire!' I shouted back, laughing.

I reached into my man bag for my 'needle', an EOD weapon, used to disrupt IEDs. The needle consists of a barrel, ten inches long and an inch in diameter, with an explosive propelling charge at one end and a set of scalpel blades, known as a flying scalpel, at the other. A wire is attached to the barrel and then unrolled all the way back to the ICP where it can be fired electronically from a safe distance.

I placed my needle as close to the IED as possible without touching it, slowly stood up and started to gather my kit.

'Dave, I've placed the needle, prepare to move.'

I retraced my steps towards Dave, swinging my metal detector as I went along the path I'd already cleared but this was the standard operating procedure (SOP) – never assume anything. By the time I'd reached Dave he was standing up and ready to go.

'Ready? Follow me.'

'Roger,' he replied.

The two of us slowly and carefully made our way back along the cleared lane to the vehicles where the rest of the team were waiting.

'All OK?' Lewis asked as we approached.

'Yep. Prepare to fire the needle. Lee, get your team into the back of the vehicles for some cover.'

I was trying to act cool but excitement surged through my body and I had to consciously slow myself down to ensure I didn't make any mistakes or short-cut the process.

'Dave, let the Danish soldiers know there's going to be a controlled explosion. Lewis, are we ready?'

With everyone safely under hard cover, Lewis prepared to fire the needle. There was always the possibility that the IED might detonate, showering the ICP and everyone in the area in earth, stones and anything else kicked up by the blast.

'Standby! Firing!' Lewis shouted as he fired the needle, which emitted a bang, like a shotgun firing at the target end.

Next, I grabbed my metal detector and retraced my steps back down to the IED, dropping off Dave on the way, all the time searching the ground again just in case something had been missed on the first approach.

A quick examination showed that the device was partly disrupted.

'Dave, needle worked. I've got exposed wires. I'm going to tape up the ends and continue clearing.'

'Roger.'

Down on my chest again, I put the needle back in my man bag and retrieved a roll of insulation tape attached to the front of my body armour. I carefully taped up the exposed ends of the wire to prevent them touching, which would allow the current to flow if the pressure plate was inadvertently stepped on. My face was now just inches from the pressure plate with the main charge possibly buried just beneath my chest, which can only be described as an odd feeling.

Bomb disposal is all about following the rules, the standard operating procedures that had been established forty years earlier when the IRA began building IEDs to target the British and attack city centres. For example, not repeating an action, find another way to do something that's not the same as what you have just done. Follow the rules and the chances were that I would live longer.

The bomb was now 'safer' but not completely safe. I had disrupted the circuit and effectively added my own switch. But until I had a full understanding of how the device was meant to detonate caution was required.

Time passed quickly and unnoticed. I was like a sculptor, probing, digging and prodding, searching for inspiration. I continued fingertipping around the pressure plate and then came across another section of wire, not what I had been expecting.

Pausing for a few seconds, I cast my mind back to the High Threat course, searching for answers but there were none. Rather than confuse the issue by over-thinking the problem I reverted back to the SOPs.

'Dave, I've found a shitload more wire. Going to have to attack it again with the needle.' I recharged the needle and placed another set of flying scalpels next to the device and again carefully withdrew. I followed the same route back, collecting Dave and searching our way back to the ICP. Lewis shouted his warning and fired the needle a second time.

It was the same procedure again: tape the ends of the severed wires and continue probing. I had now been out in the sun for a couple of hours and could feel the back of my neck burning. I took my helmet off and ran my fingers through my hair, which was dripping with sweat. I drank some water and poured half a bottle over my head. The cool water was instantly reviving, like a cold shower on a hot day.

The High Threat course took place over the winter, in the rain and snow, where my fingers were often numbed to uselessness by the cold. Then I dreamed of working in the sun but the heat on that day was unlike anything I had previously experienced. I began taping up the wires again when some sand gave way next to my arm exposing even more wire.

'I've got even more wire – this is taking the piss!' I shouted over to Dave.

'Don't get angry,' I said to myself, rebooting my focus. 'Work the problem.' Being methodical was crucial. The instructors back at the school warned us that we'd face some problems that superficially appeared baffling; the solution, they said, lay in remembering having confidence in our SOPs. The constant reference to the SOPs was like a comforting, trusted voice in my head.

The whole process was repeated again: setting up the flying scalpels, returning to the ICP and remotely firing the weapon. On the third attempt I managed to uncover the entire pressure plate and the battery pack. I took a deep breath, I was halfway home. Images of the Taliban bomb-maker carefully burying the IED in the ground and hoping to kill or seriously injure a British soldier flashed across my mind. I felt controlled anger but a sense of satisfaction that this time we were the winners.

Eventually, after another ten minutes digging, one complete side of the device was uncovered providing a clear view of the layout. At the top was the pressure plate, directly underneath was the battery pack and lastly the main charge, still perfectly preserved in the ground. The charge was housed in a 20-litre yellow palm oil container (YPOC) filled to the brim with some form of home-made explosive. It then became apparent that all of the wires I had encountered were the same piece of wire, which had just been bundled together and buried in the ground for no apparent reason.

ATOs never lift or pull bombs out of the ground by hand, none of that *Hurt Locker* bullshit. Lines and hooks are attached to the bomb or parts of it, which are then pulled out of the ground from a safe distance. If the bomb detonated or there was an anti-handling device attached, there would be a large explosion but no one would get hurt.

The main charge was destroyed in situ so there was no need for it to be removed from the ground. The firing cable was strong enough to drag the pressure plate and battery pack out of the ground and to a safe distance from the explosive charge. After attaching the hook to the firing cable and then extremely carefully resting it next to the pressure plate, I gathered my kit, collected Dave and returned to the ICP.

'Lewis, we're gonna pull the bomb out of the ground, the firing cable's attached. Get ready and I'll give you the nod when to pull.'

'OK, boss.'

'Everyone in cover?'

'Yes, boss,' Dave replied.

'Lewis, go for it.'

Lewis took up the strain and the firing cable lifted off the ground. He began to gently tug away, gradually increasing the pressure while I monitored what was going on at the target end through my rifle scope, controlling the rate of pull. A few seconds later the plate and the battery pack broke free. Lewis stepped back to steady himself and continued pulling until pressure plate and battery were dragged a metre or so from the hole.

'Stop there, it's worked, we'll give it twenty minutes and then head down and sort out the main charge. Lewis get a demolition charge ready and Dave make sure we have some forensic bags with us when we head back down.'

While my team was excited at successfully defusing our first bomb, the Danish guys looked bored to death and I couldn't blame them. We had been on the ground for over two hours and as far as the Danes were concerned little had happened.

'Almost done,' I said encouragingly to them, now relaxing with shirts off in the sun and smoking cigarettes and listening to their iPods.

'Take your time, we have nothing else to do,' one of the Danish soldiers casually responded in excellent English.

As we approached the target end I smiled inwardly – first bomb in the bag and it couldn't have gone better. As we reached the target, Dave was already holding a large forensic bag in his hand, grinning like a dog with a bone.

But the job wasn't over. Every piece of the bomb, apart from the main charge, had to be forensically bagged so it could be analysed further down the chain. A database of forensic material had been created that was pored over by teams of intelligence specialists trying to determine any patterns emerging in the different areas of Helmand. Fortunately, the Taliban weren't very forensically aware so strands of hair, fingerprints and sweat often contaminated various parts of the IED, all of which were collated and stored. The forensic material could then be compared with fingerprints or even DNA material obtained from captured or even dead insurgents. A positive match would lead to the suspect being prosecuted in the Afghan courts.

During the process of pulling the bomb out of the ground some of the sand had caved in and re-covered the main charge. I dropped back down onto my belly, peered into the hole and used my paintbrush to sweep away the sand and dirt and slowly uncovered the palm oil container, which had been slightly distorted by the mass of explosive crammed inside. I searched for the detonator, the final piece of the bomb, which could provide forensic clues. The det is the explosive item that provides the energy necessary for the main explosive to detonate.

Despite all the hard work the bomb was still not safe. Dets are electro-explosive devices, which means they can be susceptible to radio frequency (RF) interference. If RF passed through the wire there was an extremely small chance it would impart current and cause the detonator to go bang and cause the main charge to explode.

After a few minutes of peering into the hole, I found the detonator attached to the main charge via a small piece of orange commercial detonating cord. Det-cord looks like a washing line but it's filled with a powdered explosive and used to link explosive charges.

The Taliban bomber had knotted the det-cord and placed it in the main charge container before filling it with their home-made explosives (HME). The lid of the container was pierced and the det-cord was threaded out through the hole, leaving a short length exposed to which the detonator was attached with a piece of insulating tape. I was now nearing the end game and allowed myself the briefest of smiles as I reached into my man bag for a scalpel. It felt mega, I had beaten the enemy. Not in a heroic firefight with bayonets fixed, but on another level. They were using years of cunning, their knowledge of the land and their incredible ability to build bombs out of almost anything, but not on that day. No British or NATO soldier would be killed or injured by that bomb. That day belonged to us.

'Fuck you,' I said out loud.

'All OK, Kim?' Dave asked.

'Yes, I've found the detonator and I'm cutting it away from the main charge.'

I sliced into the tape and carefully peeled it back with my scalpel. Taking the detonator in my left hand I slowly cut the remaining tape away freeing it from the det-cord. The improvised detonator was made from part of a Bic biro and filled with home-made explosive.

Like much of what the Taliban built, the improvised detonator was primitive but effective. I put the detonator in a small tin to screen it from any RF and packed it away carefully in my man bag. The mission was almost complete.

'Smacking the main charge in situ, ready to move in two!' I shouted over to Dave.

I pulled in a little slack from my firing cable and reached into my bag for one of my own Army-issue detonators and carefully attached it to the end of the cable and set it aside. While I kept a lot of my bomb disposal equipment in my man bag, plastic explosive or Charge Demolition 8oz No.4 Plastic

Explosive (PE4), known within the trade as 'bang', was kept in my ammo pouches.

Each pouch was big enough to hold two 8oz sticks, which I always taped together to prevent plasticiser within the explosive from sweating out in the heat. Each stick provided 16oz of bang to ensure the job was done correctly the first time, every time. In the EOD world there is a saying that goes 'There is no job that can't be fixed without the right application of high explosives'. Basically if all else fails blow it to shit. In this case 'P' definitely stood for plenty. I took my knife from the front of my body armour and made a hole through the insulation tape and into the explosives. The plastic explosive had a consistency very similar to marzipan and was easy to cut with a knife. I sliced through the PE and inserted the detonator before placing the explosive charge on top of the palm oil container. The position of the PE meant that the explosive wave should travel downwards and away from the ICP.

'Got all your kit?'

Dave nodded.

'Sweet, then let's move.'

Back at the ICP, Lewis and the Danish commander were waiting patiently.

'Right, guys, we're all sorted. As soon as everyone's in cover we're gonna smash it. Lewis, get ready.'

I turned to the Danish officer: 'There's going to be a lot of shit kicked up from the explosion so make sure your guys are well in cover.'

'Kim, ready,' Lewis informed me.

'Wait one.'

I had one final look about to make sure everyone was underneath hard cover when I noticed a Danish soldier sitting in the open, with his camera at the ready hoping for a few happy snaps.

'Mate, get yourself down into your vehicle. There's going to be a huge explosion in a minute!' I shouted. But despite my warnings he refused to move.

'Get fucking down!' I shouted louder. The Danish soldier looked at me but was unresponsive as if to say 'I'm taking this picture.'

Fortunately a Danish officer appeared, looking slightly irritated that a very long day in the sun was being lengthened unnecessarily.

'That idiot won't get into his vehicle. We're not smacking this until he does,' I said unapologetically.

The Danish officer shouted an order and his soldier disappeared. I turned to Lewis and gave him the nod.

'Standby. Firing!' Lewis yelled.

The blast was immense. Twenty-odd kilos of explosives detonating was loud and a massive plume of smoke mushroomed into the sky. Seconds later debris from the blast began to rain down on our positions giving rise to a series of tings, bangs and twangs. An echo, like rolling thunder, rumbled around the plateau before giving way to an outpouring of laughter from the Danish soldiers, often the response to a massive explosion. It was almost like a release of pent-up tension.

After allowing the dust to settle, Dave and I headed back down to assess the damage. The explosion had left a crater one metre deep and three metres wide. The Taliban were shrewd and resourceful fighters so it was vital to check that all of the home-made explosive had been destroyed because anything usable would be collected by the insurgents and fed back into their bomb-making network. But the explosion had worked, nothing was left.

Back at the ICP, exhausted by the hours in the sun, I collapsed against the side of one of the armoured vehicles, slid down onto my arse and took off my helmet, allowing my sweat-soaked head to breathe for the first time in hours. Everything had gone to plan, just the way I had hoped and, momentarily, I couldn't help but wonder why this operation had gone so well and the last mission, which ended in Sam fighting for his life, had ended so badly. Telling myself the incident was down to luck just made me angry, it seemed too simplistic. The answer, I decided, was that there was just no answer, it was just Afghan.

Once our equipment had been packed away and all of the forensic material had been correctly labelled, we returned to PB Armadillo and waited for our flight back to Bastion. The team gathered in the shade of a compound wall and began the age-old Army practice of brewing up to fill a few empty minutes. Lee, whom I hadn't spoken to since bollocking him earlier in the day, made a beeline for me, and I sensed that he wanted to pick up where we'd left off. But he was a true professional and instead broke the ice by telling me to get a brew on.

'Come on, Kim – look after your RESA. Where's my tea? I've had a long day lying in the sun,' he said with a broad smile.

'Tosser,' I responded, laughing.

'So how was it? Your first IED. Looked good from our end.'

'Yeah, it was OK, but it took ages, way too long. There's no way I can take that long in the Green Zone.'

'Don't worry about it, mate,' Lee said encouragingly. 'You'll get faster, we're all on a steep learning curve and everyone's taking extra care after what happened to Sam.'

As Lee and I chatted, the rest of the team went into full

banter mode, ripping the piss out of each other for being either too fat, too thin, too short or too tall. Their heads were back in the game. The team were in a good place.

Forty minutes later, we were airborne, slicing through the cool evening air towards Bastion, landing within the hour. The Ops Room barely acknowledged my presence as I entered, perhaps hoping that I might be greeted like the all-conquering hero given that I had finally arrived in the world of High Threat bomb disposal. But the warm glow of self-congratulation didn't last long.

'You took your time over that one,' the SAT said, looking up at me as I stood by his desk. It was a typical piss-take, designed to bring me back down to earth, but I also knew he was right. There was no way the Taliban would allow any operator that much time on land they owned.

'Let me have your report in the next couple of hours,' he added.

I left the Ops Room deflated and feeling like a right twat. The SAT was right. I'd spent more than two hours working on a bomb that an experienced operator could have pulled out of the ground in half the time. I had become so focused on doing everything by the book that I had forgotten about the wider tactical picture. The threat of a Taliban attack high up on the plateau was remote, but I was still operating in a war zone, and that meant it was still possible.

Walking through the maze of tents within the EOD Task Force village, I went through the whole operation from start to finish, wondering what I could have done better, quicker, without endangering my life or those of my team. Around me inside their tented homes soldiers laughed, slept, played music, watched films and wrote letters home, but I was oblivious to it all. The sun had dipped beneath a distant mountain range to the west and in the failing light I sat down on a makeshift bench outside my tent, listening to the banter inside. Morale was high and I wasn't about to puncture it by announcing that the mission had taken too long.

Next time would be faster, more expert. Despite everything I felt a special pride in what I had achieved. More importantly I had taken the first step on a journey that would change me in ways I never thought possible. The war in Afghan was changing, primarily because the Taliban had grasped the effectiveness of the IED as a weapon when used in massive numbers, and bomb disposal operators were at the sharp end.

A year earlier in 2008, there were just two British Counter-IED teams in Helmand, one commanded by one of my best mates, WO2 Stu Dickson GM, a friend for at least fourteen years, and the other by WO2 Gary O'Donnell GM and Bar. Gary was one of the most experienced and respected High Threat Operators in the Army at the time. He was a family man, extremely popular and set the standard to which all EOD Operators hoped to aspire. For his courage and skill he'd been awarded the George Medal in Iraq. But his luck ran out in September 2008 while attempting to defuse a device near Musa Qala in northern Helmand. Gary was awarded a posthumous George Medal for his work in Helmand, which saved dozens of lives, not just British soldiers but also those of ordinary Afghans. His death served as a reminder that Afghan was different from every other environment British bomb disposal experts had ever been in.

Stu finished the same tour as Gary having defused over 48 devices, a record in the world of British Army bomb disposal. Stu like Gary also won the George Medal and he was something of a living legend within the world of EOD.

Never before had bomb disposal experts been so important in a conflict – this was going to be my war and it would be a dangerous and unpredictable journey, where experience or skill no longer guaranteed survival.

7

The Science of Explosives –
the Layman's Version

It's worth having a bit of knowledge about why things go bang if you're interested in the EOD world. But easy to get a bit overly scientific about explosives so I'm going to keep it relatively simple.

An explosive is a material that has the potential to cause an instantaneous release of heat, light, sound and pressure. The point at which the material goes bang is known as the 'detonation' and this is effectively a chemical reaction. Modern commercial or military grade and even some 'home-made' explosives are relatively stable, meaning that the explosive won't go bang on its own. So they need something to help them on their way to initiate that chemical reaction.

The stability of an explosive substance can alter, and often quite quickly if environmental conditions change such as temperature, humidity or even the age of the explosives (everything has a shelf life). Some of the early explosive compounds were extremely volatile and unstable and would often explode in transit or when the air temperature rose. But explosives found in most modern weapons and improvised explosive devices, if left alone, will sit there relatively happy as the world passes by them – hence why Second World War bombs buried for seventy years beneath the ground remain stable. The stability of the explosive compound is also why some IEDs found in Afghanistan may have been buried in the ground for months before being discovered.

To get the explosive substance to initiate that 'chemical reaction' the material requires an energetic shock, a 'kick'. This is achieved using what is known as a 'detonator'. The detonator essentially provides the energy to give the kick that starts the chemical reaction and results in the explosion. High explosives are categorised into two types: 'primary' explosives – the detonator – and 'secondary' explosives – essentially the main charge.

Primary explosives are extremely sensitive to heat and shock and should be handled with respect and care. They can be made from a number of different chemical compounds and an example of this is lead azide, a highly sensitive chemical compound composed of lead and nitrogen. The compound is so sensitive that it needs to be stored under water in insulated rubber containers and tests have shown lead azide will explode if dropped from a height of around eight inches.

Detonators can also be made from mercury fulminate, a compound first used in the 1800s in one of the earliest detonators. Both work superbly well as primary explosives and will initiate or explode by applying energy in the form of heat. This can be from an electrical bridge wire, if electrically initiated, or by a flame if initiated using a burning fuse (like in the old Wild West films where a cowboy would light the fuse on a stick of dynamite).

These primary explosives can also be initiated mechanically by driving, pushing or compressing the explosive, which causes friction and heat at the molecular level. The energy created will cause the compound to undergo that same chemical reaction and detonate.

A commercial grade detonator contains a very small amount of primary explosive positioned on top of a small pellet of secondary explosive, both contained within a small metal tube. The tube will either be sealed with an electrical bridge wire or left open to enable the insertion of a burning fuse. The Taliban have mastered the art of making their own detonators using containers such as a biro pen; however, the chemistry behind both factory-made and improvised is the same. They both provide that kick.

Now we come to secondary explosives. These are relatively insensitive chemical compounds, such as military-grade plastic explosives like Semtex or C4. They can be subjected to extreme force, such as being hit with a hammer or shot with a bullet from a gun and even be set on fire, without causing detonation. Secondary explosives require the 'kick' I mentioned earlier, to enable the chemical reaction to take place that will result in a rapid release of energy or explosion.

The Taliban, like the IRA, often struggled to get their hands on large quantities of commercial or military explosive and so made their own – known as home-made explosives or HME. There are various types of HME and to name them all would take forever. Ammonium nitrate and sugar (ANS) or ammonium nitrate and fuel oil (ANFO) are two common examples and both are relatively easy to produce. These compounds still require a detonator to provide that initial kick to make them explode. In some cases the HME is so insensitive they also require a small booster to ensure that the detonation wave moves from the detonator to the explosive charge.

The Taliban got round this problem by using commercial detonating cord, known as det-cord. This consists of a powdered crush-sensitive secondary explosive known as pentaerythritol tetranitrate (PETN), a compound very similar in its molecular structure to nitroglycerine and regarded as one of the most powerful explosives ever manufactured. The explosive is tightly wound with twine and covered in plastic and looks exactly like washing line. Det-cord is used as an intermediary between the detonator and the explosive charge and has a speed of detonation of over 7,000 metres per second. So if you laid a line of it from Edinburgh to London (a distance of approximately 400 miles that would take an average of seven hours to drive) and initiated the Edinburgh end, it would take just under seven seconds for the detonation wave to reach London.

So what happens to explosives when detonated? Let's look at an ammonium nitrate-based explosive. When the detonator explodes, the kick causes the ammonium nitrate within the explosive mixture to vaporise instantaneously, creating extreme heat and a large volume of gas. The heat causes the mixture to break down and release oxygen. This process kick-starts the detonation of the explosive and creates a chain reaction in which more heat, gas and oxygen is produced. This in turn fuels the burning process, resulting in more heat and gas and so on. This intense reaction takes place within a fraction of a second.

The gas produced is what causes the instant pressure wave as the explosive detonates. It is the gas or the force of the blast, known as the over-pressure, which is so damaging. If you were to further confine those explosives, perhaps within a metal container, the confinement would increase the velocity of detonation with the added effect of high-speed fragmentation. The power of this over-pressure and fragmentation can be harnessed and directed to achieve the maximum effect. For example, if you were to suspend an explosive charge in mid-air and detonate it, the explosive wave or over-pressure would be omni-directional: like throwing a stone into a puddle, the ripple effect starts in the middle and works its way out. If the bomb was buried, like IEDs in Afghanistan, the explosive force has nowhere to go but up towards the victim. The results are devastating, causing serious if not fatal injuries.

Although differences exist in the chemical compounds found in modern, industrial explosives compared with the explosive mixture found in an IED, the science behind them is very similar. The Taliban and terrorists as a whole have been able to use the science of explosives to develop a range of very simple but effective IEDs and it's the role of the bomb disposal expert to deal with them.

8

Keeping Score

The summer of 2009 was rapidly turning into one of the bloodiest periods of the entire Afghan War. Soldiers were being killed or wounded every day, sometimes several times a day, either by a hit-and-run ambush or an IED. Those who survived being blown up by an IED often suffered terrible wounds: legs torn off, at the hip, cock and balls gone, bladder shredded, intestines perforated, wounds to hands and fingers. Nothing but months of operations, suffering and an uncertain future to look forward to. All caused by a few kilos of home-made explosive, a battery and a pressure plate put together probably by a kid, somewhere in Helmand.

The first inkling that casualties had been taken was when an anonymous voice announced via the Camp Bastion loud-speaker system that Operation Minimise was in force. It was the first indication that there had been British casualties some-where in Helmand. Operation Minimise was an automatic shutdown of all unofficial communications – email, Facebook, any form of social media or satellite phone – with the outside world. No details of the incident such as the number of casualties were ever provided; that was left to us to ponder on.

Initially the announcement of Operation Minimise would stop everyone in their tracks, wondering what had happened to whom and when but as time went on the tragic reality was that we barely noticed. If anything the constant broadcasts soon grew into something of an irritation in the day-to-day running of the base.

By 2009 Bastion had more than quadrupled in size from the base that existed three years earlier. The US Marines had grafted on Camp Leatherneck, their home in Helmand, while the Danes and the Estonians also had their areas too. Also housed within the Bastion footprint was Camp Shorabak, run by the Afghan National Army, where masses of Afghan recruits were trained and housed. Bastion had all the obvious creature comforts: gyms, coffee shops and various stores where soldiers could spend their hard-earned cash, but it also housed several different headquarters and that meant an abundance of officers, warrant officers and bullshit. Bastion might have been the largest base in Helmand, but it was also the most claustrophobic – there was always someone more senior only too ready to bollock you for some unknown crime. Beyond the wire, in the smaller forward operating bases (FOBs), life was a lot more chilled and, crucially, we were often treated like valued guests.

The early summer was a grim period for the British Army in Bastion with the constant drumbeat of casualties so when the opportunity came for Brimstone 42 to spend a few weeks embedded with the Royal Danish Army inside FOB Price, one of the smaller bases in Helmand, it was seized enthusiastically. Price was regarded as a five-star FOB with arguably the best cookhouse in Helmand – salads, plenty of fresh fruit, decent meat pies and puddings to keep the British squaddies happy. It also had a fully equipped gym, a fantastic coffee shop but best of all the Danish women were stunning, and, although we never quite understood why, found the British squaddie an attractive alternative to the average blond, chiselled Danish soldier. FOB Price also served as an indirect firebase capable of raining down mortars and artillery shells on the enemy if and when needed.

The place was located on a flat desert plain, close to the main Kandahar highway, a road which rings Afghanistan and was the most important transit route in the entire country; one of the key responsibilities for the troops was to keep the highway open. Like all bases in Helmand it had a perimeter wall constructed of Hesco blocks, so that from a distance they looked like something out of a 1950s *Beau Geste* film, with permanently manned watchtowers positioned at each corner of the camp.

Accommodation consisted of the standard, white air-conditioned tents, about thirty feet in length and sixteen feet wide – some were even larger. They were supported by steel poles that bent over forming an arched roof, not too dissimilar from corrugated-iron Nissen huts sometimes seen on old military bases in the UK. The floors were made of black plastic matting and hanging from the roof was a huge plastic pipe that pumped out wonderfully cool air. The tents were identical to those in Bastion but they somehow seemed more welcoming.

The Danes were great hosts and always ensured that we had a tent to ourselves so there was more than enough room for every man and his kit. Nothing was too much trouble for them as they went out of their way to make us feel we were part of their Task Force. Likewise, I was also keen to make sure the relationship worked in the hope that whenever the Danes needed EOD support they would always ask for Brimstone 42.

A week or so into the attachment, I learned that we would be providing EOD support for the Danish battlegroup in one of the biggest operations ever undertaken at that time. Although by June 2009 NATO had been based in Helmand for almost three years, there were still large parts of the central belt, close to Lashkar Gah, the provincial capital, effectively controlled by the Taliban – or perhaps a better way of putting it was not under the control of the Government of the Islamic Republic of Afghanistan.

Operation Panchai Palang – or 'Panther's Claw' – was going to change all of that imbalance. The plan involved British and Danish battlegroups fighting through the Green Zone to secure a series of canal and river crossings, which would force the Taliban into a trap. Those who stood their ground and fought would be smashed. Once the ground had been cleared, more bases would be created, which in turn would increase and deepen NATO's security footprint in the area, at least that was the theory. It was a counter-insurgency concept known as the ink blot, where the security presence of ground troops spreads out and eventually links up to other bases until the entire area is covered.

The night before the operation, every team leader based at FOB Price attended a detailed orders briefing, involving who would be doing what and when. The orders procedure was a painstaking step-by-step process, supposedly covering every eventuality. The role of Brimstone 42 was to be attached to an engineering unit for the duration of the operation and to provide EOD support to the entire battlegroup. What this meant in reality was that as the Danes moved through the Green Zone, any IED finds would be dealt with by my team.

As the briefing drew to a close, the ranking Danish officer asked me to remain behind while dismissing everyone else. When the room had emptied, he turned to me with a pained expression: 'Kim, I want you to understand that this is going to be a dangerous operation. We are expecting casualties, probably more than anyone thinks. I want you to be aware of this. Your soldiers will be right at the front.'

As he spoke I could feel the hairs standing up on the back of my neck. His look was intense and I immediately knew he meant business. By that stage in the three-year-long campaign over 170 British soldiers had died. Attacks on NATO forces within the province were running at ten a week. Helmand was a dangerous place but it almost felt as though he was warning me that I was about to lose some members of my team.

'We know the risks, sir. My guys will be ready.'

Later that evening, after another delicious meal in the base canteen, I gathered the team together in the privacy of our tent and briefed them on the operation. The mission was going to be tough, I explained, probably tougher than anything we had experienced. I ran through the outline plan of what Panchai Palang was setting out to achieve and our role within that. We could be expected to be worked hard with the operation lasting anywhere between a week and ten days, possibly longer. Everyone was enthusiastic but also anxious.

I kept the extra detail on the threat of casualties to myself – there was nothing to be gained from telling them that there was a good chance that one of us might be killed or injured. It was lost on none of us that the last major 'well-planned' operation we had been involved in ended with Sam being seriously injured. But there was no mention of it. Instead everyone packed and checked their equipment and set about taking the piss out of each other.

Just after sunset the team made its way over to the volleyball court where the Danish engineers were battling one another almost as fiercely as they attacked the Taliban. I watched the game for a few minutes before one of them broke away and headed over to me.

'Hi, my name is Rom,' said a shirtless Danish sergeant with shaven head and a small goatee beard. He was the epitome of the cool, relaxed Danish hippy. 'You must be Kim – the ATO. You're going to be with my team. That will be your home for the next few days,' he said, pointing into the back of an armoured vehicle, which looked as though it had seen just a little too much action. 'It will be cramped and hot but you'll get used to it soon enough. Eventually. Operational kit only I'm afraid – no room for luxuries. Get your kit packed and loaded and then come and join us for a game of volleyball.'

'Seems like a nice bloke,' said Lewis as Rom walked away puffing on a cigarette.

'Yeah,' I said, 'I think we've done all right here.'

We packed our kit into the vehicles as best we could, wondering how we were expected to fit inside, and headed back to the volleyball court.

The atmosphere was so relaxed that, just for a few minutes, it was easy to forget we were on the front line of what was becoming an increasingly bitter and dirty war. My guys joined a small crowd of Danish soldiers who had gathered to watch the volleyball match. While the rest of the team enthusiastically cheered every point, Rom and I sat down for another chat. He was one of those larger than life characters often found in the military world whom you could trust with your life. He had a reputation of being a fearless fighter, with two tours of Afghanistan already under his belt. Over some excellent Danish coffee, Rom explained how our team would integrate into his crew.

'You'll have your own vehicle but it will be commanded by my guys. We'll take the lead during the operation and if we get into a contact my guys will deal with it. When we find an IED, and we will, then you take the lead and we'll provide you with cover. Happy?'

It was exactly the sort of no-nonsense relationship an IED Operator wanted to have with the parent unit and I immediately sensed that whatever happened over the next few days my relationship with Rom would only get stronger.

Then apropos of nothing, Rom pointed up at the sky where the stars shone like diamonds and said: 'The Egyptians used those very same stars to build the pyramids. Makes you think, doesn't it? They've remained unchanged for thousands of years. The same stars that Alexander the Great saw when he came through Afghanistan, if he did.'

Elsewhere across Helmand, hundreds of other troops from dozens of different units were already swarming into the Green Zone. Soldiers from the Black Watch, the Royal Regiment of Scotland and the Rifles flew into Taliban-occupied areas in what was described as the biggest British air assault operation since the Second World War. On the ground the Welsh Guards pressed forward the attack in Warrior armoured personnel carriers (APCs), while above Apache attack helicopters and heavily armed US Spectre gunships supported the ground troops.

Despite the size of the ground force taking part in the operation, the EOD element consisted of just two bomb-hunting teams, mine and another led by Staff Sergeant Oz Schmid, who was on the same High Threat course as me but deployed slightly later. There were only five British Counter-IED teams in Helmand at that time so reducing the number by 40 per cent for a single operation was a significant reduction.

The camp was awake before first light and the peaceful pre-dawn silence was soon broken by the roar of vehicles being revved into life. Choking clouds of diesel exhaust belching from the tanks and APCs added to a frenetic atmosphere as soldiers rushed around completing last-minute checks and cramming extra ammo into already packed vehicles. One vehicle broke down, creating an instant but short-lived panic as soldiers were ordered to find spaces elsewhere in the small convoy.

Even at 4.30 a.m. my team were buzzing, trying to keep a lid on their nervous anticipation at what lay ahead. Everyone wanted to get going, get out of the gate and confront the enemy and we were all gripped by the sense that we were going to be part of something special.

APCs might seem like an ideal way to go to war: no walk-ing, air conditioning, a comfy seat and armour plate designed to protect those inside from small arms fire and rocket-propelled grenades (RPGs). From the outside looking in the vehicles can appear huge but the reality was very different. Brimstone 42 was split between two APCs, the search team in one and the bomb disposal element in another. Our kit was jammed into every empty nook and cranny. Water, rations, ammo, radios, sleeping bags, our Bergens, all had to be fitted inside and by the time we had packed there was virtually no room for us. One of the joys of being the boss meant that I got to choose the least uncomfortable seat – the one by the rear door.

'How we all doing?' I asked, tightening the harness that

would keep me strapped into my seat if there was an IED strike.

'Cosy.'

'Fucking dandy.'

'Happy as a pig in shit.'

The responses all came at once.

'Guys, there's some cold drinks in the fridge if you want some, help yourself,' the Danish vehicle commander called down from above.

'Yeah, nice one, dickhead,' I thought to myself, thinking he was joking.

He bent down looking at us with a smile and said: 'Over there . . . can you pass me one?' He indicated with a nod to the corner of the vehicle. There was a small fridge, a solitary item of luxury, and it was composed of two shelves stacked with ice-cold Mountain Dew.

'If you wouldn't mind, it's one out, one in,' the Dane said, pointing to the other side of the vehicle where there were three crates of the drink hidden behind boxes containing heavy machine gun ammunition.

'Lewis, pass the man his drink,' Dave responded.

Then without warning the vehicle jerked forward, swung into its position in the convoy and headed for the Green Zone and Taliban country.

Within minutes the temperature inside was almost unbearable and must have been nudging 40°C. Everyone was dressed in full battle order, including body armour and helmets, with weapons positioned between our legs. It was like sitting in a cramped sauna fully clothed and I could feel sweat running down my neck and dripping from my chin.

Conversation was only possible by shouting above the engine noise and most of us gave up trying after the first twenty minutes. The day seemed endless and I dozed, occasionally slipping into a sleep, only to be awoken as the vehicle lurched from side to side as it bounced over the undulating terrain.

Occasionally the vehicle's radio would randomly spark into life throwing up snippets of information on the operation's progress. As the morning turned into afternoon, firefights between the forward elements of the convoy and the enemy became more frequent and intense. Elsewhere vehicles were hitting IEDs and casualties were being taken; it was obvious that a KIA was only a matter of time, given the numbers and intensity of the contacts, but when it came we were all left shocked.

While we were complaining about being hot and cramped, Lieutenant Colonel Rupert Thorneloe, the Commanding Officer of the 1st Battalion Welsh Guards and Trooper Joshua Hammond, of the 2nd Royal Tank Regiment, were killed by a huge IED detonating beneath the Viking armoured vehicle they were travelling in. No soldier's life is worth any more or less than anyone else's but the death of a CO on the battlefield had not happened since the Falklands War.

'Jesus,' one of the lads said. 'If a boss can get blown to shit it can happen to any of us.'

Armoured troop carriers offer protection from small arms fire and possibly RPGs, but not much more. An IED with a large main charge, anything more than 20kg of HME, had the potential to do some real damage. The impact of the blast on the underneath of the vehicle would send a huge scab of metal flying around inside, ricocheting from side to side until everyone had been turned into a bloody mush. Any survivors would then be incinerated in the ensuing fireball – it was a pretty unpleasant way to die. With the door closed we were both protected from the outside and also trapped.

After two days of being bounced around the inside of that

armoured vehicle I was beginning to lose the will to live. The air conditioning broke right at the beginning of the operation, turning the vehicle into an oven on wheels and the lack of air inside was almost suffocating. Meals were snatched when the vehicle stopped for long enough. Otherwise we often ended up having to piss in bottles and one of the lads even asked if he could have a shit inside the vehicle – he didn't ask twice.

The relief when the steel rear doors opened was almost overwhelming. One by one we fell out of the back of the APC, almost crippled by stiffness and squinting into the bright intense daylight. It was early afternoon but we had lost all sense of time and felt completely disorientated. The journey through the Green Zone had taken two long, punishing days of near continuous travel, only punctuated by brief rest stops. Everyone stank of old sweat and the inside of the vehicle reeked like a pigsty. My body odour was so bad that I could actually smell myself. My arse crack felt like a swamp and my hair was matted with dust, sweat and thick grease. I had spots on my forehead like boils from the dirt that had been swirling around inside the APC. I would have happily given a month's salary for a shower.

The operation had been running for just forty-eight hours but we were exhausted mentally and physically. If the Taliban had attacked us at that moment we would have struggled to defend ourselves. A day earlier the area had been the scene of a ferocious battle during which several Danish soldiers had been killed and injured but they had smashed those Taliban who had stood and fought. The twisted, bloated corpses of several dead Taliban, mutilated by the effects of modern military weapons, lay in the open ground. Clouds of black flies hovered above and the sickly rich odour of putrefying human flesh hung heavily in the air.

I wondered why no one had bothered to collect the bodies that seemed to be surrounded by dozens of red spray-painted circles.

'What's with all the red paint?' I asked a Danish officer who came over to greet us. 'Those are IEDs,' he said with a certain amount of satisfaction, 'and it's your job to clear them.'

Dozens of IEDs had been buried in a wide bank across a main transit route into one of the key areas controlled by the enemy. A warm breeze blew against my face as I stared out to the scrubby fields beyond; there appeared to be red circles almost everywhere.

'That's a massive job. We can do it but clearing this many IEDs will take days.'

'That's not a problem,' the officer responded casually. 'Take as much time as you need. We're not going anywhere. We will rest today, there's only a few hours of daylight left and we'll start tomorrow.'

I called the team together and gave them a quick brief: 'All of the red circles you can see out there are the locations of IEDs and they're just the ones the Danes have found. There could be more and they want them cleared. We start tomorrow early. So get your kit sorted, get some scoff on and get a good night's sleep.'

Our home that night was an Afghan compound with pock-marked walls and buildings scorched black by the impact of high explosive shells fired by the Danes a few hours earlier. The area was cleared by the search team, both inside and outside the compound, and we claimed a building that didn't look as if it might collapse. The smell of the dead decaying in nearby fields dulled our appetites that night and, despite the distant rumble of artillery fire throughout the night, Brimstone 42 slept soundly for the first time in over forty-eight hours, confident in the knowledge that the Danish battlegroup with their two tanks and dozens of soldiers would repel any Taliban attack.

The following morning I woke just after dawn to the sound of a tank starting its engine, a ritual that would take place every morning. The rest of the team slept soundly as I walked the compound's perimeter, looking out across the IED fields, wondering whether the task was too great for a single Counter-IED team. I attempted to count the red circles but gave up after twenty or so, convinced I had counted the same one twice. The compound was located in a blissful area, with a tributary of the Helmand river running left to right about forty metres in front of it. Either side of the river were two very basic roads. The area looked peaceful enough and my only real concern was several deserted compounds a few hundred metres away in the fields beyond the far side of the river.

I returned to where the lads were sleeping and made myself a quick brew and watched as the sun rose in the east, turning the velvet-black sky into a wash of dark-blue and orange. The sounds of distant battle began to fill the air, snuffing out the shrill sound of morning birdsong. Someone was getting smashed and thoughts of Oz and his team flashed across my mind.

'Good morning,' said a voice from behind. I turned to see Rom standing behind me, smiling broadly and drinking coffee.

'Morning,' I responded. 'Your guys have been busy finding bombs. Does anyone have any idea how many are out there?' I said, nodding towards the mass of red circles.

'We think we have marked twenty-eight IEDs so far,' he said smiling, 'but there could be a lot more.' I climbed up onto a wall to get a better view of the area to see if there was any plan or design to the layout of the bombs, but if there was I couldn't see it.

By now the rest of the team were up, cleaning weapons, washing or preparing their breakfast, conducting their morning admin, a practice that would have been ingrained in them from their time as recruits. Dressed, fed and ready to fight, I began briefing them on the plan. It was going to be another slack day for the search team – after all, the bombs had been found – but for the rest of us it was going to be a bitch.

'The Danes have done a good job in confirming and marking but let's not get complacent. It's a big job, it will get boring, we will get tired but we have to remain focused. Anyone struggling in the heat sing out and we'll take a break. They are pretty cool, they won't be on our backs but the longer we are fixed in this location the more chance we have of becoming a target. It's a straightforward enough task – one bomb at a time – no short cuts, no fuck-ups.'

The team nodded enthusiastically. After the previous forty-eight hours of armoured vehicle hell, everyone just wanted to get to work.

While Lewis got his kit together I walked over to the compound boundary and peered out into the desert.

'Right, where to start?' I said out loud.

'Why not there?' Lewis said, pointing at a red circle about thirty metres in front of us.

'Why not indeed? You guys take cover in the compound behind the wall.'

I turned on my metal detector and listened for its high-pitched whine before setting off towards the IED, tiptoeing at first before striding purposefully towards the first red circle. The area had been cleared but given the enormity of the task

I decided it was a job that needed to be done with a strict application of the basic rules of EOD – the first of which was never assume the ground is clear.

As I reached the target area I could feel my heart thumping with excitement, like a child at Christmas, unwrapping a long-desired present. I felt as though I was wholly in my element as I dug away with my trowel and carefully swept away the dry, sandy earth with gentle brushstrokes, searching for a wire, a corner of a pressure plate, anything. I was in the zone, pitting my wits against the Taliban's.

But my concentration was broken when Lewis told me with a certain amount of urgency that I needed to return to the compound. Using the Leopard 2 Tank's powerful optics, a Danish gunner had spotted several Taliban moving into a number of the compounds on the other side of the river. Looking back over my shoulder, I could see the tank barrel pointing at something in the distance and I was in its line of fire.

'For fuck's sake,' I said to myself but also realising that the Danes couldn't exactly fire a high explosive round a few feet above my head. The over-pressure would have seriously ruined my day and potentially detonated the bomb I was working on.

Feeling frustrated I walked back to the compound and seconds later the tank fired.

The ground beneath my feet shook as the shell flew across the desert towards its target and exploded a second or two later. Whatever threat had been there no longer existed. I felt nothing for those who had just died, apart from the mild irritation of being delayed in my work.

Minutes later I was back at the target, lying face down close to the IED, which I soon discovered had a pressure plate attached – no tricks or traps, and after forty minutes of coming back and forth it was ready to blow.

Lewis pressed the firing switch and unleashed a massive explosion which erupted around the valley, sending up a huge cloud of dust and debris that took several seconds to clear and when it did I realised I'd made a very basic mistake. A thick blanket of dust and lumps of earth thrown up by the blast had settled across a wide area covering dozens of the red circles. The minefield that the Royal Danish Army had so painstakingly uncovered had disappeared.

Everyone looked at me in almost disbelief. 'That's a bit of a balls-up,' I said out loud, wondering why I hadn't factored in the obvious problem of dust. I looked around more surprised than embarrassed and saw Rom walking away, his shoulders moving up and down as he laughed to himself.

The dust problem was more of an annoyance than any major drama because as a matter of course I searched everywhere I went when I was working on an IED. I worked throughout the day, moving from one device to the next, only stopping when my concentration was broken by the distant sound of sporadic gunfire.

By the end of that first day I had cleared eight bombs, one after another. Eight bombs in a day – that was ridiculous. As the light began to fade I stopped work and cleared a route back to the compound. I headed over to where the team had gathered and sat on a low wall, suddenly exhausted after almost ten hours in the sun. Lee by contrast looked fresh and relaxed and handed me a brew.

'Long day?' he enquired with a rather-you-than-me look on his face.

'Yeah, too long.'

'Go and sit down and I'll get some food on,' he added. I

was almost too tired to eat and tried to protest but Lee was insistent.

My back ached and my knees were blood-sore but I felt a real sense of achievement. Despite being exhausted I had enjoyed every minute of it. I didn't even think of the task as a challenge, it was just fun. More and more I was starting to realise that I had finally found my true role in life. It was a curious and comforting feeling but one which at that stage I felt I couldn't really discuss with anyone. If I had told my team 'This is what I was made for' they'd probably think I was a bit of a wanker.

I took a great deal of satisfaction from knowing that with every bomb removed from the ground we were potentially saving one of our own from death or injury and also beating the Taliban at their own game. Despite the dangers and hardships I faced, I also knew that elsewhere on the battlefield British soldiers were fighting and dying, a fact I was keen to remind my team of whenever they started to whinge. I slept soundly that night beneath the stars.

The following morning I was up at 6.00 a.m. and as the air around me warmed I was about to learn the full extent of the challenge confronting Brimstone 42.

Rom appeared fresh-faced with a huge grin and was sipping from a piping-hot mug of coffee.

'Morning, Kim. Did you sleep well?'

I nodded and smiled.

'That's good because when you were working yesterday my guys found another twenty devices. I think you are going to be here for a while,' he laughed and walked off to the make-shift toilet.

I did the maths. It now meant that there were around forty to sixty bombs in the area. Nothing in my training had prepared me for anything on such a scale – in fact no one in Army Bomb Disposal had ever faced such a daunting IED task.

After breakfast, I called the team together and gave them the latest news from Rom.

'Fellas, we have got a shitload of work to do here. It's far larger than I thought. There are at least forty bombs in the area but the figure could be as high as sixty. That's more than some teams have done in six months.'

Everyone's eyes were fixed on me.

'The threat will be complacency. There are no Taliban in the area and we've got the Danes watching our backs. We have to be methodical and remember our training. We'll smash this shit together. Let's be ready to work in thirty mins.'

One bomb followed the next, all identical pressure-plate IEDs, only the size of the main charge varied. The explosive was mainly HME but occasionally we would come across a Russian anti-tank mine or old artillery shells. The Taliban's ingenuity and resourcefulness seemed to be endless. The older veterans had probably fought the Russians but back then they were regarded as allies of the West and were called the Mujahideen. The guerrilla warfare skills of turning anything on the battlefield into a weapon had obviously been passed on from one generation to the next, given that they'd even man-aged to turn British-made illume or smoke shells into main charges. Illume rounds are basically shells that contain a flare pot and a parachute. When the shell reaches a certain height it would kick out the pot and chute. The empty shell would fall to the ground and the Taliban would pay local farmers and children to go out and collect the shell cases, which they would fill with HME – an instant improvised metal-cased charge.

Throughout the day, Dave gave a running commentary of

the battle raging in the British sector a few miles away. The Taliban were launching hit-and-run attacks almost every hour, sucking our guys into IED minefields, watching as someone stepped on an IED and then attacking the casualty evacuation. It was a brutal, almost cynical tactic, but it was very effective.

The fighting in the other sector was so intense that Oz's team were actually involved in more firefights than clearing IEDs and I counted myself lucky that I could practise my trade in relatively safe surroundings rather than fight as a makeshift infantryman.

Meanwhile, I was faced with the problem of what to do with the huge number of main charges we were collecting. Blowing them up in situ was a non-starter because of the problems with dust, yet the HME couldn't be left in the ground because it would be reused by the Taliban and there were too many to take back to Bastion. The only alternative was to pull them out of the ground and empty the mixture of ammonium nitrate and sugar into the Helmand river.

With the end of the day approaching I cleared a path from the compound to the river so that we could enjoy a refreshing swim. I followed the safe route back to the compound, headed over to where my kit was stashed, grabbed a towel, kicked off my boots, put on my flip-flops, my one piece of comfort clothing I carried with me everywhere, and announced that I was going for a swim. The rest of the team followed close behind and on reaching the water's edge, I dived in fully clothed.

The cool, crystal-clear water was instantly reviving and I suddenly felt energised and refreshed. It was enough to just float, eyes closed, feeling my body cool down second by second, letting the life flow back into aching limbs. I ducked my head down and washed the dirt and sweat out of my hair.

The current was quite strong and I noticed I had floated away from the compound and had to put in a few powerful strokes to get back to where the rest of the soldiers were watching me from the bank.

'Come in, the water's lovely!' I shouted while noting it was the last thing I had expected to say in Afghanistan.

One by one the soldiers jumped in while others kept watch, rifles at the ready. For the next hour or so we frolicked like carefree children playing in an undiscovered river, laughing and joking and for just a few minutes forgot about the war, IEDs and those who wanted to kill us.

Reluctantly, as the sun began its journey towards the horizon, we left the river and returned to the compound, our pace quickening as swarms of mozzies began their evening feast.

Over the next few days our lives took on a slightly groundhog day routine. The team would wake, have breakfast and then hit the bombs early, pausing when it was too hot for a reviving dip in the river, which had become as important to us as it was to the Afghans. It was instantly morale-boosting and a late-evening swim was always the best part of any day.

Every evening before we settled down to cook our rations, Lewis and I would total up the number of devices cleared, carefully noting every detail – from the approximate size and composition of the main charge, the layout of the bomb to the design of the detonator. It was a laborious process but a vital one. Every pressure plate would be photographed and forensically bagged and tagged. Any improvised detonator that hadn't been seen before was also photographed and retained for further examination.

With only a day or so left to go I was just finishing up on a device that I had rendered safe. I'd decided to leave the main charge in situ because there was another device close by and blowing both wouldn't cause me any problems. I'd just recovered the pressure plate and battery pack and had returned to the ICP to brief the team on the next move.

'Right, that's that one done. I'm leaving the main charge in place as I'm gonna blow it in the ground. The second device isn't far away, so I'm going to go back down, reload the needle and move my kit to the other device and work on that one. Everyone happy?'

Everyone nodded. I thought my instructions were pretty clear but Lewis had heard something completely different.

'Kim, where's the needle?' he asked.

'On target, next to my man bag.' I thought nothing of it at the time.

A minute or so had passed before I heard Chappy screaming at the top of his voice: 'Lewis! Stop. Stand still.' I instinctively spun around to see what was going on. Everyone was staring at the area where the majority of the IEDs had been located and cleared. In the middle of the danger area was Lewis, standing by my man bag holding the needle, with a look on his face telling the world he had just realised that he had fucked up big time. He had re-entered the danger area with no metal detector, or a searcher. He had broken all the rules. Lewis had assumed the route was clear because I had been walking up and down it all day – but as we say in the EOD world, 'assumption is the mother of all fuck-ups'. The device was safe but what if there was another bomb close by which hadn't been found? I was furious.

'Chappy, Malley, go and get him.'

The two searchers who had spent the best part of the week swimming and sunbathing went straight into action and made swift work of clearing to Lewis. Lewis returned with his head bowed, preparing for the inevitable bollocking and knowing that after all the months of training he'd made the most basic of mistakes.

'You lunatic, what are you playing at?' I shouted at him half annoyed but at the same time amused that someone could be so stupid.

'Sorry, boss – I thought you said go and reload the needle.'

'Why would . . .?' I stopped myself. There was no point in losing it.

Lewis had some great strengths. He was meticulous and usually completely reliable but so focused that he occasionally forgot the wider tactical picture.

When we got back to the compound I decided to call the team together.

'Good soldiers, soldiers more switched on and more experienced than us lot are being killed or losing their legs every day because they switched off for a moment. This is Afghan. Look what happened to Sam. If we are going to make it to the end of the tour without any more casualties we've all got to keep our focus. From now on when you walk anywhere on operations it's behind a metal detector. A path is only clear when you've personally cleared it. That's the last warning. Lewis, that was ridiculous.'

There were a few moments of silence before near-hysterical laughing erupted and the piss-taking began. Being a soldier is a human endeavour and none of us is perfect. Soldiers train to minimise mistakes and mistakes are a part of Army life but it was the magnitude of Lewis's error that made it so comical. After that incident I declared work over. Everyone was a bit tired and with the temperature nudging 37°C the river looked too inviting.

One of the Danes volunteered to clear a route to the part

of the river that had become our preferred choice for a swim. He led us through a hole in the outer perimeter wall, swinging his metal detector like a pro, while the entire Brimstone 42 team followed on behind walking the fifty metres or so of open ground to the river. While the Brits were wearing shorts with towels over their shoulders, he was dressed in his boxer shorts, helmet, body armour and boots. All I could think about was jumping in the cold water, having a moment to myself and chilling out, when I heard the faithful double tone of the metal detector.

The Danish soldier froze for a second. 'It's probably just some shit in the ground,' he said dismissively. 'I'll just check.'

After a quick check he turned and looked at me, slightly concerned.

'What we got?' I asked.

'A pressure plate,' he responded nervously.

'You are taking the piss,' I said and lowered my head in disbelief.

I looked over at the cool river and my mouth was almost salivating as if I was staring at a delicious steak meal at a fancy London restaurant. Talk about so close but so far.

'Leave it,' I said to the Dane. 'You lot, back in. Lewis, kit.' The rest of the team filed back into the compound, shoulders slumped and looking pissed off.

The process started again. I went chin down to the device and began painting the sand, forcing thoughts of swimming in the river to the back of my mind. I could feel the sun beating down on the back of my head like a hammer while large black flies feasted on the dried salt on my face. But nothing could break my concentration. A pressure plate, another one for the record books and another main charge. I wasn't going to rush. I took my time and cleared the bomb in just over an hour. As the sun dipped below the horizon and another stunning Afghan sunset unfolded in the western sky, the team had one last swim in the river, washing away the dirt and sweat.

By the end of the week we had pulled over forty IEDs out of the ground, more than many other teams had defused in an entire six-month tour, and no doubt there were many more hidden that hadn't been found. But while the operation had been successful for Brimstone 42, I couldn't help worrying about the level of threat the British Army was now facing. If the Taliban could put forty or more devices in the ground to protect a couple of relatively unimportant compounds, what else were they capable of? There were just five British Counter-IED teams in Helmand but the number of bombs being produced by the Taliban was just too many. My team could have easily spent another week in the area pulling bombs out of the ground but what would happen when we left? The chances are the Taliban would return and plant them again and so you couldn't help but wonder what was the point. The war was changing and at that point the British Army was behind the power curve and on the back foot. Simply clearing IEDs was only part of the answer and not the solution on its own. Even as a lowly staff sergeant it was clear to me that NATO needed to go after the bomb-makers, the bomb factories and then hold the cleared ground. But that would require a lot of troops the British Army didn't have or were unwilling to send.

With the operation complete the battlegroup headed back to FOB Price in a journey that took a less agonising and uneventful twelve hours. Fortunately the Ops Room back at Bastion gave us a twenty-four-hour period of grace in Price to get our kit sorted out, before the entire team along with forty-odd pressure plates, a handful of detonators and battery packs were flown back to Bastion.

The mission had been long and tough and the forty-eight hours in the back of an armoured vehicle remains one of the most gruelling experiences of my life. At times we had been pushed to the limits of our physical endurance but at the same time we learned a lot about ourselves, our strengths and weaknesses and those of the Taliban.

9

God Complex

Nothing could touch me – I was bomb-proof. Invincible. Two months into the tour and I had developed a certain swagger. I'd broken all the records for defusing IEDs and was strutting around like I was God's gift to bomb disposal. But I was actually being a right twat. There's a fine line between confidence and arrogance and if I'm honest I crossed that line on a lot of occasions. Bomb disposal is all about confidence. If you don't trust yourself no one else will – it's that simple – and if you don't, you're in the wrong line of work.

Taliban IEDs weren't difficult to defuse providing the basic rules were followed and lady luck was on your side. The real risk came from their number and the lack of build quality. One loose stroke of a brush, an exposed wire caught by a gust of wind, a faulty detonator that just happens to go bang and it could all be over. They were the odds ATOs faced every day so my action plan was to say that's not going to happen to me, I am too good. That attitude or arrogance, if you like, is really something that developed in my character while I was in Afghanistan, although as my Army career progressed I was becoming more self-assured anyway.

By the time I arrived in Afghan of course I was no longer the thick kid with the girl's name. I was the High Threat Bomb Disposal guy, the person who had the answer to everyone's problems, or so I thought. But during one brief encounter with the Taliban I realised my self-confidence had grown into a God complex.

The realisation that things were getting out of hand came while Brimstone 42 was located at Patrol Base (PB) Argyll, a small, dusty, dirty outpost very much on Helmand's front line and home to around sixty British soldiers. It was one of those days when nothing was going on and I was bored rigid. A few of the lads were sweating away inside one of the small buildings watching a recorded football match on TV, while outside beneath the blazing sun other team members had fashioned a makeshift punchbag out of a hessian sack and a piece of old rope and were having a competition to see who could hit the bag the hardest.

It was too hot to drink tea and just as I was wondering whether the day could get any more tedious a young soldier appeared in front of me.

'ATO?' he said, slightly out of breath.

'Yes, that's me.'

'You're needed in the Ops Room,' he said looking slightly concerned that he was giving someone with a more senior rank an order.

'Cheers, pal. At last, something to do.' I grabbed my notepad and headed to the Ops Room.

'Hi, Kim,' said the duty officer, a young lieutenant who had taken to calling all senior NCOs by their first names.

'Hello, boss. What's up?'

'A Mongoose call sign has reported an IED find on a patrol earlier this morning and needs it to be cleared. Your team has been given the task.'

'At last,' I said out loud.

The IED had been found by Mongoose 42A, an Estonian unit based at PB Pimon around fifteen to twenty minutes flying time from Argyll. They had discovered what they believed to be the main charge while clearing a piece of ground known as a vulnerable point (VP). A VP can be any location where troops are channelled into a specific area such as a T-junction, crossroads or a slow-down point of a road. The standard operating procedure when approaching a VP was to stop short, debus from the vehicle and conduct a search of the area.

I was now like a kid with a new toy and almost ran to where the team had been watching their match.

'We've got a job, lads. We can finally get out of this place and get some real work done.'

Within the hour we had been picked up and flown by Chinook across the desert to the vast, desolate base of PB Pimon. Its sheer size, equivalent to a couple of football pitches, made Argyll seem quite small by comparison. Pimon was a strange base and lacked the intimacy of the small PBs and checkpoints. It was austere and isolated and I always preferred leaving to arriving.

There was no arrival party at the HLS. The lads found a quiet corner to relax in for a few minutes while Lee and I went to the Ops Room for a briefing. I bounded in enthusiastically all smiles and offered a hand to a huge, stony-faced captain with piercing 'don't mess with me' eyes. He stood up from his desk and just stared at both of us. The atmosphere in the room was icy cold. There were no welcoming smiles, no gestures of soldierly solidarity. It was as though our presence had insulted them. Through their military exploits in Afghanistan, the Estonians had developed a reputation for being as hard as nails. They might have been the smallest military force in NATO, but they made up for it by being ruthless fighters.

Lee looked at me and raised an eyebrow. Finally the captain shook my hand and welcomed us to his base and explained that an hour earlier one of his soldiers had stepped on an IED while out on patrol and lost both his legs. The soldier, he went on, had earlier been part of the team that had found the IED at the VP. During the clearance operation the Estonians carried out a search of several abandoned compounds that overlooked the VP and could have been used as remote firing points. But with just a few men they were unable to hold the ground and were ordered to clear a route for another of their patrols to pass through the area. After being informed that a UK Brimstone team was being flown into Pimon to clear the device at the VP they reoccupied the nearby compounds, which had been left unmanned for an hour. It was while the compounds were unmanned that the Taliban had returned and placed another IED in one of the previously cleared buildings.

'Those motherfucking Taliban, I will kill them all,' he added.

I was left in absolutely no doubt that he would keep his promise.

Lee and I returned to where the rest of the team were waiting and I briefed them on the situation. 'One of the Estonians has just lost his legs. His brother's also based here as well. The Taliban went back into a cleared building and placed a device and the Estonians didn't clear it again when they re-entered. They're obviously pissed off so don't expect too many smiles. They might be looking for some payback so there's a good chance it could get a bit cheeky.'

A convoy of two armoured vehicles ferried us for about a kilometre along a rutted desert track to the area of the VP. The vehicles halted in a cloud of dust, the rear doors swung open and the unsmiling Estonians indicated for us to get out. The suspected IED was located on a T-junction – a classic Taliban ambush point. Any NATO vehicle moving along the track would be forced to slow down making themselves vulnerable to both pressure-plate and command-initiated IEDs.

As I climbed out of the armoured vehicle I was hit by the desert heat and the ripe smell of sewage bubbling up from a stagnant canal running adjacent to the track. The water was green and opaque. Clouds of mozzies and flies buzzed above what I assumed was human shit floating along. Some of the soldiers gagged, spat and cursed those who had sent them to Afghan. Almost from the moment I stepped from the vehicle I had a bad feeling.

We immediately swung into operation, clearing the area around the vehicles and under Chappy's supervision established an incident control point (ICP) while the Estonians looked on, appearing slightly bewildered. There was too much dead ground in the immediate area where the Taliban could make a covered approach to our position. A group of compounds around eight hundred metres away appeared to be full of murder holes (holes made in compound walls to enable the Taliban to shoot at us) and there weren't enough Estonians to properly secure the area. Despite the warning signs my supercharged self-confidence kicked in and I began formulating my plan.

There was a very tense atmosphere, not just among the Estonians but in the general area. It was simply too quiet and my gut instinct and training told me that was not good. EOD

Operators always have to look for the absence of the normal and the presence of the abnormal. There should have been some activity but there was nothing, no kids, no farmers and no one using the road. What did they know that we didn't?

The search team sat down in the shadow of one of the Estonian vehicles, relaxed but ready to fight if needed. I went through the plan with Lewis and Lee, sorted my kit, and checked that my pistol had a round up the spout in case things kicked off. The joking and banter that usually accompanied lulls in activity was absent and the anxious looks on the faces of my team and the Estonians revealed that everyone expected the day to get nasty. But I felt oddly energised by the situation, almost looking forward to it all going tits up so I could test myself under even greater pressure.

I cleared a path down across the undulating desert track to where the Estonians had found the bomb. Dave was positioned in a dry ditch running alongside the track, ensuring that I was within his ECM cover and he could give me some covering fire if needed.

The Estonians had done a good job in exposing the ground around the bomb and even from twenty metres the main charge, housed in a yellow palm oil container, was visible. I moved forward and carried out a search of the ground around the main charge but as I did so I started getting loads of metal hits on my metal detector – metal had been scattered all around and I couldn't locate the pressure plate. Something definitely wasn't right so I returned to the ICP and discussed the situation with Lewis.

Lewis already looked concerned even before I started speaking. It was hot but he seemed unusually sweaty and tense.

'I dunno what's going on here,' I said. 'I can't find the pressure plate so I'm going to smash it with a ground clearance charge.'

But Lewis remained silent.

'Come on, what's up? Talk to me, Lewis.'

'It doesn't feel right to me, boss,' Lewis said. 'The charge is on a T-junction, exactly where you would expect it to be. The ground is open, there are compounds overlooking our position and the area's deserted.'

Soldiers, especially those in bomb disposal, can be notoriously superstitious and often swayed by gut instinct, which is no bad thing, and Lewis was always one to trust his gut.

'Yeah, but there's a bomb and we ain't leaving until it's done so let's crack on,' I responded nonchalantly.

Back down at the device, I cleared an area close to the palm oil container and was just about to place the clearance charge when the ground erupted in a huge explosion about fifty feet in front of me. The blast covered me in dust and the shockwave made my eyes water. I coughed and spluttered and then shouted 'RPG!' as the explosion rumbled away.

Seconds later what felt like the entire Taliban insurgency opened up with every weapon in their arsenal. Bullets were fizzing past my head and thumping into the ground around my feet, sending up splashes of dust and dirt. Tracer rounds ricocheted off the ground with a loud *peeow* and rocketed skywards. I lay down, trying to make myself as small a target as possible. The crack of bullets flying overhead sounded like an endless firework display and for a few, brief seconds I felt trapped by indecision. Were the Taliban aiming at me or was I caught in the crossfire? The Taliban often opened fire with AK47s on fully automatic and accuracy went straight out of the window, with rounds flying everywhere. RPGs were now exploding in front of me and behind me and I felt as though I was at the centre of a maelstrom, unable to think clearly. It wasn't fear exactly, just a state of confusion, as though I had lost the power to make a decision, almost like suddenly finding yourself in the middle of a violent, crashing storm.

After what seemed like an eternity, the Estonians began returning fire, using every weapon they had, from assault rifles to the heavy machine guns mounted on top of the APCs. The firefight went into overdrive and I was caught in the middle. Then when the realisation hit home that neither side was actually aiming at me, I was almost able to relax a bit and started to think a little more clearly.

The Taliban had moved into the same compounds that had given me some cause for concern when we first arrived. It was impossible to see any enemy, just the muzzle flashes of the weapons firing from murder holes. Rather than feeling fear I was fascinated. I watched the muzzle flashes, almost felt the crack of the bullets passing overhead and then heard the distant noise of the gun being fired.

Rather than make a run back to the safety of the Estonians, I decided to carry on laying the ground clearance charge, forcing the noise of gunfire to the back of my mind. My concentration was again broken by Dave's shouting.

'Kim, Kim – we're in contact!' he shouted as he took cover in the ditch. 'We're being shot at.'

'Well fire back!' I shouted. Dave looked surprised and then began firing his SA80.

I continued excavating only for the Estonian commander back at the ICP to demand that I return, or at least get into cover.

I quickly finished laying the charge, grabbed my metal detector and returned along the cleared path back to the ICP, occasionally ducking or dropping to one knee every time some bullets came my way.

Lee was standing by an Estonian officer, who was attempting to control his troops' rate of fire.

'What's up?' I said, slightly provocatively.

Lee went to answer but was interrupted by the Estonian.

'We're in contact, we need to leave now,' he answered in a thick eastern European accent.

'Shoot back. They're miles away. You've got snipers, right? Then let them solve the problem. I'm here to clear that device. You get on with sorting the enemy out. They're not going to try and outflank us. They are eight hundred metres away across open ground. We've got armoured vehicles. You've got us out here to do a job and we're going to do it. I'm not coming back here tomorrow when we can get it completed today. Accept the fact that we're in some sort of contact and give me some cover.'

Lee gave me a wink and told the search team to start engaging the enemy. It was like letting a greyhound out of the cage as the searchers ran, dived into their defensive positions and began firing at the enemy with small, controlled bursts.

While the Estonian officer began barking orders at his men, Lewis fired the clearance charge. The shockwave swept back up the track towards us, a short, sharp, crisp explosion. A few minutes later, with the battle still raging, I returned to the IED. The blast had ripped open the palm oil container but there was no HME, only shipyard confetti, metal gearing and nails.

'What the fuck,' I said out loud. 'How is that supposed . . .?' It then dawned on me that the IED and subsequent attack was part of an elaborate, well-planned Taliban ambush, and we had walked right into the middle of it. The question for me was: who were the Taliban after? Was it the Estonians or were they targeting ATOs? There had been some intelligence suggesting that the Taliban wanted to kill a bomb disposal operator. After all, we were effectively spoiling their fun.

'It's a come-on!' I shouted across to Dave who was busy taking carefully aimed shots at the compounds. At this point, and I still have no real idea why, I started laughing.

With the situation becoming increasingly hairy, I decided to head back to the ICP picking up Dave on the way.

'You OK?' I said standing over him. 'Shall we head back?'

But by the time we got back to the ICP one Estonian vehicle had already left.

'Where's the other vehicle?' I asked.

'It's gone. You were taking too long,' a large monosyllabic Estonian NCO responded.

'So how's my team meant to get back to the PB?'

'Walk,' was the one word response.

Lee had the situation under control, explaining what had happened with the vehicle and how we were now going to get back. There was not enough room for everyone in the one remaining APC so half the team took cover on the safe side and tried to return fire as it slowly withdrew back to the patrol base.

The vehicle should have been going at walking speed but it got faster and faster and our walk soon turned into a jog. The Taliban, possibly thinking that they had us on the run, appeared energised by our departure and their rate of fire intensified. Rounds pinged and twanged against the vehicle's metal hull, which seemed to cause the driver to increase the speed so that our jog turned into a run.

By the time we arrived at the PB we were on our chin-straps, and too exhausted to give the Estonians shit for their crap driving. Despite their exhaustion the team was buzzing, each with his own war story. They had been in contact and survived. Everyone was smiling and laughing. 'Did you see how close . . . Did you see that RPG . . .'

I slumped against the wheel of one of the vehicles to catch my breath and thought about what had happened over the last couple of hours. It was my first serious contact and the bullets had been landing dangerously close but I wasn't in the least bit scared. There was no rush of adrenalin and certainly no fear – not what I had expected. Was it the God complex kicking in? My actions had almost been reckless. Had I been injured or killed other soldiers would have had to put their lives at risk to extract me. But what was I supposed to do? Was it better to be fearless or scared? What would keep me alive longer? I wasn't sure. But there had been barely time to think.

Later that evening, we were back in PB Argyll and at what was the start of a sustained period of intense activity – one job after another, not really knowing where we were going or who we were working for. The workload had gone through the roof and days, sometimes weeks, merged into one continuous deployment, where our only rest was when we lay down on our beds. While the IED teams were being worked into the ground, the infantry were getting hit hard, sometimes losing two or three soldiers in complex IED attacks. But throughout that busy period I never doubted that I would survive, I didn't even think I was going to get injured and while morale in Brimstone 42 was high, in some units we visited it was rock bottom, usually because they had just lost someone. IEDs had now completely reshaped the way the war was fought. A year earlier perhaps 5, maybe 10 per cent of all attacks were IEDs; now it was up to 50, and higher in some areas, and the victims weren't just soldiers but also civilians – men, women and worst of all children.

Those who survived were often damaged, both mentally

and sometimes physically by what they had witnessed. Seeing someone you know turned into red mist in front of your eyes literally seconds after you'd just been in conversation with them was a terrible, traumatic experience often made even worse by being told to pick the bits up that were left and put them into a bin bag so that something could be sent home.

At the same time as what was happening in Afghan, politicians back in the UK were using the Army as a political football. Labour claimed we had enough of everything while the Tories said they would give us more of everything if they were in power – which we of course knew was a crock of shit. As a soldier you just have to learn to suck it up. There's no point in moaning or thinking you're hard done by; after all, we're all volunteers.

Over the next few weeks my God complex intensified. I was drawn to danger like a drug. The most enjoyable jobs were the most dangerous. After I'd found one bomb, I'd go searching for another, then another, always looking for the next challenge.

But that all changed a few weeks later when my team became embedded with a British unit located in the district of Nad e'Ali. The main British base sat in the centre of the district and was known as FOB Shawqat and was the site of what was rumoured to be a nineteenth-century fort first occupied during the period known as the Great Game, when Britain fought a sort of covert war against the Russians for control of Afghanistan. It served as a kind of hub base around which were a series of satellite patrol bases that supposedly helped to secure the area. The small, less well-protected PBs needed to be resupplied with food, water, mail, ammunition and fresh soldiers by armoured convoys at least a couple of times a week. The convoys used roads and tracks largely over-watched by either NATO troops or our Afghan allies and so were regarded as 'secure' in that it was unlikely the Taliban would attempt to plant a device under the eyes of enemy troops. But there were also large sections of roads that were insecure and these had to be cleared by ground troops every time they were used by a resupply convoy. The result was that a simple forty-five-minute drive between FOB Shawqat and a satellite PB would often take several hours.

During one early morning operation, Brimstone 42 was tasked with providing EOD support for a resupply mission to a small base called checkpoint Hagi Lim. The team was split between two Mastiff armoured vehicles positioned at the back of a convoy, ready to move forward to deal with any potential IEDs. The convoy left Shawqat in the predawn dark and I was asleep before our vehicle was a hundred metres from the gates. The Mastiffs are a major improvement on the ageing Bulldog armoured vehicles, which were largely regarded as deathtraps by the troops. Mastiffs were wheeled and had a V-shaped hull that helped deflect an IED blast and thereby reduced the chances of death and injury to those travelling inside.

Earlier that day another Mastiff vehicle had struck an IED on a so-called 'secured route'. No one was injured even though the vehicle was a write-off but the fact that the Taliban could plant a device on a secured route had put everyone on edge. It was simply impossible to search every inch of every road – to do so would mean that resupply operations would take days. So only unsecured areas, such as a bend in a road that couldn't be overseen or vulnerable points (VPs), were searched. The searching of insecure roads, tracks or VPs was known as Operation Barma – a technique designed by expert search engineers to ensure the entire area is cleared using the trusted metal detector.

An hour or so into the resupply mission the troops in some of the forward vehicles debussed to conduct another Operation Barma. The terrain was not demanding, classic Helmand Green Zone, with a canal running along one side of the road and a maize field on the other, but there was a small bridge that needed to be crossed and hence was identified as a vulnerable point and so had to be cleared.

The soldiers moved into their formation and began searching. There were a few new guys on the operation who had been flown in as battle-casualty replacements and the resupply operation was the first time they had been out on the ground. The replacements were very young, just eighteen, fresh-faced and scared shitless. Some almost had to be coaxed out of the vehicle and ordered to take part in the clearance. Every soldier had to be able to execute confidently an Operation Barma and so the commander presumably thought no time like the present.

The search progressed slowly. So slowly in fact that I had woken up and fallen back asleep, along with most of the rest of my team. But things got interesting when the lead searcher saw a flash of light cross in front of his path as he moved along the track, assuming at first that it was the silvery back of a lizard or some other reptile dashing into the undergrowth. He raised a fist in the air, the universal military sign to stop, dropped to one knee and spotted a shiny piece of metal. He moved closer for a better look when the ground in front of him moved, almost lifted up, not by much but enough for him to notice. It was a command-pull IED, which is initiated by the terrorist pulling a piece of string attached to the firing switch.

He didn't know why but the bomb hadn't detonated. But it was clear that at the end of the piece of string leading away through the maize field was a Taliban bomber trying to kill British soldiers. The bomber had tugged the string so hard the switch had been pulled out of the ground. It was an unbelievable stroke of luck. The switch that was meant to allow the current to flow was composed of two metal washers attached to two pieces of wire and a gentle pull on the string should have brought the washers together. The bomb would have caused carnage had it detonated. Anyone not killed instantly would have been blasted into the canal, and given all the kit they were carrying, would have probably drowned.

Chappy got his team sorted and began his brief: 'We are going to do a horseshoe isolation because we're not going to be able to cross the canal. You will be looking for some kind of string or wire, probably going off somewhere into one of the compounds beyond the maize field, at least that's where I'd be if I was them. The threat is coming from our left, so we don't have to worry about the right flank. The infantry will be providing us with cover, using small arms and the armoured vehicles. If they see any movement in those compounds they'll fucking smash them. Questions?' Everyone seemed happy, although a little tense.

Chappy turned to me. 'Kim, my team will lead – I'll put Malley up front. He can find anything. My concern is who's on the end of the command wire and where?'

He was right to be concerned – his men would be focusing on the ground and their spatial awareness would be severely curtailed. So they would be dependent on the professionalism of others for their safety.

The searchers set off and headed into the maize field, which was like entering a waist-high jungle. The crop was still damp with morning dew and the cloying soil stuck to the soldiers' boots, making progress cumbersome. Chappy pushed up to 150 metres from the compounds before turning ninety degrees right. He continued searching for another 50 metres and then he found the kite string. It was either a brilliant piece of planning or amazing luck.

He beckoned me forward. 'Kim, what do you reckon? Command wire?'

I made a quick assessment. 'Yep, definitely. Well done. Good find.'

The rest of the team moved back to approximately 30 metres beyond the device and hopefully out of the immediate danger zone. I pulled a few of the maize stems out of the ground to create a working area, dropped down flat onto my stomach and got to work. The wet earth felt cold but not uncomfortable beneath my chest as I examined the kite string, which needed to be cut, and like most things in the EOD world, any form of cutting is best done remotely.

I always carried with me a specialist firing device, about the size of a hip flask, containing a detonator and a length of shock tube. I laid the det next to the string and then laid out the shock tube. At the other end of the shock tube was a striker, like a mouse trap, which when fired would light the shock tube and cause the detonator to explode and cut the string. It was all done in a matter of minutes and with the device now isolated there was no way the Taliban were going to be able to detonate the bomb.

With the search successfully completed, Chappy made his way back to the road and established the ICP behind the lead Mastiff while under the watchful gaze of the infantry, who had their weapons directed towards the compounds. I was conscious of the time the clearance was taking. The longer the convoy was stationary the more of a target it became. In many ways the Taliban were opportunists who had an almost irresistible desire to attack – it was almost comical in its predictability. Sit anywhere long enough and they would have a go.

Dave and I inched our way forward to the location of the switch discovered earlier. I suddenly saw the two metal washers sticking out of the ground, almost touching each other. 'Jesus – I didn't think they were that close.' A breath of wind or a heavy footstep could have caused them to move and detonate the device. I immediately shouted 'Stop!' Although the string had been cut, the device was still active and primed. This was not a scenario I had practised in training but rather than be deterred or even scared I felt as though this was the challenge I had been looking for. Stepping as softly as possible, I moved back along the track and searched a path to an area where Dave and the infantry escort could get into cover.

'Wait here and don't move,' I said before disappearing back towards the bomb. I inched my way around the switch, taking several pictures of the device in situ, primarily for my report but also if anything was to go wrong at this point and I got wasted there would be some sort of record of what I was dealing with when I was killed.

I very carefully placed the needle next to one of the wires while at the same time chuckling to myself on how ridiculously dangerous the situation had become. The kite string had somehow become caught between the two washers, which had prevented the bomb from exploding. It was the equivalent of a hand grenade with the pin nine-tenths hanging out and was possibly the most dangerous situation anyone in the EOD world could ever encounter.

Despite the risks, I was never scared, my hands didn't shake and I felt no surge of adrenalin, something that always happened during the early part of the tour, and at one point I was actually laughing at the sheer danger I was facing. It did occur to me that this wasn't the normal response but I decided not to dwell on my behaviour. I searched my way out of the target area and back to the ICP making sure that the firing cable did not get tangled. Lewis fired the needle and after I gathered my equipment I made my way back to the device.

I taped the exposed ends of the cut wires and began sweeping the dirt away with my paintbrush. After a few minutes the yellow palm oil container that contained around 20kg of HME was exposed. It was a massive bomb, designed to kill and not maim. The main charge was destroyed in situ and twenty minutes later the convoy was back on the move. As the APC bounced along the track I noticed my team all staring at me, serious and concerned.

'What?' I said to Dave and the others.

'You were laughing, boss,' Dave said, looking very worried.

'What? What are you on about?'

'You were laughing when you were taking a picture of the device. That's not right. That thing could have gone off at any time and you were laughing. Do you really think that's the right response? What we do is dangerous. It will always be dangerous and it will never, ever be funny.'

'Come on, lighten up. You have to admit that was funny. I mean what else are you supposed to do when you come face to face with something like that?'

But it wasn't funny to them. I knew I shouldn't be laughing but there was nothing I could do. If that was my subconscious response to the stress then I was happy to live with it.

The engine noise soon killed off the conversation but the mood didn't lighten. I closed my eyes and tried to relax and attempted to convince myself that it was sometimes healthy to laugh in the face of extreme danger.

Ten minutes later we arrived at the checkpoint only to be

greeted by a Scottish sergeant major gobbing off about how late we were. His comments were aimed at us and I mumbled the words 'wanker' as the team gathered around. A huge roar of laughter erupted and the sergeant major looked furious but said nothing.

The following morning we were lifted out of FOB Shawqat and took an uneventful flight back to Bastion. I made my way to the Ops Room and walked straight into Jim, the Task Force SAT.

He greeted me with a handshake and asked how the job went.

'You know, same shit, different day. Just another three pressure plates and an odd command-pull that the Taliban couldn't even bury properly, nothing really.'

Jim's demeanour changed as the clumsy words fell from my mouth. He grabbed me by the arm and led me out of the Ops Room.

'Oi, dickhead, stop being an arse.' His face was so close to mine I could smell the coffee on his breath. 'Every one of those bombs can kill you. Respect them or I'll pull you off the ground. If you become a danger to yourself, you'll be a danger to the team. Now wise up.'

I wandered back to my tent with Jim's words ringing in my ears. He was right and I didn't blame him for his reaction. I hadn't lost the plot, I'd just grown used to living with fear. I'd become immune and in Afghan fear kept you alive. 'God complex?' I said to myself as I lay down on my bed. 'Don't be a twat. You're just a lucky arsehole at the moment.'

10

Where the Fuck's the Bomb?

It should have been just an ordinary Monday. One of the many ordinary, routine, dull days on a six-month journey that eventually becomes blurred by time and forgotten. Instead Monday 20 July 2009 has been seared into my consciousness.

Brimstone 42 had been based in FOB Price for a week or so conducting routine bomb disposal missions. Much of the previous evening had been spent preparing for a move to FOB Keenan, another of our preferred bases, for another Counter-IED task that also should have been routine. A local Afghan had reported the presence of a home-made bomb in a field close to Keenan and Brimstone 42 was being sent to clear it. The Afghan, who we were told was a farmer, was willing to identify the device's location, but also wanted to be paid.

So-called 'walk ins' were relatively rare in Helmand and something that was actively encouraged. The local population often knew where the IEDs had been placed but were usually too scared to report them to NATO forces for fear of punishment by the Taliban. So when an IED was reported by a member of the local population the EOD Task Force would pull out all the stops to get a team to the location as soon as possible. But 'walk in' IED finds also needed to be treated with caution because a Counter-IED team could find itself walking into a well-planned ambush.

The team was ferried to Keenan courtesy of an RAF Chinook, landing around 0800 hrs, still in time for a quick second breakfast. Waiting for us on the edge of the landing area was Major Sam Plant, the officer commanding C Squadron Light Dragoons, an armoured recce unit equipped with Scimitar light tanks. Major Plant was the base commander and the archetypal cavalry officer. Very laid-back, efficient and public-school educated. He had officer-style big hair, occasionally wore glasses and was always very welcoming and helpful. My team spent so long at Keenan that he almost regarded us as his own IED detachment but this time no smile greeted our arrival.

'Morning, Staff,' he said sombrely. 'You need to call your Ops Room urgently.'

My first thoughts were that I had fucked up. Had I produced a shit report, had someone complained about a job – worst of all, had my team missed a bomb?

'This is Staff Sergeant Hughes. I've been told to check in.'

'Wait one,' said a voice at the other end.

'Staff, this is Major Eldon Millar.' He sounded serious but not angry. Major Millar was the officer commanding the EOD Task Force. I waited for the bollocking coming my way.

'. . . I've got some bad news,' the phone crackled and his voice faded briefly. He said something about Captain Dan Shepherd.

'Sorry, sir, I lost you for a second. It sounded like you said Captain Dan Shepherd. Can you repeat that?'

'I'm sorry, Kim. Dan died this morning while working on a device in Nad e'Ali. He was killed instantly. I wanted you to know as soon as possible. I know you spent a lot of time together on operations recently.'

Suddenly my world contracted. I didn't know what to say or how to respond. Dan was very relaxed but professional and had a really great relationship with his team. He was only twenty-eight, just married, with a whole life ahead of him. I had known him for a couple of years and was his DS on the Joint Service IEDD course. But we had grown closer in Afghan after we worked together on an operation to clear a deserted bazaar in a small village in the Nad e'Ali area during Operation Panchai Palang. It meant little to him that he was an officer and I was an SNCO; there was mutual respect, a common bond and a genuine friendship. I had only spoken to him a few weeks ago and now he was dead and it didn't seem possible.

'OK, sir, can I ring you back? I just need five minutes,' was all I could think of to say.

'Yes, sure,' replied Major Millar, 'but be prepared, you will be moving from your location to clear the area where Dan was killed.'

I put down the phone, walked out of the Ops Room and headed over to a corner of the HLS. It was almost like a dream, one of those occasions in life when you ask yourself 'Did that just happen?'

Over on the opposite side of the square the rest of my team were relaxing in the sun, laughing and joking and smoking cigarettes.

I dropped onto my haunches and held my face in my hands. A tear ran down my cheek. I wanted to scream and shout at the top of my voice. Dan was gone. A good bloke, a good

ATO, a loving husband, the perfect son and a good mate now gone. For what?

Lee the RESA wandered over. 'What's up, mate?'

'Dan Shepherd was killed this morning,' I said hardly believing my own words.

'Shit.' Lee's face dropped. 'What happened . . .?' but his sentence trailed away. 'I'll tell the lads.'

'No, it's OK, mate. I'll do it,' I said, 'just give me a minute.'

By now the team sensed something was wrong and I saw no point in delaying the inevitable.

'Lads, I've got some really bad news. Captain Dan Shepherd was killed this morning in Nad e'Ali. I know you all knew him and liked him. Take a few minutes but be aware we've still got a job to do here and at some stage, either today or early tomorrow, we'll be flying into Shawqat to clear the area where Dan was killed.'

Even when I said it – Dan was dead – it didn't seem real.

I walked away from the team and was met by the OC. 'Everything OK, Staff?' he asked.

'No, sir. We've just lost one of our operators.' He could see that I was upset, broken almost.

'I'm so sorry to hear that. I sensed something was wrong when the call came in from Bastion. Look, forget about this task here for the time being. There's no rush and besides your Ops Room are telling us that you're on the next helicopter out of here to Shawqat for a more urgent task.'

'It's OK, sir. I think I'll need to keep the lads busy for the rest of the day.'

After another brief chat with the Bastion Ops Room, the plan was confirmed. We would be leaving first thing in the morning for Shawqat. I would be working with the operations warrant officer to carry out a post-explosion investigation and to make sure what was left of Dan and his kit were removed from the battlefield. I couldn't think of a worse job but at the same time I wanted to do it.

I called the guys together again. 'We are staying here to complete this task then flying out tomorrow to clear the area where Dan was killed. Everyone needs to be focused. If we don't do this someone else will so let's get it done. We're going to pull these bombs out of the ground or we're going to blow them in situ. They're in the middle of a farmer's field but if he doesn't like it he can fuck off.'

I was angry and not in the mood for shit from anyone. The team silently got their kit ready.

A platoon of soldiers from the Light Dragoons were ready and wanted to get on with the job. They were accompanied by a small detachment from the Afghan National Army, who were co-located at Keenan, an interpreter, known as a Terp, and the Afghan who had reported the IED. He was dressed in an ANA uniform in the hope that any Taliban watching us wouldn't be able to identify him. He bore the classic features of the Pashtun warrior. He was tall, around six foot, with brown leathery skin, a hook nose, dark-brown, serious eyes and bearded. He could have been anywhere between thirty and sixty years of age. He said little and eyed us suspiciously – part of me wondered whether we were being lured into a trap. I wasn't in the mood to be messed around.

By 9.30 a.m. the temperature was at an almost unbearable 37°C. As the patrol left the compound and began snaking its way through the fields towards the target there were so many questions. What had Dan being doing? Had he made a mistake? Was the device booby-trapped? I thought about his family and his wife, whom he adored and how right at that moment would be waking up to that dreadful knock on the door and nothing would ever be the same again. I thought of my own son and how he would cope if I was the next ATO to die. Up until that point our tour had been relatively easy. After the incident with Sam we had pulled together and grown stronger. Sam was in hospital back in the UK. He was out of danger and making steady progress on what was going to be a long road to recovery. Harry had managed to put the incident behind him and was back to his old self. The operations had come thick and fast but we had coped and all grown to relish the challenge. But Dan's death hit us all like a low punch, leaving everyone on their knees.

The countryside surrounding Keenan was stunning, with wonderful contrast between the desert and cultivated fields of green young crops, criss-crossed with an elaborate array of irrigation ditches that had been feeding the soil for centuries. The sky was a perfect, cloudless, deep blue. It was a scene of simple rural beauty but it meant nothing to me and only seemed to fuel a deep anger burning away in the pit of my stomach.

After about twenty minutes of moving randomly across fields, the patrol arrived at the location of the suspected IED, an undulating field of about an acre in size where the green shoots of a crop, possibly wheat, were forcing their way through the sun-baked soil. A few hidden birds sang away out of sight, while high above a pair of combat jets took ownership of the sky ready to strike on demand.

'So where's the device?' I said to the Terp, a young eager-to-please Afghan, with bright eyes and a ready smile. The farmer was pointing to the middle of the field and before the Terp could relay his answer, I interrupted: 'That's no good to me. I need an exact location, otherwise I'm going to be wandering around that field like a twat.'

The man just carried on pointing into a general area.

'Tell him to go and point out where it is otherwise he doesn't get paid.'

He slowly stroked at his beard but his expression remained inscrutable – he wasn't giving away any clues. The thought that we might be walking into a trap was never far from my mind. The field had been ploughed some weeks earlier and the broken soil had hardened like lumps of concrete. If there was an IED in there, finding it was going to be a real balls-ache.

Lee and Chappy got the rest of the team to clear a working area, the Light Dragoons established a protective cordon while Dave and I moved to the edge of the field. Dave took up a position beneath the shade of a tree in full bloom and I began the search, aiming for the approximate location given by the Afghan.

I searched for more than an hour up and down, backwards and forwards, almost in lanes and found nothing. I could have sent the search team in but after what had just happened to Dan I felt an overpowering need to keep them safe. Every time the Terp asked the Afghan farmer to be more specific he just waved his finger contemptuously in the area I was standing in.

With time passing quickly, Lewis and I decided a ground clearance charge might prove successful in either uncovering the bomb or causing it to initiate. He quickly got to work attaching small 50g pieces of plastic explosive along a length of garden bamboo cane 1.5 metres in length. The explosive was linked together by det-cord with a detonator attached at one end, which in turn was attached to a firing cable.

I returned to the field with the bamboo cane and laid it on the area to be cleared before withdrawing to where Lewis was waiting. Lewis flicked the switch and the charge worked like a dream. The sound of the explosion echoed around the surrounding countryside and thick, grey smoke and dust billowed into the sky.

Back at the blast site there was nothing to indicate the presence of an IED and I was just about to give up when I spotted a piece of black plastic next to my boot. It was a low-metal pressure plate that I hadn't been able to detect with the metal detector. At that stage of the war the Taliban were using two types of pressure plate, low- and high-metal. The metal content in the low-metal pressure plate had been reduced to the bare minimum, making them more difficult to detect. I brushed some of the mud and dust away with my hand exposing a three-litre palm oil container filled with what I immediately recognised as an ammonium nitrate and aluminium mix known as ANAL – home-made explosive and a one-time favourite of the IRA. I was three inches away from being the second bomb disposal operator to be killed in twenty-four hours. I stood there frozen with disbelief, wondering whether I'd made a mistake or whether I'd been too preoccupied with Dan's death. A very bad day had just got a lot worse.

Rather than mess about trying to disarm and extract it I decided to blow it in situ. The sound of the ground clearance charge would have acted like a clarion call to all the local Taliban and besides I wanted to get over to Nad e'Ali. After the device was destroyed the Afghan, who appeared to age visibly the longer we spent in the sun, took the patrol to another area a few fields away where he claimed there was a second IED. Again he stopped short of the actual location and speaking through the Terp said that the IED was along a sloping path channelled between two trees, which screamed 'walk this way'. As far as I was concerned it was the perfect ambush point. So how did he know where the bomb had been buried? I asked. But he simply shrugged and said, 'Others had told him.' I wasn't happy trying to search with my metal detector downhill towards the location of the device because the ground was wet from being irrigated, and a low-metal plate IED could easily be missed. Again another ground clearance charge was used – this time with slightly less explosive.

But when Lewis fired the charge there was an almighty explosion and the trees just disappeared. A 20kg main charge had detonated which produced a huge crater and would definitely have killed anyone who stepped on it. The explosion was so powerful that the Counter-IED team and half of the Light Dragoons were covered in dust. A few laughs broke out; the funereal atmosphere seemed to be lifting. We cleared another two devices that day before eventually heading back to Keenan hot and tired but also relieved that the hours had been filled with useful work. I'd hoped to find more. I wanted to be kept busy. The last thing I wanted was the team sitting around reflecting on what had happened to Dan.

As we walked through the gate, Major Plant greeted us and congratulated the team on a job well done. But none of us were really in the mood for small talk.

'Thanks, sir. We'd better get on with our admin and I have a couple of reports to write.'

Usually post-op admin is a pain in the arse but that day everyone stayed busy. While I wrote up my reports Lewis sorted out his kit, replenished his explosive and dets. He automatically did the same with my kit. He could see I wanted to be left alone. Dave recharged his batteries and ensured all of his ECM equipment was in good working order as did the searchers, while the RESA wrote up his search log in conjunction with the search commander.

With the report almost complete, Lewis and I began writing down the details of the bits of devices recovered. The dimensions of the pressure plates, colour and length, if there were any wires and what kind of tape was used were all carefully logged.

Later that evening when our work was done, Lewis made a quick brew, which was drunk in silence, both of us no doubt thinking about Dan and how on any other day it could have been one of us.

Dave appeared with a towel under his arm and said, 'We need to go for a swim and I know where. Come on – any idiot can be miserable.' We followed him through a maze of tents until he reached a huge tank filled with water where the rest of the team were laughing and joking.

It wasn't long before my thoughts again turned to Dan – difficult questions surfaced. Had his body been recovered? Was there anything left to recover? Sleep didn't come easily that night and when I did doze I dreamed of death. I woke at 5 a.m. unable to sleep any longer. In a few hours' time I would be confronted with the evidence of Dan's last moments on earth and I was dreading it.

11

Losing a Mate

An early flight on an empty Chinook took us into FOB Shawqat, the main British base in the district of Nad e'Ali. The usual banter that filled those idle, empty minutes was absent. No one smiled. Dan was dead. And we were going to try to find out what killed him. Nothing good would come from this day and we all knew it.

As we dragged our kit from the Chinook I was met by the Operations Warrant Officer (OPSWO) from Bastion and Major Danny Rae, who was OC of Weapons Intelligence Section (WIS, pronounced WIZ), a mixed unit of Royal Military Police, Intelligence Corps and Ammunition Technicians or ATOs, whose role, among other things, was to conduct post-blast investigations. The WIS unit would attempt to find out what happened through interviews with eye-witnesses and examining the evidence. It was often an unpleasant, difficult job.

Stilted pleasantries were exchanged but there was no real attempt at small talk. Then out of the blue the Operations

Warrant Officer announced, 'Right, I'm going to be running this operation.'

I gave him a look that said: 'What are you on about?'

'Yeah, I'm going to be using your team. You won't be doing this task.'

'You what?'

The OPSWO continued but I wasn't really listening. I had spent the previous evening wondering how I was going to feel being confronted by the scene of Dan's death. Now he was telling me I wasn't needed and he was taking over my team.

'You know what, that's not happening. If you want to use my team then I'm going to be there as well. You don't know them. They don't know you. If you have to be there then we'll do it together.'

The OPSWO immediately sensed my anger and despite outranking me rightly assumed that this was a battle he wasn't going to win.

'Yeah, sure, Kim, whatever you want. I just thought you might want to sit this one out.'

Chappy, who'd been listening to the conversation, was almost as angry as me and said, 'Is he for real?'

'Look, Chappy. It is what it is. We're just going to have to deal with it. We need to really focus on the task, no distractions, and do what's best for Dan.'

We had barely been in Shawqat ten minutes and already emotions were running high. Fortunately a runner from the Ops Room appeared and announced that everyone taking part in the recovery operation was immediately required to attend a briefing.

The Shawqat Ops Room was a huge wooden-framed room, reinforced with steel girders and designed to withstand a direct hit from either a mortar or rocket. Inside, the air was hot and stale. Clerks and officers tapped away on computers as we gathered around a large planning table covered with maps and aerial photographs of the surrounding area. My eyes were immediately drawn to a large red pin placed on a track about three kilometres south of the FOB. The location where Dan was killed. A surge of anger rose up inside me. 'He had a name,' I wanted to shout. 'Why don't you use his name instead of a red pin?' I was still raw, still hurting and nothing bad was meant by the red pin. Whenever there was a contact IED a red pin was always used to denote the location – it was standard practice.

The plan involved a small convoy of Mastiffs transporting the Counter-IED and WIS teams to a rendezvous point 700 metres from where Dan had been killed. A platoon of Welsh Guardsmen would also be on the ground to provide some added security. The blast site would be cleared of any further IED threats and then the WIS commander and his evidence team would begin their work, scouring the area for every shred of evidence.

With the briefing over, I headed out into the daylight where my team was waiting, eager to get on with the job.

'Dan's IEDD team is still on the ground. They've been there for twenty-four hours securing the scene. Just be aware that they've had a shit time.'

Almost as soon as I'd finished the brief the OPSWO appeared.

'Kim – everything OK?'

'All fine with me.' My response was a bit childish and I regretted it immediately.

'I mean with us, you and me.'

'Look, mate. Dan was a mate of mine. My team knew him and worked with him. As shit as this job is they want to do it and they want me leading them. With all due respect, they don't want you. So let's just get on with it.'

The OPSWO nodded, the penny had finally dropped.

As we made our way over to where the Mastiffs were waiting, we walked past a makeshift gym where some members of the Welsh Guards were relaxing, lifting weights, listening to music, laughing and joking. They weren't being disrespectful; they might not even have known that Dan had been killed. But it served as a reminder of how we had all grown used to coping with death. If you didn't know the person who had been killed, you barely took any notice. The death of a British or NATO soldier was a daily occurrence and none of us had the emotional capacity to mourn them all. You had to pick whom you shed tears for if you hoped to keep your shit together.

The convoy of Mastiffs slowly trundled out of the camp, along an arrow-straight dusty track and into the Green Zone. The journey to the drop-off point took about twenty minutes and by the time we arrived it was almost 10.00 a.m. and burning hot. The search team swung into action conducting one isolation after another, effectively creating a cleared box into which the Mastiffs moved, waited and moved on again. The whole process was repeated until the searchers made contact with Dan's team who had already cleared and established an ICP.

Once out of the vehicle, I quickly orientated myself with the ground. A field full of maize ran along one side of the track while on the other was a series of orchards fed by an irrigation ditch which hand-railed the left side of the track. Water was bubbling along irrigation ditches, birds sang in the trees and the sky was a clear, beautiful blue. But less than a hundred metres down the track was where Dan had taken his last breath.

Soldiers with blank faces and sad, tired eyes lined the track keeping guard as they had done for more than twenty-four hours. They looked at me almost suspiciously as we retraced Dan's steps towards the location where he was killed.

One of the last soldiers to see Dan alive was slumped against a wall. He'd been awake throughout the night, refusing to sleep, determined to keep the area secure. The soldier, a corporal, had been providing top cover in an armoured vehicle and had been watching Dan right up until the point he was killed.

I dropped down to one knee, next to where he was resting, eyes closed, and gently asked if I could have a chat for a couple of seconds. He went to stand but I told him to remain seated. He explained that he had been watching Dan through his antique Army-issue binoculars.

'It was a basic no-dramas pressure plate IED,' he said. 'Dan was lying down on his stomach working on the IED. Everything seemed to be going OK. He was fully in control of the situation. He stood up to go and get his hook and line and then returned to the IED and it looked as though he was trying to attach his line to something.'

This all made sense. Dan was doing this so that he could pull something out of the ground from a safe distance.

'As he was doing this there was a huge explosion. When the dust cleared he was gone.'

Based on the information provided by the corporal it seemed to me that Dan was carrying out some sort of manual action on the device when something went terribly wrong; what that was I had no real idea.

Following the explosion, Dan's search team had gone down to where Dan had been working, hoping that he might have escaped serious injury. But his body had taken the full brunt of the blast. His death was instantaneous. The search team had little option but to gather up Dan's remains in what were effectively bin bags. No wonder they all looked traumatised.

The next stage was to isolate the target area, which was conducted by myself, the search team, the OPSWO and the WIS major following on. Malley led, moving out to the right-hand side of the target and around eighty metres beyond the point of the blast.

Pieces of Dan's shredded uniform were scattered across the ground along with pieces of mangled EOD equipment. His combat helmet lay on its side, dented and almost cracked in half. I wanted to pick it up, partly out of respect but also wanting to keep it safe, but it needed to be photographed in situ by the WIS team along with everything else. Dark-brown patches of dried blood stained the area around the scorched black crater. His body armour had also been torn to pieces and I felt my stomach turn as I imagined Dan's last seconds.

Any pieces of foreign debris that could possibly be linked to the bomb were collected for further analysis. But there was little of anything that could provide real intelligence. Almost nothing was left of the IED apart from small pieces of yellow melted plastic, the remnants of the container.

The more we searched, the closer we came to the conclusion that Dan had just been a victim of bad luck. The device was probably faulty in some way, possibly with a loose wire that caused the bomb to detonate when Dan was attempting to attach his line. It was possible the device was booby-trapped but there was no evidence to suggest that was the case. From the size of the crater, 1.5 metres in diameter, it was estimated that the main charge was around 20kg – Dan wouldn't have felt a thing.

As the day progressed, the blast area became increasingly busy with evidence collectors taking pictures of the scene and the surroundings to help with the final report, while other members of the WIS team began collecting Dan's equipment. A narrow dusty track, almost like an alleyway bordered on one side by some trees, ran close to the site of the explosion and hanging in one of the branches was a piece of Dan's uniform.

'Bits of clothing up there. All going to have to come down,' I said to one of the RMP corporals.

But he shook his head dismissively. 'Nah, we're not going to bother with that. Not important – won't give us anything.'

'You will get it,' I snapped. 'Were you listening to the brief? Everything, every little thing comes back. Nothing gets left behind.'

The RMP soldier looked sheepish and said nothing.

'Fuck it. I'll get it.' I jumped onto a wall and shinned up the tree trunk with my rifle slung across my back. The piece of uniform was darkened by dried blood and had stuck to the branch in the baking heat.

'Bag it. Remember, we leave nothing behind,' I said sternly while handing it to the corporal.

'OK. Sorry, Staff.'

I had expected to see some of Dan's equipment, his metal detector, an EOD weapon, a patch from his uniform, and if I'm honest more of Dan – but there was nothing. The main charge must have been massive. The only large piece of Dan's equipment left was the helmet.

Once everything had been bagged and the exploitation of the area complete, everyone involved in the operation, including Dan's team, moved south of the blast area and back to where the Mastiffs were waiting. The OPSWO departed so that he could get back to Bastion and begin preparing the report. Before he left we shook hands and thanked each other and both agreed that it had been one shit day.

It was now dark and as we waited for the order to move back to Shawqat it dawned on me that back in the UK everyone in British Army bomb disposal would want to know what had happened. By now they would know that Dan was dead but the questions would soon become rumours and in our world that was best avoided at all costs.

I pushed open one of the heavy armoured roof hatches and stood up, the top half of my body exposed to the night air. The Milky Way was like a spray of glitter across the dark, inky-black sky. It was beautiful, almost breathtaking and it felt good to be alive. For a few brief seconds, I gazed in awe at the sky above, forgetting briefly about the day, before pressing the speed dial on my satphone. A few seconds later and 3,600 miles away at the Felix Centre, Lee Ridgway answered.

'Hi, mate, it's me,' I said, my voice heavy and lacking any real emotion.

'Kim, how are you?'

'Pretty grim, mate. You must have heard Dan's died.'

'Yeah, but that's all we know.'

'Me and the OPSWO have just done the post-blast where he was killed. I can't speak for long but I don't think Dan made a mistake. It seems to have just been bad luck.'

I was probably breaking all the rules but Lee was teaching the next set of ATOs who were due to be heading out as the next relief in place – they needed to know what had happened. Quite rightly they would be asking searching questions, with the main one being whether they are being trained correctly.

'Listen, mate, I'm going to have to go, things to do . . .' and I ended the conversation abruptly, not really knowing what to say. Within a few minutes the Mastiffs were on the move back to the FOB. It was difficult to leave the place where Dan had died. It almost felt like a betrayal. I wanted to stay and guard the area because we knew the Taliban would be back to examine their handiwork and congratulate each other on a job well done.

By midnight that evening we had been choppered back to FOB Price. I climbed into bed in a daze, not knowing what to think, about Dan, the shit day, tomorrow, the day after. I closed my eyes and waited – one thing that was certain, death would visit my dreams.

Dan was the 187th British soldier to die in Afghanistan. Before the British Army left a further 267 would be killed in action.

12

Blown Up

The last thing I remembered was listening to John Legend through my iPod headphones. The 26th of July had been a long and unusually hot day. The heat had sapped my strength and I was about as knackered as I could remember. The armoured vehicle was crammed full of dirty, sweat-soaked soldiers, but I cared not. I closed my ears and relaxed. Thoughts of cold beers and peaceful days – I was in my time.

The team had been based at Keenan for a few days, dealing with IEDs as and when they were found by the troops running the patrol base. It was bread and butter work, just what was needed to keep everyone ticking over after a period of intense activity.

Mornings were spent sorting out equipment and making sure reports were up to date – a process loosely referred to in the Army as 'admin'. Lunch beckoned, an event that should never be missed by anyone either based in or passing through Keenan. The food was always fresh and cooked by chefs who took a real delight in watching others enjoying the effort of their labours. I was sitting down to a lunch of cold chicken and salad when a young private soldier appeared and apologetically explained that I was required to attend a briefing immediately. The rest of the team, now well versed in reading the signs of a fast-ball mission, finished their meals and headed straight for our accommodation to await my orders.

A Danish infantry unit call sign Echo One One Alpha based at Patrol Base Barakzae had found a suspected command-pull device in an area known as the Witch's Hat. The bomb was located 800 metres from the PB in a critical location on the track. It was disrupting patrolling activity and so they needed it cleared ASAP.

The Witch's Hat had a reputation as a Taliban bomb magnet. Dozens of IEDs had been found in the area and several soldiers had been killed and injured. It had been given the name by soldiers because all the tracks in the area converged into one main route, in the shape of a witch's hat and right at the peak sat PB Barakzae. But soldiers manning the bases did not have a clear line of sight down the main track, which meant the Taliban could plant IEDs on the routes into and out of the PB with relative ease. Although the mission appeared to be simple enough, areas like the Witch's Hat had to be treated with extreme caution. The Taliban, like most guerrilla groups, would usually only plant IEDs in areas where they got results, and the Witch's Hat was definitely one of those.

Back at our tented home I briefed the team on the plan. Everyone was familiar with the area's notoriety and they all shared my concerns. It had been a week since Dan had died and everyone was still a bit raw. The incident hadn't been discussed since we left Shawqat and no one mentioned his name. In an ideal world we should have chatted about Dan, how his loss affected us and talked about our own fears. But we didn't and instead his death hung over us like a dark shadow for the rest of the tour.

The Chinook dropped us off on a dusty HLS a kilometre south of PB Barakzae that could have been anywhere in Helmand. As I was orientating myself to the terrain, a small convoy of four Danish armoured vehicles appeared from over a slight rise in the undulating desert landscape.

The convoy's commander explained that his soldiers had already secured the area after they found a long length of kite string attached to an IED. He explained that the IED was located on a Vulnerable Point, a narrowing of tracks that channelled anything moving by vehicle towards the device. The ever-vigilant Danes had searched along the length of the kite string until they found what they believed to be the battery pack and firing switch, at which point they cut the string, believing the device was safe and waited for the Counter-IED team to arrive.

'Impressive,' I said congratulating the commander on his soldiers' efforts, but also warning them of the potential dangers of walking the length of a command wire or string and snipping it. The string could have been booby-trapped, pressure plates could have been placed along its length and they could have found themselves walking into a come-on. Better wait for us next time, I suggested. The Danes took my advice with good grace and my team set about clearing the IED and by just before 7.00 p.m., as the evening light was beginning to fade, the job was finished.

Kit was eagerly packed away and the team split itself between two armoured vehicles for the quick trip back to the HLS and onwards to Keenan in the hope that we might still be able to get an evening meal. Given my seniority, I bagged the best seat, the last on the right looking into the vehicle. Space was always at a premium and any spare room was filled with kit, ammunition boxes, radios, batteries or water. Everyone was supposed to be strapped into their seats by belts which crossed your chest but these had been largely ignored because they were either broken or too difficult to adjust. Likewise most of us had removed our helmets the moment the rear doors slammed shut. Despite the squeeze, the noise, and the overbearing heat inside the vehicle, I lay back and closed my eyes and quickly slipped into a well-earned power nap.

The vehicles sped eastwards following an unmarked route that hand-railed the main track back to the HLS and on to the patrol base. The convoy was just two minutes from the HLS when my vehicle struck an IED. The bomb, thought to have been around 20kg of home-made explosive, detonated almost directly beneath where I was sitting. The force of the blast threw the 18-ton vehicle several feet into the air. Everyone inside was thrown out of their seats, smashing into each other while boxes of ammunition, radios and equipment fell down on top of us. At some point I must have smashed my head against the reinforced armoured sides or been clipped by an ammo box because I went from being asleep to unconscious.

'Kim, wake up, wake up . . .' Chidders was shaking me, his face a few inches away from mine and there was real fear in his eyes. My vision was blurred and Chidders's voice was muffled, like he was shouting with a gag in his mouth. LCpl Matt 'Chidders' Chiddley was the search team's second-in-command. He was one of the most reliable soldiers in the team – fit, bright and utterly professional. The vehicle's interior lighting had failed and soldiers fumbled around in almost complete darkness, coughing and spluttering as dust filled the cabin.

'Kim, are you OK?' Chidders shouted again as though he was speaking to someone who couldn't understand.

'ARE. YOU. OK?'

'Yes, yes. For fuck's sake. I'm fine,' I said, spitting dust and blood from my mouth.

My ears were ringing like an alarm bell had gone off inside my head. I felt drowsy, almost as if I were drunk or had just woken from a long sleep.

One of the top hatches was opened from the outside and I could see for the first time the carnage inside the vehicle. There was kit and equipment everywhere. Ammunition boxes had spilled open, radios and cables were hanging from the sides and food was strewn across the floor.

'What's going on?' I said, utterly confused.

'IED strike. The vehicle's knackered and I think you were knocked out. You were thrown all over the place. Do you feel OK?'

Before I could answer, a sharp, almost blinding pain, like the world's worst hangover, began to career through my head. Just as I was starting to get a grip on what had happened I felt a sharp, stabbing pain in my right leg, which had been wedged beneath my seat by a dislodged ammunition box. Reaching down I could feel that my leg was wet and initially I thought I had been injured in the blast. I brought my hand to my face expecting to see blood and gore but it was just water from a broken water bottle. I sighed in relief. 'Thank fuck for that.'

Chidders grabbed me again. 'Are you hurt? You were out for a bit.'

'I'm all right. Stop looking at me like that. Jesus. I'm OK.'

I pulled myself out of my seat, yanking my headphones out of my ears in the process but as I tried to stand, my legs buckled. I stumbled and a hand reached down through the top hatch and grabbed my arm, helping me climb unsteadily up onto the top deck.

I spat again, wiped dust from my eyes and rubbed the back of my neck, which had started to ache. The Danish vehicle was a write-off. One of the tracks had been completely ripped off and the wire storage cages blown to pieces. Mangled pieces of kit and equipment were lying all over the place. I turned around and could see the blast crater still smoking about twenty feet from where the vehicle had come to rest. Twenty kilos of home-made explosive packs a very powerful punch and on another day could easily have taken out the entire vehicle and all of us inside.

The search team were already on the ground moving quickly and efficiently, clearing two routes, one on the left and one on the right of the damaged vehicle. Everyone knew exactly what to do and they worked as single unit.

'Everyone OK over there?' Chappy shouted.

'Yeah, all fine, mate. ATO's got a bit of a sore head but that's it,' Chidders said, now more relaxed and almost laughing.

I still wasn't quite sure if I had been knocked unconscious but that did not stop everyone treating me as if I was a serious casualty. I kept telling everyone to chill and attempted to coordinate the search, making sure all areas were being cleared.

After a few minutes, I tried to stand again to get a better look at what was going on but almost immediately my legs gave way again.

'Kim, just stay put, the medic's coming,' said Chidders.

My body felt as if it was no longer obeying orders. Nothing like this had ever happened to me before. My head was really thumping as though there was a massive build-up of pressure ready to burst and I was just about to lie down when a Danish medic leapt up from the ground.

'Hi, my name is Anders. I'm a medic. How are you doing?' he enquired.

'Yeah, I'm fine. I've just had a bit of a head rush. Make sure everyone else is OK.'

Anders then turned to Chidders and asked what had happened. 'There was the explosion and while I was checking if everyone was OK, Kim still had his eyes closed. He got thrown around the vehicle, banged his head and hurt his leg.'

The medic returned his focus to me, studying my pupils with a small torch before checking my neck and back. When he finished I tried to stand for a second time only for my legs to give way again. Anders grabbed my arm and looked very unimpressed. 'Right, stay there. We're getting you off the ground.'

'I know,' I responded, 'we're all heading back to Bastion after this job.'

'I mean we're getting you off the ground now. I'm calling a chopper in. You're going to be casevaced.'

'You're joking. I'm fine, I'm just a little light-headed.'

Anders ignored my protests and told the small group of soldiers, who had now gathered around the damaged vehicle, that I needed to be carried off. I was passed from one soldier to the next until I was on the ground. Still feeling unsteady and light-headed, I sat down resting my back against the side of the damaged vehicle. My stomach began to turn and I was convinced I was about to puke when a spine-board was dropped by the side of me.

'I'm not getting on that,' I said to Anders, making it sound as much like an order as possible.

'Look, you might outrank me but you're a casualty and while you are in our patch you will do as you are told. Understand?'

At least he's got the balls to stand up to me, I thought. 'All right, whatever.'

'You're not a critical casualty but you've hurt your head, you were unconscious and you've collapsed twice. I don't know what has happened to you. I can only do so much. You could have a concussion or a more serious brain injury. We need to get you back to Bastion so the experts can have a look. It will be a lot easier if you let me do my job.'

The spine-board felt like some form of medieval torture and my misery was complete when Anders insisted that I wore a neck brace. It wasn't long before the piss-taking started and the cameras came out.

Anders began sending through a nine-liner, a specific message format that provides vital information to the surgical team back in Bastion as well as to the airborne medical units.

He returned his attention to me. 'You are a Cat B casualty, help is on its way and you'll be back in Bastion very soon.'

'I'm not leaving my team on the ground,' I said indignantly and saw the medic's eyes roll to the back of his head.

Even my guys were getting pissed off with me now. 'Kim, just do what he says. We'll be following you into Bastion a little later,' Chappy said, clearly fed up with my antics. Next Anders placed a drip in my arm, checked my pulse and listened to my breathing before ensuring I was firmly strapped to the board.

'Make sure all my kit comes off the ground, especially my man bag. It's got my weapons and explosives in it,' I said to Chappy, still trying to act as if I was still in command.

As darkness closed in around us, two US Black Hawk helicopters arrived. One hovered menacingly above providing over-watch, scanning the ground surrounding the convoy below, while the other dropped quickly onto an HLS marked with green smoke. Almost immediately four members of my team grabbed the spine-board and quickly carried me through the dust cloud and slid me into the waiting arms of two US medics.

'I'll be back in a few hours!' I shouted, feeling like a bluffer with a fake injury.

The medics were part of team PEDRO, the special forces-trained combat search and rescue team. The two medics began frantically checking every part of my body for unseen injuries. One of them rolled up my sleeve and began stabbing my left arm with a needle in search of a vein.

'Sorry, dude,' the US medic responded with a southern drawl, 'I'm trying to get an IV line into you.'

'What like this one?' I lifted my right arm to show him that a drip was already pumping saline into my body.

Despite my protests and my insistence that I was fine the PEDRO boys took no notice. They had dealt with dozens of soldiers with far worse injuries, looking after casualties who'd lost legs and arms or had been shot while claiming that they were fine. Twenty minutes later the chopper was landing on the HLS at Bastion. I lifted my head and saw the blue flashing lights of the base fire engine standing by for any untold emergency. I felt like a complete fraud and only hoped that I wasn't holding back a chopper from some poor sod who really needed it.

Even though the HLS was about forty metres from the Bastion hospital, I was lifted into the back of a waiting ambulance for the twenty-second journey. The hospital door swung open and suddenly the air felt clean and medicinal. Occasionally a face would appear in front of me, telling me that I was fine and everything was going to be OK.

Next Major Millar, the OC of the EOD Task Force and the Operations Warrant Officer appeared.

'Kim, how are you?' the OC asked, concern spread across his face.

'I'm all right, sir. Honestly I'm fine.'

But I must have looked pretty bad because I was filthy, covered in dust and had various tubes going into my arms and winced with pain every few seconds.

As I was wheeled away I shouted back to the OC, 'Boss, have you got my pistol and rifle? There are explosives in my man bag.'

'Don't worry, Kim,' the OC shouted, 'it will all be sorted.'

The stretcher trolley smashed through another pair of swing doors and a team of medics descended on me, cutting my clothes off, in an instant ruining my brand-new combats, which I had just been issued with after weeks of waiting.

The doctor, a specialist in battlefield trauma, who was used to dealing with bullet wounds and multiple amputations, turned to me: 'You were in an explosion?'

'Yeah.'

'So what hurts?'

'Just my head, mate, my leg and my ears are ringing.'

'OK, but what else?' the doctor asked as if they expected me to say: 'Oh, I forgot to say I was missing a leg.'

'No, that's it. I've told everyone I didn't need to come here.' The doctor looked almost disappointed, as if I had somehow let him down by not being more seriously injured.

'Right, CT scan. Let's go. He has a head injury, he might have internal bleeding!' the doctor shouted after a few moments' thought.

After the scan another two doctors began poking and prodding me. One pressed my knee and I winced.

'Does that hurt?'

'Yeah,' I responded.

'Right, X-ray,' the doctor said and another medic immediately appeared with a portable X-ray machine.

Every time I said anything hurt it was X-rayed. It was a case of 'No, that's not broken, what else hurts? Your pelvis? Right, X-ray' and these were real-time images that immediately appeared on a screen.

Within twenty minutes of arriving at the hospital I was put through a CT scan and most of my body was X-rayed. It was extraordinary. I had never realised up to that point just how good the medical care was in Bastion.

Eventually the doctor turned to me and effectively told me what I already knew: 'Good news, there's no internal bleeding but you do have a concussion so we are going to keep you in hospital for observation for the next few days.'

Once everything had calmed down and I was 'in the clear' one of the doctors pointed to a phone and told me to ring my next of kin and tell them that I had been injured. It was, they said, far better that I do it than some anonymous voice on the end of a phone. It was a call I didn't want to make. My wife was my next of kin but my marriage was over. I thought about what to say for a few seconds before calling home.

'Hi, it's me. I'm fine but I've had a bit of a smack. I'm OK, a lot of overreaction, but I'm in hospital for a few days. There's nothing to worry about. Can you let my folks know?'

That was about the extent of the conversation. I could sense concern but the chat was minimal.

An hour later and I was on a general ward surrounded by soldiers with dodgy backs, twisted ankles and infected mozzie bites. I felt as if I was being punished for some unknown crime. Most of the real battle-injured, those soldiers who'd been shot or blown up, were on the Intensive Care Ward, where they would spend a few hours before being flown back to the UK. We were the semi-professional injured. I drifted in and out of sleep that night, suddenly being woken by what I thought was a loud bang and thinking I was reliving the explosion, then realising the noise was from more wounded troops arriving.

A day later my team arrived back in Bastion and the joking began. Oz Schmid was one of the first to visit and took the piss out of me relentlessly. But alongside the humour, everyone knew, including me, that I'd had a lucky escape. A week earlier Dan had been killed and now I was lying in a hospital bed with concussion. Soldiers, ones unluckier than me, had been killed in almost identical IED strikes to the one I had survived. It wasn't lost on me that maybe this was something of a wake-up call. I'd spent the last few weeks really pushing it, going after bomb after bomb, thinking I was invulnerable, and that somehow the rules didn't apply to me. But at that moment lying on my own with time on my hands, it began to dawn on me that luck as well as skill was going to be needed if I was going to survive Afghan.

13

R & R

R & R – rest and recuperation – two words guaranteed to bring a glowing smile to any soldier's face. R & R usually kicked in about halfway through the tour, a two-week break from the horrors of Afghanistan, a chance to forget about killing and getting killed and a milestone in anyone's tour of duty. But unlucky soldiers got their R & R slots at around week eight of a six-month tour, which meant they would have four hard, solid months to do when they returned to Helmand. Conversely there were also soldiers that spent four months deployed before they got a break. With 10,000 troops in Afghanistan all requiring a two-week break, the whole R & R schedule needed to be carefully managed. No unit could be left too short of manpower to complete the mission. The general feeling among soldiers in Helmand in 2009 was to survive up until the R & R date and you were halfway home.

After three days in a Bastion hospital bed, doctors gave me the all-clear to return to work on the condition that I didn't deploy on the ground for two weeks. I had a perforated eardrum and if it was going to repair properly then flying in choppers was out and so was being close to things that went bang, not ideal for those employed in EOD. The two possibilities open for a non-deployable ATO were either training fresh troops arriving in Helmand or working in the Ops Room as a watch-keeper, not something I relished.

I entered the Ops Room apprehensively, wondering how I would be greeted. I was still convinced that a lot of people within the Task Force thought I was a bluffer, feigning injury to get a few cushy days in a comfy bed. But I needn't have worried.

'Kim, welcome back. Glad to see you're fit again,' the OPSWO said as I entered the Ops Room. 'Got some good news. We're sending you and your team on R & R early. Your search team will stay here and go on R & R next month. But we've managed to find your team a slot. Frankly you're no use to us here if you can't go out on the ground.'

He smiled at me with a look that said I should be delighted but I wasn't. I left the Ops Room feeling pissed off and concerned about the whole R & R situation. My team was now being split up after three months of living in each other's pockets. The REST element would be working with another ATO and if anything happened to any of them I'd blame myself.

Then there was my failing marriage. Being a typical bloke I'd done a pretty good job of not facing up to the problems at home, convincing myself that I needed to focus on the job. But the time had come to face the music and frankly I felt more comfortable facing the Taliban.

Later that afternoon, I told Lewis and Dave that R & R had been brought forward and their reaction could not have been more different from mine. They chatted and joked like a couple of kids who'd been told that Christmas was coming early.

With a certain amount of dread I then phoned home. While just about every other soldier's partner would be getting the balloons out and family round to see their hero husband or son, my wife simply said, 'Are you planning to stay here?' It wasn't a long conversation.

The following morning the long, arduous and painful process of trying to leave Bastion began. Everyone departing was given their passport and mobile phone, if they had one. The talk was about holidays in the sun, seeing the kids and shagging wives and girlfriends. Seemingly endless sheets of paperwork were completed following a ten-hour wait, where vast quantities of fat-rich snacks and weak coffee were consumed in a futile attempt to relieve the monotony.

Later that evening the assembled mass of troops were shown a film of what soldiers should expect to experience after arriving home from a war zone. The film began with how the average soldier assumed he might be greeted by a wife he hadn't seen in three months, a scantily clad wife dressed in a negligee gagging for sex. And then there was the reality: a wife who's been stuck at home for the last three months, been driven mad by the kids, who was more likely to say: 'Right, you look after them now. I'm going out with my mates.' It got a lot of laughs but everyone got the message.

While Dave and Lewis willed the clock on the wall of the 'departure lounge' to speed up, I was almost overcome by a deep sense of impending dread and the grim surroundings didn't improve my mood. The hanging around and waiting prior to boarding the flight was typical RAF bullshit and bordering on spiteful. It was as though someone really resented sending soldiers home and, to make matters worse, that day wasted waiting to fly out counted as one of the R & R days. In the long hours I arranged for Lee Ridgway and Stu Dickson, two fellow ATOs, to pick me up at the airport. Both knew my marriage was in trouble and realised that if they weren't there to meet me no one would be.

Finally the moment of departure had come, a civilian aircraft had been chartered to fly from Bastion to Cyprus and then to Heathrow. It was just before midnight and although the soldiers were exhausted by the endless waiting around, there was an end-of-term atmosphere on board the plane. Everyone but me cheered as the engines roared into life and the plane accelerated into the empty black sky. Bastion, the one place on the planet where I had felt comfortable and relaxed, faded away into the dark.

After the aircraft departed Afghan airspace the captain announced that it was now safe to remove body armour and helmets. The troops cheered and cheered again when beer started to be served, just a can, but my mood refused to lighten. During the long flight home I kept my thoughts to myself, head plugged into my iPod trying to hide from the world of shit waiting for me.

When we reached Cyprus the aircraft flew over beautiful, white, sandy beaches with couples and families playing in the sea. It was another world occupied by people who had no knowledge of a bloody war being waged a couple of thousand miles away while they were sunbathing and eating ice creams. Happy couples, women and blokes on hen and stag weekends, lapped up the sun and cheap package tours while young men were being blown to pieces fighting to, supposedly, protect their freedom and they knew nothing about it. I felt a surge of anger as I stared out of the window.

Twelve hours later the aircraft landed at Heathrow where

Light scales kit — we only took what we could carry, and nothing more.

Working on a PPIED buried just in front of a small bridge. This was the first and last occasion in which I used the remote controlled robot called Dragon Runner, shown here on my left. My metal detector is positioned on my right. Note the stones, which were placed by the Taliban to warn locals that IEDs were laid in the area.

Brimstone 42 – Malley, Robbo, Lewis, Harry, me and Chappy relaxing in the Helmand river outside FOB Waheed, in June 2009.

Marijuana was grown by farmers and sold to the Taliban. The illicit drugs market helped fund the Taliban campaign against NATO.

Chappy and me on the only piece of grass we saw in our entire tour.

Lewis and me on Operation Panchai Palang. The Danish vehicle in the background was our home for the first part of the operation.

Bridge Micky (*left*) – Day 2 of Operation Tufaan Dakoo. The hole in the foreground shows the position of the main charge, a 105mm illumination shell, of the command-pull IED. The bridge had been closed with rolls of razor wire, but the Taliban had managed to swim across and place the IED at the base of it.

These two metal rings (*right*) made up the firing switch. When the string is pulled, the two contacts are forced together, allowing current to flow and causing the device to function. On this occasion the device failed.

Cutting off the Taliban's line of sight with smoke.

Briefing a journalist during a clearance operation.

Bomb-making equipment found during Operation Panchai Palang.

The Taliban used a variety of commercial, military and improvised detonators.

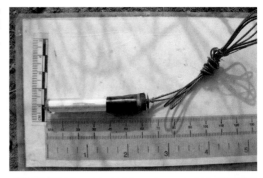

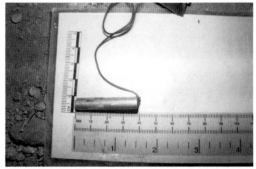

My search team clearing part of Pharmacy Road, one of the most dangerous areas in Sangin.

The various stages of uncovering an IED. The pressure plate is sealed with a plastic bag to protect it from the elements. The actual explosives are contained within a British 105mm illumination shell.

Painting the sand – the classic pose of an ATO using a paintbrush to expose an IED.

Speaking with Bob Ainsworth, the Defence Secretary, and Alan Johnson, the Home Secretary. Little did I know that my brief chat would be headline news twenty-four hours later.

Chappy and me checking a Taliban flag pole to see if it is booby-trapped. Taliban flags became popular souvenirs among the troops but the insurgents quickly exploited the situation and started to protect the flags with victim-operated IEDs.

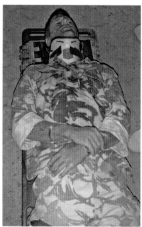

Left: 26 July 2009 – the damage caused by an IED to a Danish armoured vehicle. The blast occurred when the vehicle drove over a PPIED at the Witch's Hat near PB Barakzai. *Right*: I was the only casualty, and a very reluctant one. Minutes after this picture was taken, I was airlifted off the battlefield by a US Blackhawk helicopter.

Receiving the George Cross from Her Majesty The Queen, 8 June 2010.

400 soldiers, still dusty from the Helmand deserts, were afforded a certain celebrity status as they marched through the terminal to cheering friends and relatives.

I said goodbye to Dave and Lewis and walked through arrivals to the grinning faces of Stu and Lee, and finally at that moment it almost felt good to be home. I hugged them both and almost immediately they started taking the piss out of me for losing loads of weight courtesy of the Afghan diet, the odd bout of diarrhoea and cutting around Helmand with 50kg on my back. For the next ten minutes or so we stood there chatting, catching up on gossip and having a laugh.

During the drive home the conversation turned to Afghan, the devices and whether I had any further news on what had happened to Dan. Then Stu, in his thick Scottish brogue, ventured into the area we had all been avoiding.

'So what's happening?'

'With what?' I replied.

'With home.'

'It's been difficult,' I said with mild understatement. 'The marriage is on life support, we hardly talk any more and when we do most of the conversation is about our son.'

It was probably the confirmation they had been expecting and the chat died away for a few minutes before Stu announced that he had booked a couple of bed and breakfast rooms in Blackpool for the middle weekend of R & R.

'Brilliant,' I said, 'a weekend with the lads, that'll be something to look forward to.' My spirits felt slightly lifted.

'Sorry, mate, the girls are coming as well.'

During my time in Germany and after our son was born, my wife and I separated a couple of times when things were bad but always came back together for my son's sake. Part of me hoped that might happen again.

We first met in 1998 when I was home on leave from Catterick and she was working as a clerical assistant at my mum's company. I was aged nineteen and she was a bit younger. We started seeing each other and the relationship became what people call 'serious'. I passed my Ammunition Technician's course and was posted to Fallingbostel in Germany. We continued our relationship at a distance, which appeared to work when my tour of duty in Germany was extended for another three years, and it was at that point that I fell into the same trap as so many young soldiers. After going out for a while we were now going to be separated. But we could stay together if we were married and so it was during a wet afternoon in Weston-super-Mare that I made a proposal of marriage while sitting in a Lidl car park after having secretly bought an engagement ring from a cheap high street jewellery shop. Within a few weeks a date had been set, a venue had been booked. From memory my overriding emotion at the time was 'Fuck me, that was quick.'

By the age of twenty-three I was shacked up in a grotty three-bedroom Army quarter and about as unprepared for married life as was possible. By contrast my wife revelled in the 'slippers by the fire' aspect of marital bliss and almost immediately I began missing going out with my mates. She wanted kids, I was still growing up and wanted to enjoy life. The marriage was a car crash waiting to happen.

All too soon we were in Kineton and the car pulled up outside my house. Stu and Lee said they would wait with my kit while I said my hellos.

As I walked through the garden, I could see her silhouette in the kitchen. My heart rate increased and I found myself half hoping that she would welcome me with open arms. I knocked on the door rather than using my own key and was greeted with the smallest of smiles. We hugged and kissed, but only on the cheek, and exchanged pleasantries. It was perfectly polite but nothing more. There was friendship but no passion, no love. But my spirits soared when I saw my son and my dog Sabot. I hugged them both and felt emotional about something apart from death and injury for the first time in months.

A few minutes later Lee and Stu sheepishly appeared at the back door of the house, said a quick hello to my wife and dumped my bags in the kitchen before heading off. An awkward silence filled the room for a few minutes before she told me that it was my son's feeding time and she disappeared into another room leaving me and my bags stranded in the kitchen wondering what was going to happen next.

'Jesus, I miss Afghan,' I muttered to myself. In the world's biggest shithole I had a purpose. In my own house I felt unwanted and useless.

I went to the bedroom and began unpacking, slowly, not knowing whether I should be using a spare bedroom. Did she want me in the same bed? Nothing felt right or comfortable. I went to the bathroom, splashed some water on my face and looked in the mirror. This was meant to be my R & R – the time when I could rest, clear my head and go back to Afghan refreshed and with the best possible chance of surviving the next three months.

Downstairs I sheepishly asked whether I could feed my boy. It felt as though I hadn't seen him for years although it had actually been around twelve weeks. He recognised me but probably not as his father. He had grown so much and it suddenly struck me that I was missing out hugely on his life and development.

The small talk between me and my wife was stilted and

awkward and only seemed to emphasise the unbridgeable gap that had grown between us. Later that evening my son went to sleep and an awful silence descended.

'How long does he sleep for?' I asked, almost immediately regretting the question given that as his father it's something I should know.

'A couple of hours, depends,' she replied.

'OK, shall I take the dog for a walk?'

'That would be nice.'

Just about every other soldier on the flight would have been dreaming of that exact moment: away for three months, kids asleep, a chance to catch up on some shagging but instead I was walking the dog, on my own, on a dark, empty street inside an Army housing estate.

For the next few days we carefully skirted around each other, avoiding intimacy and each other's personal space. The weekend in Blackpool loomed ever closer. My wife's parents had agreed to look after our son but there was no sense that the marriage was salvageable.

I thought constantly about Afghan, how the war was progressing and what I was going to do when I returned. The war was on the TV news, with the focus being on casualties, but my wife never asked me once what it was like and to be honest I was pleased she didn't.

The Blackpool weekend finally arrived and although we were staying in a cheap, tacky hotel close to the sea and the amusement arcades, I was delighted, until I walked into the bedroom and was confronted by the double bed. We'd slept in the same bed at home but we'd also had our son and the dog to occupy our time. Now it was just the two of us. I felt as though I was being punished for some unknown crime.

The six of us sat down for a tense dinner where the chat was polite but stilted. Then it was off to an Australian bar, which I had hoped would be the highlight of the evening but my wife wasn't happy. She had barely said a word all night. I took her to one side and asked if we could have a chat.

'Look, we are going to be here for a couple of days so maybe we should make an effort for the other guys and put our differences aside, what do you think?' She just stared at me. I'm not sure if it was the way I came across or if she had just given up, but she walked off without saying a word and the two other wives followed.

My mates were obviously concerned.

'What's up, mate?' Stu asked.

'Nothing, mate, just a domestic,' I sighed. The girls had decided to go their own way and so we began having a laugh and getting pissed, exactly what I needed. We bumped into our other halves in a couple of bars and on one occasion I tried to make casual chit-chat but my wife was having none of it and completely blanked me.

Later that evening we arrived back at the hotel. Stu rushed up to his room while I chatted to Lee in the bar as we had one last drink.

Stu reappeared looking slightly awkward: 'We're sleeping in the same room tonight, mate. My wife and yours are shacking up.'

'What? Don't be silly. We can stay in the same room as each other. Let's not ruin the evening.' I was more concerned about ruining Stu's night than anything else and thought I should try to reason with my wife. But my pleas fell on deaf ears.

I spent the night with Stu feeling that I would have been better off spending my R & R in Bastion hanging round the NAAFI and watching films on my bunk.

The following day we met up on the seafront for breakfast.

I went over to my wife and hoped that last night could be put behind us but I was wrong. She refused to speak to me.

'Fuck this,' I said loud enough for everyone to hear and stormed off.

The guys ran after me and tried to get me to come back but I was furious and my mood wasn't helped by a severe hangover.

'I'm done with it, mate. This was meant to be a weekend away for all of us and it's shit. It's over.'

The drive home to Telford was torturous and not a single word was spoken or a glance exchanged. We collected our son on the way, which softened the atmosphere, but only slightly. When we got to the house I went straight to the bedroom and moved all my kit into the spare room, where I slept for the rest of the week.

On the last day of my R & R, just after I finished packing my bags and explaining to my son that I wouldn't see him for a while, I turned to my wife. 'Look, I don't want a row before I get on the plane,' I said softly, 'but it's obvious we can't let this situation hang over our heads while I'm away – it's not fair on either of us.'

She looked straight into my eyes and said, 'I think we're finished.'

'Yeah,' I said. 'I think we are.'

Neither of us tried to save what was left of our marriage. We both knew it had run its course.

'So where does that leave us?' she added.

'I'll move my kit out when I return from Afghan.'

She nodded and turned away, bringing to an end possibly the worst R & R anyone could ever wish for. I was both physically and mentally exhausted, exactly the opposite of what I was meant to be. Slowly, on the last day, I began to feel the full impact of what a failed marriage meant. Was I going to be able to see my son regularly? How was I going to be able to pay maintenance? Only the prospect of returning to Afghan and reuniting with my team seemed to lighten the mood.

I spent the last few hours playing with my son, squeezing as much time as I could out of what was left and knowing there was the very real prospect that as I left the house I might never see him again. I gave him one final hug, kissed his head one last time before turning to my wife.

'Right, I'm off.'

'Yeah fine,' she said with a half smile. There were no hugs or kisses, no warmth, not even a 'Look after yourself'.

I walked out of the door and turned back to wave looking at them for one last time before climbing into Stu's car and heading off to RAF Brize Norton for the flight back to Afghan. Stu and Lee tried to chat but my monosyllabic responses ultimately stymied their well-intentioned efforts and the majority of the journey was completed in a tense silence.

I said goodbye to the guys and walked into the departure lounge and immediately clocked Dave and Lewis – both of them were smiling and looked well rested.

'How did you get on?' I asked Lewis.

'Fucking mega. I was on the piss for most of it and can't really remember what happened. Brilliant time.'

Dave was also full of it. Both had ripped the arse out of R & R, exactly what young soldiers should do.

'How was yours?' Lewis asked, with a knowing smile, expecting a detailed account of a married man's two weeks of endless sex and home-cooked meals.

'Yeah, fair to middling, mate.' I had no intention of

dropping a massive downer on either of them. The last thing they needed was to think that my head wasn't in the right place.

The RAF TriStar climbed into a glorious English summer sky and for the first time in two weeks I began to relax. I plugged myself into my iPod, closed my eyes and smiled to myself. Afghan was just fourteen hours away and I couldn't wait.

14

Sangin – Death in the Wadi

If there was one place in Helmand feared and loathed by soldiers in equal measure it was Sangin, a scruffy, lawless, violent town in the north of the province. Sangin was the nexus of the drugs trade in Helmand and until the British arrived in 2006, it was largely in the hands of warlords, who had a vested interest in keeping the British out.

By 2009, the town had become a graveyard for British troops. Its streets, narrow alleyways and bombed-out houses had become soaked in the blood of British soldiers and the more soldiers that were sent the harder the Taliban fought back. The Sangin Taliban were rumoured to be the fiercest in Helmand – rather like the South Armagh IRA in Northern Ireland. They showed no fear and were not intimidated either by the modern Western soldier or his formidable weaponry. It was rumoured that Sangin was used as a testing ground to 'blood' Taliban volunteers in battle. Those who survived progressed up the ranks or were sent to other parts of the province in the belief that if they could survive Sangin, anywhere else would be a breeze.

The three years of war that followed the arrival of the British Paras in 2006 had left its scars on the town. Most of the homes close to the main British base had been abandoned or turned to rubble. The rest of the town was a sprawling maze of archetypal Afghan compounds with sixteen-foot-high, mud-baked walls channelling soldiers into killing zones carefully constructed by the Taliban.

In the centre was a bustling bazaar selling just about everything from Chinese motorbikes to electric fans. Shopkeepers would offer beguiling smiles to the British soldiers and their Afghan colleagues. But the handshakes and the friendly waves couldn't hide the town's true nature. Sangin was evil, there's no other way to describe it. You might argue that a town can't have a human character trait but I assure you it can. For the British squaddie, there was nothing good in Sangin, nothing redeemable. It was hate, pure hate and it was all directed at us.

I returned from R & R on 12 August 2009. Stepping off the Hercules, I was immediately greeted by the unforgiving furnace-like heat of Bastion in high summer. By the time I got to the EOD Task Force Ops Room I was soaked in sweat and feeling dehydrated. Dust coated the back of my throat and clogged my nostrils. It was only a matter of time before my snot turned black.

'Kim, welcome back,' Jim announced as I entered the Ops Room. A few unfamiliar faces turned and looked at me.

'You're going to Sangin,' he announced matter-of-factly. 'Oz is down with chronic shits and we need to send another team in ASAP.' Oz must have been seriously unwell if another team was being sent in. For some reason Oz regarded Sangin as his patch and had become something of a legend among the unit based there.

'Sangin, of all the fucking places,' I thought to myself. Everyone was getting smashed in Sangin, the infantry, the IEDD teams, even choppers were coming under fire. Officers, noncommissioned officers, rookies and experienced soldiers on their second Afghan tour were being killed or losing their legs every day.

'When?' I fired back, my mind racing.

'Tomorrow morning. You leave on a 5 a.m. flight. Make sure your team's shit is squared away. The area's been a bitch the last couple of weeks.'

The UK already seemed a world away and now I was going into Sangin — it was more of a mind fuck than culture shock.

Malley was the only one in the tent and he greeted me with a smile that didn't last long.

'Go and round up the rest of the guys — we're back out tomorrow. I want everyone here in thirty mins.'

The team hadn't seen each other for almost two weeks and I suppose we had all gone a bit soft — R & R does that. It tricks soldiers into believing that they will be rejuvenated and ready for another three months in the arsehole of the world but in reality it's just a reminder of what's being missed.

As soon as the word 'Sangin' was announced the room fell silent. There were no complaints, no whingeing. But their faces told another story. They were wondering whether we'd make it, whether in a week's time we'd still be together and that was anybody's guess. I wanted the guys to be kept busy so I ordered a thorough check of everything.

'I don't want to get there and find we've left something behind. Bring everything you think we'll need plus any goodies you want.'

We were ready and waiting at the Bastion HLS at 4.00 a.m. for a 5.00 a.m. flight. Those who smoked sucked on their cigarettes, inhaling deeply. Others chatted and a few loud laughs split the early morning silence.

Over in the east, night began to give way to day and then one by one we climbed on board an empty Chinook along with several young ashen-faced battle-casualty replacements, whose first test of war in Afghan would be Sangin. The chopper's wheels lifted and Bastion fell away, disappearing into the predawn gloom and I wondered whether I would ever see it again. It would take around forty minutes to fly from Bastion but it would be like entering another world. Sangin boasted a 360-degree front line and firefights with the Taliban were so routine that only the most serious were acknowledged. It was often said that the only good thing about Sangin was leaving.

One of the RAF aircrew on board the Chinook was manning a mini-gun, an electric multi-barrelled machine gun capable of firing up to 6,000 rounds per minute. He frantically scanned the ground below searching for the Taliban. The Chinook banked left and right as it swung towards the town. The RAF loadmaster, chewing nervously, indicated by lifting a finger that it was one minute to landing before the chopper dropped out of the sky onto the HLS. Above, two Apache gunship helicopters bristling with weaponry provided over-watch.

The British base was called FOB Jackson and it sat astride the cool, green waters of the Helmand river. On one side of the river was a large concrete-grey building called the Fire Support Tower, which bore the heavy scars of months of battle. Bullet-riddled sandbag-filled holes where windows had once been and soldiers' graffiti provided a commentary of who had served, fought and died in the base. On the other side of the river was the battalion headquarters, effectively a mortar-proof hut where the commanding officer and his operation team lived, planned and plotted.

A large concert building, also pock-marked with the signs of recent battle, housed the stabilisation team, whose official job description was to bring security and normality to the area. The irony wasn't lost on the soldiers serving in Sangin – who had dubbed it a 'Town Called Malice'. The building was rumoured to have once been owned by a drugs lord and its garish mirrored walls and ceilings suggested as much.

Across from the HQ was a small memorial dedicated to those who had died fighting in the town. There was also a large sand-coloured tented dining area, soldiers' accommodation, showers, a makeshift gym and a vast HLS, about the size of a football pitch. Long-drop toilets, contained within wooden cubicles and best avoided in the heat of the day because of the overpowering stench, were dotted around the area ensuring that the smell of human shit was ever-present. The entire complex was surrounded by a huge Hesco wall.

In summer the temperatures easily topped 37°C during the day and dropped to a slightly less stifling 26°C once the sun had set. The one, possibly the only, benefit of Sangin was the Helmand river. The soldiers called the river 'morale' on the basis that their morale soared every time they went for a swim. The river had become a meeting place where the guys could relax, wash their clothes and forget about the war and the constant threat of death for a few short minutes. It was the only thing that made Sangin bearable.

Fresh rations were a rarity and the dreaded diarrhoea and vomiting sickness or D & V, which had afflicted soldiers in Afghanistan since the days of Kipling, remained the soldiers' curse. The problem had become so bad that a separate quarantine area had been created where those disabled by illness were under orders to remain until they were disease-free.

The streets close to the base were deserted due to the non-stop fighting, but the design and layout meant that they were almost impossible to secure. The Taliban routinely sneaked in under the cover of darkness and laid bomb after bomb, some just yards away from the base, almost every day. Every road, every street, every step had to be cleared by soldiers whose only defence against the IED was the metal detector. Bombs were hidden in walls and trees, in rubbish dumps, abandoned buildings, dead animals; it was one big minefield.

The base was now home to the 2nd Battalion, the Rifles, an infantry regiment, reinforced by small sub-units of troops from across the Army. The Rifles were recruited from across Britain and had been formed from the amalgamation of the Light Infantry, the Royal Green Jackets, the Devon and Dorset Regiment, Royal Gloucestershire, Berkshire and Wiltshire Infantry. The battalion was commanded by Lieutenant Colonel Rob Thomson and roughly two companies of soldiers, around two hundred men, were based at FOB Jackson, along with a platoon of soldiers from the Royal Regiment of Fusiliers, who had been drafted in as reinforcements. The rest of the unit was split among numerous other patrol bases in and around the town.

From the HLS my team was taken to our home for the next week – an airless, mortar-proof bunker, composed of Hesco blocks and a reinforced roof, known as a 'Hesco House'. The air inside was fetid and smelt of someone else's sweat. Each bed-space contained a cot enclosed within a mozzie net and a few hanging shelves. It wasn't much but it was enough and none of us intended on spending much time inside. The buildings were oven-hot during the day and only mildly cooler at night. Sleep was often impossible, unless you were utterly exhausted, which most of the time we were.

After dumping my kit, I made my way to the D & V quarantine tent to find Oz and get as much of a brief as possible on what Sangin was likely to have in store. Serving in Sangin was hard enough but trying to do it while throwing your ring up was something else. Just outside the tent, which was Army green and about twenty-five feet by twenty-five feet, was a long-drop latrine, and nearby pallets of water and rations being baked in the sun. It was as if those inside were being punished for being sick.

Inside the tent was the nauseating stench of human shit and vomit. There were six beds, occupied by three, waxy-white, sweating soldiers, wearing shorts and T-shirts and looking as though death would be a welcome outcome.

Oz had spent the last few days shitting water and looked terrible. He was hollow-cheeked and had acquired a grey complexion. He looked as though he had lost at least half a stone in weight. A medic who seemed to be reluctantly attending to the needs of the sick told me not to shake his hand, get too close or touch anything and my time was limited to just a few minutes.

'Hello, mate.'

Oz pushed himself up onto his elbows. 'Kim, welcome to the gayest town in Helmand. You'll have fun here,' he said, swatting away flies buzzing around his mouth.

Although ill, Oz was still on good form. The conversation lasted for just a few minutes, before the smile slipped from his face and his eyes hardened.

'You can't afford to fuck up here, mate. You've got to make sure your guys are switched on. Terry watches everything. Do the same thing twice and he'll have you.'

Oz had become a legend in the Rifles and everyone from the commanding officer down seemed to worship him. For most of that day, everywhere I went I was told how Oz did this or Oz did that. How there was no job he would refuse and how his work had saved dozens of lives. No pressure then, I said to myself, wondering quite how I was going to fill his very big boots. I wouldn't have to wait long.

Later that evening I attended a briefing for an operation due to take place before first light the next day. The briefing took place in the airless Ops Room where electric fans were working overtime but made little difference to the stifling heat.

The operation was called Ghartse Khers. Every mission had a Pashto as well as an English name to demonstrate that all operations were 'joint' and run in conjunction with the Afghan National Army. The operation was a search and clearance mission along one of the main roads into the town centre, called Route Carrot. Not surprisingly the brief from the intelligence officer indicated that the chance of attack was high, with the main threat coming from IEDs.

Over the course of an hour, the company commander leading the operation explained how all routes would be led by experienced soldiers clearing paths with metal detectors and any IEDs were to be confirmed and cleared by Brimstone 42. Once the company had reached Route Carrot, my team would take over and conduct the clearance. At one end of the route were two compounds called Eagle 12 and Eagle 13, which would also have to be cleared. On paper it was a fairly routine, no-dramas mission and a good opportunity for the team to get a feel for the area. The Rifles were being supported by a platoon of soldiers from the Royal Regiment of Fusiliers, partly because so many of their own had been killed and injured in the last few months and it was their men who would lead the operation and face the most risk.

Reveille was 3.30 a.m. and, after a quick brew, those taking part in the operation wearily made their way to the assembly point, the base's rear gate, by 4.00 a.m. The last few minutes before departure were spent checking weapons and radios. The glow of cigarettes in the predawn darkness illuminated the youthful faces of soldiers prematurely aged by the stress of war. There was little if any banter. Everyone knew that the likelihood of taking casualties was high. They had all seen friends suffer appalling injuries and die. And for most of them the odds of getting out of Sangin unscathed were shortening by the day.

At 4.30 a.m. we set off, in single file, out into the night, following the footsteps of Lance Corporal James 'Fully' Fullarton, a tough, super-fit soldier from Coventry. Fully was call sign Hades One Zero, the lead search man and his job was to search a clear, safe path from the base, through a wadi to Route Carrot.

The first part of the patrol followed one of the tributaries to the Helmand river and within about ten minutes of leaving Jackson we were shin-deep in water. Although wet, I was pleased with Fully's route choice because, as far as anyone knew, the Taliban hadn't found a way of placing IEDs in a river. Silently snaking its way along the river, the column of troops stopped, started, stopped. Clouds of mosquitoes buzzed into my mouth and dined on my face and arms. Every now and then I turned around and checked on my team, making sure we were still together.

After several hundred metres, Fully led the patrol out of the water and into the wide, dry riverbed, known as a wadi, which served as a road for locals and British alike. The Rifles had used the wadi on numerous occasions but were cautious enough to vary the route whenever possible. It was still dark but the first signs of a new dawn could be seen over in the east where the sky was lightening. I instinctively became more cautious and felt my grip tighten on my rifle. The Taliban didn't have any night vision equipment so their attacks were largely confined to daylight hours. I turned again to check on the guys behind me when the earth shook beneath my feet. In that fraction of a second before I heard the explosion I knew what had happened. The sound of the blast pierced the silence and everyone stopped as if suddenly frozen. It was 4.56 a.m. The operation had been active for just twenty-six minutes.

The now-familiar sound of home-made explosives detonating was unmistakable, like thunder reverberating around the valley. The first word that entered my consciousness was IED. Everyone instinctively dropped to the ground and took cover, while Dave listened into the net for any reports of casualties. I expected a call at any moment but I didn't want to act until I was needed. There was probably enough chaos and confusion without me throwing my oar in.

A few minutes later news rippled back that there had been a casualty and an HLS needed to be cleared and marked. Straight away the search team led by Chidders, who was now the commander, went into action, slick and fast, clearing an area large enough for the MERT to land.

Dave, listening to the radio, turned to me and whispered, 'Hades One Zero is down.' Fully, the lead search man, had stepped on the IED.

I began to go through the various options in my mind. I was itching to get forward, possibly to conduct a post-blast investigation, or see if I could help in any other way when I heard another massive explosion. I looked over at Lee, my mind now racing. Something had gone very badly wrong.

A few minutes later a platoon sergeant appeared out of the gloom, rifle at the ready and sweat running down his face from beneath his helmet.

'Kim, I need your team up at the front,' he said breathing heavily. 'We've had two IED strikes and we've now got multiple casualties – it's a cluster fuck.'

I turned to Lee just before we set off. 'We need to be careful, mate. We haven't isolated this, we don't know what we are walking into.'

The team moved along a line of silent soldiers, stepping over the legs and bodies as they lay in cover watching intently for enemy movement. We must have been some hundred metres from the point of the blast and it seemed to be taking forever when suddenly we came to the edge of the wadi. It was now dawn and birdsong filled the air as the sun began to bring some warmth to the early morning chill. A faint mist hung just above the river, while over to the east, fields of corn swayed gently in a warm summer breeze.

Eventually I reached the head of the column. The pungent odour of recently detonated explosives hung heavily in the air and the ground where the IEDs had been triggered was still smoking. Soldiers were lying on the ground as if frozen by fear and at first it was impossible to tell who was dead or alive. My heart pounded as the enormity of what was unfolding hit home.

Peering through the weak dawn light there was a small mound, almost like a bundle of rags, scorched black and red. Then slowly, very slowly, an arm rose into the air. It was a soldier, horrifically wounded, covered in blood with the lower half of his body missing. He seemed barely conscious.

Then a loud piercing scream split the air and as I got closer I realised it came from a female medic lying in a crumpled heap with one leg so badly damaged it appeared to only be attached by a few sinews of connective tissue.

'Why aren't you helping your mates?!' I shouted, enraged by the lack of activity.

The sergeant turned, his face filled with rage and fear, but before he spoke I knew what he was going to say. The soldiers were in an IED minefield.

15

Painting the Sand

Someone once said when you're in a minefield tread carefully and try and get to the other side. It was sound advice and something that flashed across my mind as I began formulating my plan. Dead, dying and wounded soldiers were trapped in an area of hell about a third of the size of a football pitch. It was always advisable to assume that where there was one IED there could be two and if there were two, then . . .

'Fully was lead search man,' the sergeant said, breathing heavily and breaking my concentration. 'He stepped on an IED. Both legs gone above the knee. We tied tourniquets around what was left of his legs and got him onto a stretcher. As we started the evacuation, one of the two stretcher-bearers triggered another IED. They are both Fusiliers and we think they are dead.'

As he spoke, the haunting sound of the Muslim call to prayer echoed around the valley. The sound of the explosions would have already alerted the Taliban. There was time to get the dead and injured out but not much.

'That's one of the lads,' the sergeant continued, point-ing at a soldier who was clearly dead. The young Fusilier had lost both legs and an arm and the force of the blast had bent what was left of his body in half. 'We think the other stretcher-bearer was blown into the reeds.' He pointed at a piece of ground about twenty metres away. 'We haven't been able to make any contact with him and no one has been any further forward than this since the second blast.'

The sergeant's eyes were wide and empty. His hands were trembling and his white, mournful face was spotted with dirt and blood.

'We have three more casualties,' he said. 'The medic who has sustained a bad leg injury and two other soldiers with unknown injuries, but they're conscious and don't appear critical. No one is moving. The sergeant major has ordered everyone to stay still.'

The brief took no more than thirty seconds. It was a shock-ing scene but I felt no real emotion, just a sense of appalling waste. The priority was to get the wounded out and back to Bastion; dealing with the dead would have to wait.

Fully was the most severely wounded and had sustained multiple injuries. He had been blown up twice and was barely conscious. He was already in shock and had lost a lot of blood from the double traumatic amputation. The female medic was awake and, although in a lot of pain, she did not appear to have life-threatening injuries. A few feet away the team were standing silently awaiting orders.

'Malley, you need to search up to Fully. Take the infantry medic with you and search a wide path, quickly but don't rush, then search a working area. Make sure you spray-paint your cleared paths so they're obvious.' All clear lanes were marked with spray-paint so that soldiers entering a danger area knew where to stand. It was a slow process but the only real way to ensure that everyone stayed inside a safe area.

Paddy, one of the searchers, who was also a trained medic, began to clear a path to the wounded female medic to prepare her for evacuation.

'Work quickly, lads, but be careful. No more casualties today,' I said as they got to work. 'Chidders, we need to bang out an isolation. We have to be sure there are no other wires running into this area.'

'Roger,' replied Chidders and within a matter of seconds he'd briefed his team and was slowly moving in a wide arc around the target. But then progress was slowed almost immediately when they discovered a network of wires running into the target, which added even more confusion to an already fucked-up situation.

Malley had made his way to Fully where the medic went to work on him. His condition was critical. Still alive, but only just.

'We need to get him out of here ASAP!' the medic shouted. 'Fully, Fully. Can you hear me? We've got you, mate. We are going to lift you out of here and take you back to Bastion.'

Fully was barely conscious. He was slipping away.

More soldiers arrived and Fully was placed on a stretcher for a second time before being carried out of the killing area to the HLS for a rendezvous with the MERT.

Paddy had by now made his way to the injured medic. He was trying to keep her calm and pleading with her not to move when Sapper 'Foz' Foster, who was clearing the ground around Paddy, shouted: 'Kim, we've got another IED!' He was pointing at the ground near where Paddy was kneeling over the casualty.

'Right, come back to me. Then clear me to the device and I'll deal with it,' I said, ensuring that my voice sounded calm.

Foz approached me swinging his metal detector from side to side. He then did a very military 'about turn' allowing me enough room to walk in his footsteps right up to the IED.

The bomb, buried in the gravelly bottom of the dried riverbed, was less than an arm's length from Paddy. He was hunched over the casualty, sitting on his ankles and tying a field dressing around a horrendous, gaping leg wound. When I reached him, he looked up at me as though saying: 'What am I supposed to do, I'm not trained for this.'

The female medic was in a bad way. The muscle hung from her shinbone and the bottom half of her leg was barely attached. She had lost a lot of blood and was going into shock.

'You're doing fine, mate. Stabilise the wound so we can get her out. Do what you can,' I said before getting to work on the IED.

EOD training dictated that in an ideal world a cordon should be thrown up and everyone evacuated but that wasn't going to happen because there were simply too many injured and dead people on the ground. It was crucial not to over-complicate a very dangerous situation. I had to work on what was known. It was a Category A scenario – meaning there was a grave and immediate threat to life. There was no time to conduct the usual EOD procedures of clearing devices remotely. The rules had to be ignored. I had to conduct what's called a 'manual action' – get inside the bomb, cut the wires and pray it wasn't booby-trapped. It was a risk but a calculated one. I had trained for this very situation. Back in the comfort of the Felix Centre you wished for the chance of dealing with a Cat A scenario; now here it was as real as the sun in the sky.

I dropped down, lying flat on my stomach and slowly ran my Hoodlum – a small handheld metal detector – over the ground and almost instantly got a metal hit. A high-metal pressure plate buried just below the surface of the dried riverbed. The injured medic's screams had become a whimper. She was slipping away. I looked up at Paddy and he mouthed the words 'Not good'.

I searched around for part of the device, a wire that I could attack. It didn't take long. I allowed myself the briefest of smiles as I uncovered a length of white twinflex wire. I pulled my snips out from the front of my body armour, held my breath and carefully cut one of the wires. There was something reassuring about the snip sound and I felt totally in control. I quickly taped both ends of the exposed wire. By cutting the wires I had effectively put a 'switch' into the system, making it safer than it had been a few minutes earlier.

Digging deeper, I found a pressure cooker filled with explosives and pieces of scrap metal, whatever Terry could throw into the mix. The bomb, although still a threat, was now safe and the evacuation of the injured medic began. Just as I began to feel that we were getting a grip on the situation one of the searchers announced that he'd found another IED.

'Christ. Right, mark and avoid. I'll deal with it.'

I turned to Lewis who was monitoring events from just outside the killing area. 'Get the satphone out and ring Bastion. Tell the SAT there have been two explosions, we've got injured and dead and multiple devices.'

I brought my metal detector into action once again, clearing a path to the IED, where the corner of a pressure plate had been exposed. I followed the same procedure again. Searched and located a wire, which I was just about to cut, when Foz shouted that he had found a third IED.

'Roger. Mark and avoid and I'll deal with it after this.'

I cleared a path up to where Foz was kneeling over a pressure plate.

'Nice one,' I said patting him on the back. Once again I used the same procedure to locate, cut and tape the wires.

Then the shout went up again: 'IED Find.' The bomb was found by one of the search team clearing a route to the second stretcher-bearer who had been blown into a reed bed at the top end of the area now identified as the main killing zone.

'Another one. Jesus. How many are there?' I said out loud. 'Roger. Same procedure. Mark and avoid. I'll deal with it after this.'

The devices needed to be cleared if we were to evacuate all of the casualties and dead safely. Over the next fifteen minutes, three more IEDs were found bringing the total to seven. The size and design of the main charges varied. Five of the charges were contained in pressure cookers and two were in plastic containers. The bombs were all impregnated with pieces of scrap iron and steel, such as nails, nuts and bolts. They were designed to kill or at the very least cause horrendous injuries – on both counts the Taliban had succeeded. The design and layout of the minefield was quality. Someone had really done their homework and my gut told me that the Taliban's top bomb team in Sangin must have designed the ambush.

In between clearing the IEDs, I also took photographs of where casualties had been taken, both the wounded and the dead. The evidence gathering was crucial. There would be a follow-up investigation and it was Brimstone 42's responsibility to get as much information and detail from the scene as possible.

As daylight crept into the valley the ground-sign, the disturbed soil left behind after burying an IED, was becoming more obvious and exposed – there were bombs everywhere, at least ten. Only those which represented a threat to our movement were dealt with.

Within thirty minutes of the first explosion the four wounded soldiers had been evacuated and we prepared to move the dead. Time was now running out and it was surprising that the Taliban hadn't turned up to take us on. As I surveyed the area I felt something wasn't quite right. I'd been so focused on the mission that the obvious hadn't occurred to me and then the penny dropped. No power packs. Pressure plates, main charges, wire and dets had all been located but no power packs. Not one. But the bombs were live. So what was going on?

I retraced my steps to the site of the earlier explosions and began to sift through the rubble in the craters. No batteries, just wires everywhere. I traced a wire to see if it was connected to a battery somewhere in the distance but discovered that the wire had been spliced onto another wire. Initially I was baffled, then I realised that the wires from all the devices were connected to a central power line. Each device had its own main charge, pressure plate and detonator but they were all powered from a central source. The IEDs were wired in such a way that one could explode while the others could remain intact – exactly what had happened earlier that morning.

The Taliban could arm or disarm the entire IED belt or minefield by disconnecting the battery. Once disconnected a tank could literally be driven over the pressure plate and it wouldn't function. This gave the Taliban freedom of movement right across the wadi without fear of stepping on one of their own devices. But when they saw British or ISAF forces were on the move up the wadi they simply reconnected the battery and the whole area became a live minefield. As a tactic it was outstanding and something never seen before in Helmand.

The minefield wasn't something the everyday Taliban could throw together on their own. Its design required a detailed understanding of electronics as well as talent. The Taliban were getting help. But from whom? The Pakistanis? The Iranians? If anyone knew they weren't going to tell us.

Following the casualty evacuation, the pace of events began to slow down a little. It was now time to retrieve the dead. I stood for a second, just a few feet from one of the fallen, trying to take in what had happened, the carnage and loss. What a fucking waste.

The platoon sergeant, who'd first led us to the scene of the explosion, shouted over to me. 'Kim,' he said getting my attention, 'I need that lad's dog tags.'

My heart sank and Lewis's head spun round, his eyes caught mine and his expression said it all. I stopped and paused, steeling myself for the inevitable trauma. 'Just get on with it,' I said silently and cleared a path to where he had fallen.

The bomb had caused appalling injuries. What was left of his body was battered and torn beyond recognition and stripped of all dignity. His was not a soldier's death.

'Your guys don't need to see this. Move them back,' I told the sergeant.

I dropped down so that I was kneeling by his side, grabbed his body armour and rolled his torso onto one side, holding part of his body with my legs to prevent him from rolling back. The Rifles' standard operating procedure stated that dog tags should be placed inside the body armour. I unzipped the pocket on the front, containing the ballistic plate, retrieved his tags and threw them over to the sergeant. I breathed a sigh of relief and prepared to stand when the sergeant said: 'Hang on, Kim, they've got to stay with the body. I needed his number for ID purposes so that I can confirm he was KIA.'

I lay with the dead soldier by my side, hoping that his death had been quick and painless. I thought of home, my son and vowed at that moment that I would survive this shithole. After what seemed like an age, the sergeant, who had taken a note of the soldier's name and Army number, threw the tags back. I placed them back in the pocket and made sure they were secure, knowing all too well the value these have to bereaved parents back home. Parents who within a matter of hours would have their lives blown apart and broken forever.

I was trying to do the best job I could for him and bring some dignity to his passing. I pulled my legs back and very gently rolled his body back and patted him on the shoulder as if to say, 'Rest now. Your job is done.'

16

Aftermath

The centre of the killing zone was dominated by two large blast craters just a few feet apart. The ground around them was stained with blood that had dried into the wadi and turned a dark-brown colour. Blood-soaked field dressings and bandages lay trodden into the ground. The smell of death hung heavy in the air.

The two dead soldiers remained undisturbed, one in the reeds, the other in the open, almost as if they were peacefully sleeping. The rest of the soldiers involved in the operation had barely moved or spoken a word for almost an hour. Bastion had already been informed of the identities of the dead. It flashed across my mind right at that moment, as I slowly, carefully walked back towards the dead, that someone, somewhere in the UK, dressed in his best military uniform was going to make that dreadful journey to the next of kin. There would be that knock on the door, a moment of confusion, then disbelief and anger followed by unimaginable sorrow and pain.

'We've got to get this lad into a body bag and back to

Bastion,' I said to the platoon sergeant. 'I'm afraid I won't be able to do it on my own.'

A young soldier, possibly only eighteen, stood up, his eyes red with tears, his face contorted with grief. One of those killed was his best friend. He was sobbing, almost uncontrollably, but there was no sense of shame. There were times during that harrowing morning that almost everyone felt like crying. He walked towards me as the sergeant handed me a body bag.

'It's all right, mate, I've got this, your sergeant will help.'

'No, I want to help, I want to carry him out of here,' the young lad said, wiping away the tears. 'He was my best mate.'

The dead soldier was carefully and gently manoeuvred into the body bag. I was determined that the dead were treated as respectfully as possible given that we were still in a tactical environment, a minefield and no doubt being watched by the Taliban. Four soldiers came forward and lifted the black bag, each grabbing a handle. No one spoke. Another four from the same platoon were lifting the other dead soldier out of the reeds at the same time. The rest of the search team stood motionless in respectful silence until the dead had been carried out of view to the HLS where another chopper was inbound.

A gentle, warm wind blew through the reeds while songbirds began celebrating the start of a new day. Summer mornings in Helmand were always stunning and began with the promise of something fresh and uplifting. But it was difficult to imagine anything good coming from this day.

I turned to the sergeant major and the company commander and asked whether the operation was going ahead or being aborted.

'Sir, what do we want to achieve here? Are we going to press on?'

The company commander, a major, his eyes filled with sadness and fatigue, said, 'We're binning it. We've just learned that Lance Corporal Fullarton didn't make it. He died on the helicopter. Keep it to yourself for the moment. I don't want the rest of the company to know until we are back in Jackson.'

The suddenness with which death came in Afghan was always shocking. An hour ago the dead soldiers had been vibrant and carefree, full of life, smiles and fun. Now those same sons, husbands and brothers were dead and everything they were and everything they were going to be was gone. But now was not the time to be angry or sad, these emotions would have to be stored for another time. There was still work to be done.

I gathered my team together. 'Right, the op's been shit-canned. We're heading back to Jackson but I'm going to smack the main charges in situ before we head back. Everyone stay focused and don't move beyond the cleared areas. No more dead soldiers today. Everyone happy with that? Good. Right, give me all the bang you've got.'

I turned to the platoon sergeant: 'You need to get all of your blokes out of the area. Once I fire these I will no longer have control over what happens and three minutes later there will be a huge explosion.'

Lewis and David began emptying out their day-sacks, gathering sticks of PE, detonators, det-cord and anything else I might need. The plan was to destroy all the main charges in one big explosion with a ring-main composed of det-cord, linking as many of the main charges as possible but there was only enough for four charges. The remaining three would have to be blown individually. Small amounts of PE were positioned close to the remaining three main charges with individual detonators and burning fuses.

Seven IEDs had been found and two had exploded. The Taliban knew that the area was used by soldiers as a transit route into the main town from the FOB – the wadi was vast and the routes taken by the soldiers were chosen at random and never repeated. But to counter this the Taliban simply laid more bombs.

Chidders began pointing them out: 'Look there's another, and another – this is ridiculous. I've never seen anything like this.'

There were at least another six, possibly more buried in an arc across the wadi. Part of me wanted to stay and defuse them all but I also recognised that the soldiers needed to get back to the safety of the base and besides, the Taliban weren't going anywhere – there were always going to be more IEDs. After lighting the fuses, Chidders and I headed back to where the rest of the company had gathered.

'Everyone get your heads down, there's going to be some big explosions!' I shouted, ensuring that everyone followed the command.

The first explosion was massive. Four main charges detonated at the same time. The shockwave passed over us and a cloud of smoke, dust and debris mushroomed into the sky. A few seconds later the remaining three main charges detonated one after the other in a series of equally spaced explosions. Usually there was a cheer from the soldiers when an IED was destroyed, but not that day; there was nothing to celebrate.

The company returned to Jackson on the same route that we had come, the front man searching the ground with his metal detector, ensuring that the Taliban hadn't returned to bury more bombs. The men moved solemnly in single file, following the footsteps of the man in front, many with their heads bowed and lost in thought.

One by one we filtered back through the gates. Just ninety minutes earlier we had gathered in the same place, excited about the day ahead. But in the time it takes to play a game of football three soldiers had been killed, another three injured, one seriously, and God only knows how many traumatised.

Weapons were unloaded in silence and exhausted soldiers dragged themselves back to their sleeping quarters with some facing the daunting task of packing away their dead mate's kit. After unloading our weapons, I called my team together, away from the comrades of the dead.

'Is everyone all right? I know none of you were injured but it's been a shit morning and we've all seen some pretty messed-up stuff.' The soldiers nodded and mumbled. 'But we can't afford to dwell. Let's talk later. Anyone who has any issues or concerns, come and see me. We're a team and it's at times like this that we need to look out for one another.'

Everyone was probably traumatised by the morning's events but we just had to suck it up. If we were pulled out someone else would have to come in and cover for us.

I threw my body armour and weapon on my bed and sat on one end. I was physically and mentally drained. It had been a long, difficult day, probably harder than anything we had imagined but the team's professionalism had shone through. The months of training in the cold and wet, the endless lessons, getting things wrong before we got them right, had all paid off. Probably for the first time in my career I understood why the British Army is so good at what it does. I don't think any of us had realised how far we had come as professional soldiers until that day.

Just a few years ago, I was a kid going nowhere, knocking around with wasters whose only goal in life was to get pissed and smoke weed. I could have easily gone the same way. But

I chose to join the Army and was given a chance. The Army offered me a choice, gave me a sense of direction and purpose and now I was leading a team doing some of the most dangerous and demanding work that can be done in a war zone. If I'm honest, I almost felt elated. I had come face to face with a situation so unique that had someone suggested it at Bomb School they would have been laughed at. But the ambush had also shown how adaptable and versatile the Taliban had become. I took a few gulps of water and then realised I needed to give Bastion a full brief on the situation.

I raced across to the Jackson Ops Room and dialled the EOD Task Force's number on a secure line.

'Jim, it's me – I'm off the ground.'

'Right, tell me everything,' he responded.

I talked him through the task, step by step: the casualties, the risks, the layout of the IEDs. The conversation lasted for a good hour and at the end of the call he said he wanted an initial report emailed back to the HQ within the hour. Specifically, he was interested in the nature of the device, and how it could be armed and disarmed to provide freedom of movement for the Taliban and the local people, while targeting ISAF troops. He stressed that the detail in my report would be essential. No one had seen anything like this before and my report needed to be disseminated across ISAF as soon as possible. The Sangin IED was now battle proven, as far as the Taliban were concerned, and very soon it would be appearing across Helmand.

I commandeered a laptop and began typing, looking at my notes and recalling the incident. Ninety minutes later I hit the send button and the report was on its way to Bastion and the UK. Just forty-eight hours later the Sangin IED was being run as a new scenario at the Felix Centre on the High Threat course back in the UK. The reach-back was amazing; the guys on the course would be told: 'This is the latest device to come out of Afghan, look and learn.'

The following morning we were up again before first light on another job as if nothing had happened. Fortunately, there were no casualties and we returned with smiles on our faces. But there would be more casualties, sooner than most of us anticipated.

17

Pharmacy Road

Over the next couple of days, patrols were kept to a minimum while the battalion licked its wounds and said goodbye to the dead. My team filled its time doing admin, sorting out equipment, replenishing our expended stores, hitting the gym and washing away blood from our combats in the Helmand river, the one place on the base where smiles were still seen.

The soldiers based in Sangin had seen too much death, too many of their friends blown to pieces. Fear was the dominant emotion in FOB Jackson, fear and wondering who would be the next to be killed. Four months into the tour and the Rifles were exhausted and they still had another two months to push. Six months in Sangin was simply too long. Those who survived would be scarred, probably for the rest of their lives.

It was mid-August and most of the soldiers had at least another ten weeks to serve before their tour came to an end. Ten weeks equated to somewhere between fifty and seventy patrols and on every one they expected to be attacked and take casualties. Some of those who had been killed and injured in the last couple of weeks had been sent out to replace soldiers who had been killed or injured earlier in the tour – battle-casualty replacements needing battle-casualty replacements.

For those inside Sangin it felt as though the world was against them. The base was isolated and surrounded by Afghans, who were effectively indistinguishable from the Taliban. They wore the same clothes, spoke the same language and offered the same smiles. We never really knew who our enemy was and rarely saw them.

I attended the morning briefs in the Ops Room with the various company commanders and other attached units to see what the plan was for the day and whether we would be needed. But the demands upon us were limited to a few hours of Counter-IED training and the rest of the time was spent in a kind of limbo, waiting for the next IED find or explosion. The week rolled on and morale began to climb back to its original level. Soldiers began to return to the river to swim in larger numbers, play and relax and forget about tomorrow for just a few hours.

Four days had passed since the wadi chaos. It was Thursday 20 August 2009, and the team was enjoying a brew outside our Hesco home when the Ops Room runner appeared. He was breathing heavily and looked flustered, 'Sir, I mean Staff, the CO needs you in the Ops Room now.'

The team looked at me but no words were spoken. They rose as one and began to gather their equipment.

Entering the Ops Room it was immediately clear that something was seriously wrong. Heads turned and looked up at me from computer screens; there were no smiles, no welcome. The chief of staff, a major in the Rifles, called me over to his desk.

'Staff – we had an IED strike about fifteen minutes ago. An infantry search team call sign Yankee 31 based at PB Wishtan were supporting engineering call sign Hades 31 Echo in this location, here . . .' He pointed to an area called the Pharmacy Road. He explained that a soldier had stepped on a suspected pressure-plate IED and was dead. As his team tried to recover his body they identified what they believe was another pressure plate.

He continued: 'The QRF was despatched with a quad bike and trailer. They were intending to use the winch on the quad to drag the body out of the danger area. The winch was attached to the soldier and as the QRF commander moved back to the quad bike he triggered a second IED and was also killed and another soldier was seriously injured. Both have been recovered but we need to recover the body of the soldier killed first.'

'Yes, sir,' I replied before being beckoned by Lieutenant Colonel Rob Thomson, the Rifles' commanding officer. The CO had become used to dealing with death but I immediately sensed this incident had hit him particularly hard.

'You've been briefed?'

'Sir,' I responded.

'Your thoughts?'

'I'm not going to mess about, sir. I'm going in and I'll get your boy out. We'll clear the area later, but getting him off the ground's the priority.'

'Good,' the CO responded.

Pharmacy Road had gained a well-deserved notoriety in Sangin. It was if you like the most dangerous area of the most dangerous town in Afghanistan. It wasn't so much a road but more like a thirty-foot wide, winding, 800-metre-long minefield, linking two patrol bases called Wishtan and

Tangiers. On either side of the road were twenty-foot-high mud walls, occasionally opening up into other streets or alleyways, almost like rat runs. The ground favoured the Taliban and gave them almost complete freedom of movement. They could move into the area under the cover of darkness and at times during the day and plant IEDs with impunity, and thereby turn the road into a long, continuous nightmare.

In an attempt to restrict the Taliban's movement it was decided to block off the side roads and alleyways with huge Hesco blocks. The strategy was sensible enough but would only work if every side road or alleyway was closed, and there were dozens of them. A so-called super-sangar, a fortified rocket-proof lookout post, had also been built to provide additional cover in the immediate area and was manned 24/7. The sangar worked to a certain extent and provided a sort of visual link between the two PBs. But the Taliban were clever. They knew every inch of the terrain and careful use of the dead ground often allowed them to get to within twenty metres of the sangar.

The whole area had a no-man's-land feel to it. Sangin was once a thriving community but in the three years since the British had arrived, hundreds of compounds and houses had been turned into rubble after almost a thousand days of continuous war. Now only dogs, cats and rats occupied the ruins.

PB Wishtan was just a few kilometres from Jackson, but travelling by road was simply too dangerous and the only option was to fly in by chopper. By 0950 hrs we were in the air on board a Chinook, heading for Wishtan. The Sangin Taliban would often take potshots with RPGs at the critical moment when helicopters were slowly landing or taking off. The flight lasted just a few tense minutes and everyone was relieved when we landed in Wishtan. At the edge of the HLS were four soldiers carrying a body draped in a Union Jack flag and containing the remains of one of their comrades. All were ashen-faced and looked totally crushed.

Charlie Company, 2nd Battalion, the Rifles, had just lost two soldiers: 18-year-old Private Johnathon Young, who had only been in Afghanistan for eighteen days and Serjeant Paul McAleese, who up until the moment he died was a living legend within the regiment and the son of one of the SAS soldiers who stormed the Iranian Embassy in London in 1980. We later learned that it was Serjeant McAleese's body we had seen being loaded onto the Chinook.

The company Operations Officer, a captain, who knew both the dead men, briefed Lee and me on recovering the body. Brimstone 42 would be escorted to the target by another platoon who would provide us with additional close protection while we got to work.

Events moved quickly and by 10.30 a.m. the area where the two soldiers had been killed was reached. Chidders quickly organised an isolation of the target area while Dave and I began developing a plan to extract Private Young's body.

To achieve a thorough search of the area the search team had to blast holes through various compound walls, a process known as Explosive Method of Entry (EMOE), using half a bar mine containing 4kg of high explosive. The bar mine was essentially a massive lump of explosive designed during the Cold War to stop a 40-ton Russian tank. Although tanks weren't a threat in Afghan, the bar mine was ideal for blowing holes in two-foot-thick walls.

Once the isolation was complete I established the Incident Control Point (ICP) thirty metres around the corner from the dead soldier. The search team, their job complete, rested against a wall while Dave and I prepared for the next phase of the operation.

'Ready?' I said to Dave.

'Roger,' he replied and I set off, searching my way around the corner and up to the site of the explosion, leaving a yellow spray-painted path in my wake. The place had taken on a ghostly appearance as if Private Young had been lying there, untouched, for months. Although tragic there was also something curiously peaceful about the scene and I almost felt like an intruder. Remnants of first-aid equipment, bandages, first field dressings and tourniquets littered the area along with pieces of military equipment that had belonged to the two soldiers – all of it was covered in the same dust.

The blast had left his light support weapon bent and mangled. An Army-issue boot containing the remains of a foot had come to rest by a wall. Everything was photographed in situ before being recovered.

I attempted to visualise the last few seconds of Private Young's life: where he was standing, where the bomb had been positioned, what he was doing prior to stepping on the pressure plate. Then I slowly moved forward sweeping my metal detector and almost immediately began to get hits from fragments of metal and equipment damaged in the blast.

Dave positioned himself in a cleared safe area by a small stone wall while I continued moving slowly forward to where Private Young had died. I stared at his body, battered and torn by the violence of the blast. Another day, another dead soldier. I felt almost nothing apart from a deep sense of waste and wondered how many more dead soldiers I would see by the time my tour was over.

18

The Fallen

The dead soldier lay on his back with his arms outstretched at 90 degrees in the shape of a cross. Most of his body armour had been destroyed apart from a flap of fabric that covered his face like a veil, possibly sparing me from seeing the injuries to his head and face. Beneath him the ground had been stained dark-brown with blood that had been absorbed into the dirt.

I paused and took some comfort from knowing that his death must have been instantaneous, and carefully continued searching up to where he was lying. As I got closer I could see a pressure plate lying by the side of the body. It was immediately clear that the plate was from the first explosion and not an additional device as Serjeant McAleese had initially suspected. It had probably been blown out of the ground by the explosion. After searching around Private Young's body I spray-painted the secure area's perimeter, knelt down and fingertip-searched around the pressure plate, confirming that it was unconnected, before placing it in a forensic bag.

Back at the ICP a Royal Military Police captain, whom I'd previously met in Germany earlier in my career, had now arrived to conduct the post-incident investigation. All events in which soldiers are killed are investigated by the RMP. We shook hands and chatted briefly before I turned to the team: 'I know it's not a nice job but I'm going to need a hand with the body.'

One of the lads from the Rifles, who was sitting on the quad bike, stood up and handed me a body bag.

'I'll help,' he said solemnly.

'It's OK, mate, we'll do it,' I said, hoping to spare him from any further trauma.

Lewis and Malley both volunteered to help but their faces revealed their true feelings – no one gets used to handling the dead.

'We're going to move around to where he is lying following the cleared path. We'll then put him in the body bag as quickly and respectfully as possible and then bring him back here and the quad will take him to Wishtan.'

In single file, with our weapons slung across our backs, we made our way around the corner followed by the RMP captain, who needed to take notes and pictures of the scene for his report. There was a feeling, something like embarrassment, as we caught each other's eyes when manoeuvring the dead soldier into the body bag. We stumbled and struggled, underestimating the difficulty of lifting a lifeless, damaged body into a large black sack. Soldiers dropped their heads or turned away, looking at anything but us. A few flicked stones into the dirt or sucked heavily on cigarettes. The dead soldier was carefully lifted onto the quad's trailer. Everyone was silent as he was slowly driven away to Wishtan.

'He was a good lad,' said a young red-eyed Rifleman from

the same section as the dead soldier. 'He'd only been in Afghan a couple of weeks and only told me this morning that he was missing home so much. What a waste. His whole life was in front of him.'

As the search team began clearing the alleyway and a wider area around the blast zone, a message came through from the Wishtan Ops Room stating that an RPG had been fired into the base and had landed on the HLS. The warhead hadn't exploded but no helicopters would be able to land until it had been cleared.

'Chidders, an RPG has been fired at the PB. It's gone blind. You finish up here. I'm going back to Wishtan to sort it out. We'll RV back at the base.'

I got on the radio to the Wishtan Ops Room: 'Hello, Zero, this is Brimstone 42; we've recovered the body. The pressure plate was part of the first device, my call sign is en route back to your location to sort the UXO. Out.'

'Hello, Brimstone 42, this is Zero. Don't worry, we have a combat engineer who will deal with it. Out,' the Ops Room watch-keeper responded.

A combat engineer can undertake certain demolition tasks, like blowing tracks off a vehicle, but an unexploded RPG was a bit out of his league and it sounded like some sort of chip-shop lunatic looking to make a name for himself.

As I walked through the gate accompanied by a soldier who had been acting as my escort, I could see the engineer crouched over the RPG preparing what looked like a demolition charge. He was so engrossed in his work that he didn't notice me peering over his shoulder.

An RPG consists of two elements: a high explosive warhead and the tail unit, containing a rocket motor to propel the grenade during flight. Both contain an explosive material, but once fired, the tail unit becomes inert as its propellant charge is expended. After the RPG was fired, no doubt by a Taliban chancer hoping for a lucky strike, it had hit a wall and the warhead and tail unit had separated. The warhead was nowhere to be seen and the tail unit had come to rest on the HLS decking, and was a threat to no one. He was about to destroy the tail unit with more plastic explosive than was actually contained within the RPG. The blast would have blown a massive hole in the decking of the HLS, rendering it useless.

I leaned over his shoulder and picked up the tail unit. He jumped up and looked at me like he was about to shit himself.

'Christ,' he said, clocking my ATO badge.

'What are you playing at?'

'We've got to blow this,' he added without any great conviction.

'You're about to blow a fucking great hole in the HLS and put it out of action for an inert tail unit, you twat.'

I was absolutely furious. Maybe he was bored, maybe he hadn't done much on his tour but he was clearly big-timing it and thought he was going to get the chance of blowing something up when all he would have done is bounced the tail unit across the compound.

'Idiot,' I thought as I walked over to the Ops Room.

I was still seething as I entered the dark Ops Room, which was lit by a single fluorescent lamp hanging precariously from the ceiling. Maps with red dots signifying IED strikes hung on the walls and in the corner was the obligatory filter coffee machine gently bubbling away.

I almost threw the tail unit on the desk in front of the company second-in-command, a young Rifles captain. It landed with a clunk, which made him jump a little.

'HLS is now clear, sir.'

'Oh right, we were told it needed to get blown up.'

'Does it fuck, sir. It's inert,' I said and wondered if I was coming across as a bit of an arrogant arsehole. Just as I decided I was going to head back out onto the ground, a message came over the radio announcing the search had finished.

My team trooped back in through the main gate looking tired and sad. In the past four days they'd had to deal close up with the deaths of five soldiers. Up until that point none of them had ever seen a dead body and recent events were beginning to take their toll.

I had been told to expect a lift back to FOB Jackson later that evening but there were no specific timings. I dumped my day-sack next to one of the compound walls and made a makeshift pillow, lay down and closed my eyes. I must have been dozing for just a few moments when there was another explosion.

My stomach turned and my mind raced. The blast must have come from the area where we had been working an hour or so earlier. There were no soldiers on the ground. Had something been missed?

19

Chocolate Fireguards

The echo from the explosion bounced off the walls inside Wishtan. I sat up and instinctively grabbed my weapon. 'IED,' I said out loud.

Lee and I raced to the Ops Room only to be met with looks of barely disguised hostility as we entered.

'What's going on, sir,' I said to the Rifles captain, who had a look on his face that basically said 'Wankers'.

'An explosion has just taken place in exactly the same area that your men supposedly cleared, Staff.' His tone was direct and uncompromising.

My heart sank.

'The question for you, Staff, is what is going on?'

The awkward silence was broken by a message over the radio confirming that there had been an IED strike in the cleared area. Thankfully there were no casualties, only the bucket of the combat engineering digger had been damaged.

Instantly I looked at Lee as if to say 'Did you clear that area?'

Our credibility as a Counter-IED team was now in doubt and I felt as though I'd just been slapped in the face with a bag of shit. A wave of panic surged through my body.

'Right, sir, we need to find out what happened. I'm going out to see what's going on.'

'Yes, you do that, Staff,' the captain said when what he really meant was 'Now go and do your job properly.'

As we walked out of the Ops Room I turned to Lee. 'This can't be happening. Are you sure you cleared the ground properly?'

'Yes. No doubt about it. We all went in there – you, me, everyone. All with metal detectors.'

Fifteen minutes later we were back on the ground in the location that had been cleared two hours earlier. The digger that detonated the IED had been flattening the earth torn up in the two earlier blasts by repeatedly dropping its earth-moving bucket on the ground. It was during that process that another IED was detonated.

I didn't want to admit it but I was convinced I already knew the truth. Somehow we had missed an IED. Accidents happen in Afghan. Sometimes IEDs weren't detected. But a search team missing an IED was a different story.

'Right, Lee, Chidders. Point out exactly the area you cleared earlier.'

'We cleared that area,' Chidders added and I could tell he was getting pissed off with my questions.

'Yeah, and I've been all over that as well. But we need to be objective about this. We somehow missed a device, all of us, and we now need to find out why that happened. The buck stops with me. I'll fight our corner but I need to know how and why this happened.'

Utterly confused, I couldn't help but begin doubting

myself. I had never missed a device before, either in training or on ops. Something had gone seriously wrong.

I turned to the team. 'The area needs to be searched again. There are engineers working here and they need to be confident we have done our job properly.'

I led the way and we cleared the seat of the explosion while the engineers and soldiers from the Rifles watched us suspiciously. It was absolutely vital that the infantry trusted us. If the trust was somehow lost then we might as well pack up and go home.

There were no clues as to what had happened. On the face of it, the search team's drills had failed. But the facts just didn't seem to add up. There was always the possibility that one person could miss a device – but the area had been cleared by the whole team.

Firstly the search team went into the area conducting several sweeps, checking walls, the churned-up ground and mounds of earth, which had clearly not been touched in months. Nothing was found, which didn't make us feel any better.

The team returned to base by 1615 hrs and Lee and I headed to the Ops Room. Again people were looking at us as though we were a bunch of arseholes. I approached the Operations Officer who had earlier doubted our competence and waited for him to finish a phone call on the secure line.

'Sir, the area was cleared. We found no evidence of IEDs. I don't know what's happened. My team stepped all over that area. I even took the RMP in there.'

Then I had a thought, a possible reason why the IED couldn't be detected.

'Sir, give me five. I'll be back.'

I grabbed the two pressure plates that had been placed in forensic bags earlier and headed out of the Ops Room.

In an area free of any pieces of metal, I threw the pressure plates on the floor and ran my metal detector over the top of them. Nothing, not a sound. Everyone stared at me in disbelief.

'Chidders, give me your metal detector.'

I ran the second metal detector over the plates. Again nothing. I turned the metal detector to its most sensitive setting, something rarely done because you simply get too many false readings. But only then could the faintest of bleeps be heard.

I opened my penknife and sliced the pressure plate open and pulled it apart. This went against standard practice. IEDs are usually kept intact to preserve any forensic evidence. Inside I could see that the metal content had been significantly reduced. This was something new, something never seen before in Helmand. No one wanted to say it at that moment but the Taliban had made an IED that was almost, but not entirely, impossible to detect. Our equipment, the militarised metal detector, which had saved the lives of thousands of soldiers, had become, as one of the lads pointed out, almost as much use as a 'chocolate fireguard'.

An hour later, we were back in FOB Jackson. I told the team to get some rest and headed to the Ops Room. As soon as I walked through the door I was accosted by the battalion's chief of staff.

'What's the story with the pressure plate?'

I explained everything and watched as the blood seemed to draw from his face.

'I need to reassess this with my team and my HQ and find out what the score is, sir.'

'I want to know what you plan to do about this in thirty minutes.' There was no room for manoeuvre in his voice.

'Sir, I need to do some more tests to make sure we've got our heads around this and speak to my boss.'

'Fuck that, Staff,' he responded. 'I want to know in thirty minutes whether you can detect these things. I want your plan of action.'

Back at the Hesco House, Lee was already checking the search team's specialist equipment to see if it performed any better but the results were the same. I explained that the Rifles' chief of staff was demanding answers and we had to formulate some sort of plan.

Lee turned to me. 'Nothing works, Kim. Soldiers from this base will be doing an evening patrol in about an hour and at the moment they have no protection against these IEDs.'

'What are we going to do now?' said Malley.

'What can we do?' added Chidders. 'This is bad.'

'OK, lads, don't worry, this is above our pay grade. I'm heading back to the Ops Room. Have a think about our next move.'

The chief of staff had his hands on his hips with a look of thunder on his face. He wanted to blame someone for what was turning into the world's biggest nightmare and I was his target.

'Well?' he said, now not even referring to my rank, which was starting to piss me off. We'd worked our bollocks off since we arrived, saved the lives of his men and done whatever we were asked and I wasn't about to be treated like an idiot in front of the battalion Ops Room because the Taliban had made an undetectable IED.

The room fell quiet and all eyes were on me.

I threw the pressure plate onto the table in front of him.

'We can't detect them, sir. We've used all our kit but the metal content is too low. This is not an issue with my team, you need to understand that. This is not a failure of drill. The Taliban have made a pressure plate that can't be detected.'

His face was gripped with confusion. 'You must be able to. You're the so-called experts.'

'Sir, there's not enough metal in these bombs to be detected. My team has used all our equipment, which is more than any infantry unit has got, and we're not getting any hits.'

He closed his eyes and breathed deeply, then turned and headed to the CO's office. One by one the rest of the Ops Room went back to work. I hung around for half an hour or so and then returned to the rest of the team. They were despondent and not without reason. If the Taliban had developed a pressure plate that couldn't be detected then specialist searchers were almost redundant.

'Listen, Terry has obviously been quite clever here but he's not as clever as us. We'll work something out. Tomorrow we need to get among the Rifles and start training them on how to spot ground-sign and make sure they know where Terry is going to place bombs.'

It was a seminal moment in the Afghan War and once again the initiative was with the Taliban. As an EOD Operator I couldn't help but feel some grudging respect for what they had managed to achieve. The Taliban were adapting. Like all 'successful' terrorist organisations the insurgents tended to repeat successes and rethink failures. They had seen how metal detectors were used to detect bombs.

Within the hour Patrol Minimise, which was effectively no patrolling unless of urgent operational necessity, was put in place in Sangin and other areas across Afghanistan. Over the next forty-eight hours, the Rifles were taught how to improve their ability to identify ground-sign and how to avoid being channelled into killing areas. If there was an obvious crossing-point over a river it was also likely to be an area where the Taliban would place a device. If the only option was to wade through five feet of water, then tough, suck it up, they were told, and get your feet wet. But the soldiers also knew that they could know exactly what the Taliban were up to only to be smashed by some random, undetectable IED – that was the nature of the war in Afghan.

Early on in the tour most of the IEDs found had all the components placed together. The battery pack, containing most of the metal, would be placed next to the pressure plate, which was positioned on top of the main charge. But the Taliban changed this set-up and began to vary their tactics.

There was little choice but for soldiers to change their tactics too. They adapted to the new threat surprisingly quickly and came to rely more on their operational awareness and how to spot ground-sign rather than relying on the bleep of a metal detector.

Over the next few weeks we found more low-metal devices but also high-metal ones too. The next generation of IEDs contained no metal at all. Bare wires were replaced with conductive carbon rods removed from D-Cell batteries and crush-sensitive explosives replaced the need for any power sources or switches. However, by the time these devices started to appear towards the end of the tour, search teams were equipped with ground-penetrating radar which could be used to detect non-metal objects.

Just as the Taliban adapted we were forced to adapt too.

20

Boredom and Bullshit

Someone once said, 'War is Hell.' There's no doubt about that, but perhaps they should have added that war can also be boring, intensely boring. For many soldiers, bomb disposal teams included, a lot of what people describe as 'war' is actually hanging around waiting to do something, to fly somewhere or to get a briefing from somebody. The hardest moments came between the periods of intense activity, when there was time to think and question, when you might wonder whether you were going to make it home and see your family again. Fighting boredom was often harder than fighting the Taliban. Everyone sent to Helmand was trained to fight, taught how to spot an IED and could deal with a traumatic amputation. But there was no preparation on how to cope with the lengthy lulls in operational activity when there was literally nothing to do. Boredom was like a virus – it could undermine morale and team cohesion – but occasionally a little bit of boredom was exactly what was needed.

After the Sangin period, Brimstone 42 returned to Bastion in the hope of a few days' rest and a period of downtime before the next mission. The team arrived back in Bastion looking like the Dirty Dozen, unshaven, stinking, body armour stained with blood, sweat and dirt and our weapons hanging off us like we'd just finished a week-long firefight.

Lee and I went straight into the Ops Room only to be greeted with looks of hostility by new members of the EOD Task Force HQ who'd recently arrived from the UK. While we were covered in shit they would be sitting in an air-conditioned tent, dressed in pristine combats, well rested and clean-shaven, enjoying one of their posh selection of coffees courtesy of the mountain of welfare parcels stacked in the corner. Neither of us were in the mood to take any shit from anyone, irrespective of rank, and we looked at the Ops Room staff as if to say 'Fucking oxygen thieves, you don't know what war is', while they looked at us as if to say 'Who do you think you are, the SAS?'

Lee and I briefed the chain of command, although there wasn't much more to say than had already been said. They knew the score, had seen the reports and were aware that the team had been through a punishing week.

The first evening back in Bastion I asked everyone to make sure they were in the tent by 2000 hrs so we could go through a debrief of the previous week. Everything was covered, what worked, what didn't, how we might approach things differently in the future. It was all constructive. No one was singled out for any criticism.

I then asked whether anyone had any issues with what they had seen. One by one I went around the room asking Lee, Dave, Malley, Foz, Chidders, Lewis, Harry and Stu. No one wanted to admit that they had been deeply affected or traumatised by what had happened in Sangin. But I think we all were. Watching a soldier disfigured by mutilation die a slow, painful death was traumatising. Every member of the team probably all had nightmares, I certainly did, but none of us openly admitted that we did and no one was going to say: 'I can't do this any more.' So like men everywhere around the world, we locked those dark thoughts away. 'We'll deal with it when we get back home,' I added and everyone nodded in agreement.

The following morning we laid into our personal admin big time, getting clothes washed and equipment exchanged. Sangin felt like a world away and the banter flowed. The piss-taking was merciless and no one was spared. Music was played at a loudness designed to piss off the camp rats who never ventured beyond the wire. Occasionally someone would stick their head into the tent and ask for the volume to be lowered. The response varied depending on the rank of the complainant. Staff sergeant or lower would be told to fuck off, while apologies would be made to those of higher rank but the volume would be increased almost immediately once they were out of earshot.

Once personal admin was out of the way, we headed to Camp Leatherneck, the part of Bastion owned by the US Marines, where you could get a pretty awesome Frappuccino or a coffee or buy something none of us needed from one of the large US servicemen's stores or Postal Exchange, known as the PX. From Camp Leatherneck we got a lift back to NAAFI and killed some more time drinking coffee or Mountain Dews, gradually ticking off all the things we promised ourselves during those dark days in Sangin.

After dinner it was back to the tent to watch a film, read or just chill. But by the second day the 'Bastion bullshit' started to creep in. It was the same pattern every time we came back to Bastion. Often in the first twenty-four hours, the lads would cut around in shorts, T-shirts and flip-flops – it was an opportunity to relax, forget about the war, and try to air your feet. But our attitude and mode of dress would start to get under the camp rats' noses. Complaints would be lodged and I'd be called into the Ops Room and asked to sort it out. Unfortunately for us the bullshit factor went through the roof with the arrival of a new sergeant major who loved pointing his pace stick at anything and everything, as if he was some Guards sergeant major outside Buckingham Palace.

He had arrived while we had been out on the ground and I first came across him when I went into the Ops Room a few days after I arrived back from Sangin. I was in super-relaxed mode and probably looking a bit scruffy. He stood up and looked at me with complete disdain as I entered. I was about to offer my hand when he said, 'Can I help you?' But what he actually meant was 'Who are you and why are you coming into the Ops Room dressed like that?'

Perhaps I was being a little petulant, but I walked straight past him and went over to the new SAT, WO1 'Sandy' Little, and shook his hand. Sandy was a straight-talking Scot with a great sense of humour. He was a seasoned operator who understood the soldiers and their needs. I could feel the sergeant major's eyes burning into the back of me as he looked at Sandy and me chatting like old friends.

A few hours later as I was coming back from the showers I clocked him pointing his pace stick at one of my guys while dishing out a bollocking.

'What's going on?' I said angrily.

'Is he one of yours?'

'He's part of my Counter-IED team. If that's what you mean.'

'Well, he's incorrectly dressed. This is a military camp. Discipline is important and he doesn't look like a soldier.' It was a typical comment from a 'Z' sergeant major, someone who has to justify his existence by carrying a pace stick around with him.

'He's spent the last ten days pulling bombs out of the ground, dodging bullets and living with the shits. His uniform is being washed and he's in shorts for a couple of hours because he's got bollock rash. I told him to dress like that so he's fit to go back out on ops in a few days' time. If you have a problem with him take it up with me, sir.'

The sergeant major looked lost for words and could see that I wasn't going to back down. After a brief stand-off he said, 'I'll let it pass on this occasion but things are going to change around here.' This was the bullshit that gradually came to infect Bastion and some of the larger FOBs in Helmand.

The first signs of boredom began to appear just forty-eight hours after we returned to Bastion. Almost in unison, the entire team began checking and repacking kit, cleaning their weapons, testing pieces of equipment, which were in perfectly good order. The banter died away and morale gradually started to dip. I became twitchy and irritable and later during that second morning I headed over to the Ops Room and asked for the team to be placed on QRF. The QRF teams were on thirty minutes' notice to move and had to be ready to deploy almost immediately. Teams could be bounced around Helmand from one FOB to another for up to a week and the days would fly by. The work was often dangerous and always demanding but it was what a bomb disposal team had been trained to do.

As I walked into the Ops Room, an IED find came across the J-Chat system, a secure version of an instant messenger. A unit somewhere in Helmand wanted an EOD team urgently flown into their location.

I dashed back to my tent and ten minutes later every member of Brimstone 42 was standing outside the Ops Room, ready to be deployed. The SAT appeared and said, 'What are you doing?' looking half confused and half pissed off.

'A ten liner's come in. We're ready to go. We're on QRF.' My team were standing there like a pack of hounds that had just picked up the scent of a fox, desperate to get out onto the ground. The Ops Room staff looked on in confusion with a look of 'Why do you want to go beyond the wire?'

The SAT waved us away as if we were irritating children. 'You're not going out on this one. The infantry are going to mark and avoid it. You lot are meant to be having some downtime. The war isn't going anywhere and Terry hasn't stopped making bombs. If you want something to do I'll get the sergeant major to give you tasks – there are always plenty of Bastion duties going.'

Bastion duties could be anything from working in the cookhouse as a dogsbody to sentry duty in one of the watchtowers. It was more of a punishment than a duty and the EOD teams were often seen as an easy target. Usually teams on downtime were pretty safe but by asking to be placed back on QRF I had signalled that we were available again and that made us vulnerable to being pinged for duties. It was a perception thing. EOD teams did most of their work beyond the wire, in isolated bases away from headquarters, and so a lot of the camp rats only ever saw us when we were chilling or knocking around Bastion in shorts and flip-flops. Hence they thought we were having an easy life while they were sweating their nuts off fourteen hours a day in the Ops Room.

Suitably warned, we headed off to the training area, partly to combat the boredom but also to escape the clutches of the sergeant major and his list of duties. Lee and I created complex scenarios and really put the team through its paces, challenging them with all sorts of possible situations, from multiple-IED attacks to leadership tasks. Over the next few days we smashed first-aid training, range work and spent more time on the Barma lanes, practising and refining new metal detector skills, than I thought possible. EOD teams were used to being worked hard, we wanted to work hard and we were trained to work hard. The problem was no one trained us to deal with boredom.

After four days, Sandy announced that we were back on the QRF and the following morning Brimstone 42 flew out of Bastion back to where we felt most comfortable – beyond the wire.

21

They Want to Kill Me

If there's one abiding golden rule by which every bomb disposal expert should live by it's this: Never do the same thing twice. Once an ATO starts setting patterns he becomes an easy target for terrorists. The Taliban were masters of observation. They would sit and watch, mentally noting how EOD teams worked and what tactics were used and whether they were becoming predictable. For predictable read lazy. It was vital not to give the Taliban anything, otherwise they'd use it against you. The IRA were the same. Set a pattern and you were a marked man.

But not setting a pattern in Afghan was easier said than done. If you've got to pull twenty bombs out of the ground in a relatively small area you are going to end up repeating yourself – it was inevitable and one of those classic situations where the theory in training didn't chime with the reality on the ground.

Many of the ATOs based in Afghan in 2009 believed – it was an unwritten rule if you like – that if you did the same thing twice you were in danger of being targeted. Follow the rules and the chances are you would survive – use the robot (if it works), never pull anything out of the ground by hand – that's what a hook and line is for – and always cut wires remotely. But the reality of operational life in Afghan meant that many of the standard operating procedures weren't followed, not through carelessness or laziness, but because of the environment and the nature of operations.

A classic example was the bomb suit. In theory, every Counter-IED task should be conducted with the ATO wearing a full bomb suit complete with 50kg of woven Kevlar and armoured plate. But in Afghan, where the temperatures would routinely reach 45°C and there was a 360-degree front line, the bomb suit was a non-starter. Anyone wearing a suit would succumb to heat exhaustion within half an hour and its weight meant that you were unlikely to be able to move anywhere quickly if you came under attack.

The Taliban had a pretty efficient intelligence-gathering operation running in Helmand in 2009. Much of the local population were sympathetic to the insurgents' cause and those that weren't were often placed under enormous duress to help them. Intelligence on the movements of British troops, such as numbers, vehicles, weapons and tactics were of enormous value to the Taliban.

Counter-IED teams were not immune and one of the main problems faced was dicking – being watched. The teams had to assume they were being dicked all the time. Every time an ATO was killed or injured, either one of our own or an allied country, an investigation would be conducted to establish what went wrong and adapt our tactics, techniques and procedures (TTPs) to try and prevent it from happening again.

When IEDs really started to be used in large numbers at the back end of 2008, the Estonian troops began taking a lot of casualties. Their modus operandi was simple: walk down the road, disable the device and pull the bomb out of the ground. It was a tactic that worked well for a while until the Taliban dickers got wind of what the Estonians were doing and began booby-trapping the devices. It was a tough lesson for the Estonians to learn.

It was also vital, of course, that when a British Brimstone team came into a FOB to relieve another, the two teams had a comprehensive handover. I would sit down with Oz or Captain Dan Reid or whichever operator was taking over and go through every bomb I had cleared in the area. Over a brew, in a quiet corner of the base, every relevant operational detail would be discussed: the design of the bombs, the areas being targeted, the type of explosive, detonator and power source being used, the procedures used to neutralise them, the approach to and the time spent clearing the device, even the placement of the ICP and cordons were covered so they couldn't be targeted as part of a secondary attack. The level of information was sometimes overwhelming but it was crucial if an ATO new to an area was going to make an accurate threat assessment.

Another consideration that formed part of the assessment was identifying the Taliban's target. Was it the infantry or a Counter-IED team? The idea was that no two bomb disposal teams would ever operate in exactly the same way in the same location. But there are only so many options available and sometimes there might only be one possible route to the bomb. Circumstance might force two different teams to operate in a very similar way. I got around that potential problem by the abundant use of smoke grenades, so much so that Brimstone 42 was sometimes known as 'Team Smoke'.

The Army has several different types of smoke grenade

used for signalling and screening. Signalling grenades are used to attract attention, such as a helicopter coming into land. Screening grenades produce an excessive amount of smoke in a very short period of time, making a smokescreen and allowing troops to move freely without being seen. Screening grenades come in two different types: training and operational. The training variant when thrown produces smoke by burning a large smoke composition pellet within the grenade body, whereas the operational grenade has a central burster that, when thrown, explodes and discharges red phosphorus, which burns and produces smoke.

On one occasion I mixed up the red phosphorus grenade and normal training smoke. I should have thrown the grenade twenty to thirty metres away from where I was working but instead I dropped it at my feet. By the time I realised what I'd done it was too late. Red phosphorus was thrown everywhere but by a stroke of luck none landed on me. After witnessing the effects up close, I realised red phosphorus grenades were no use for providing an effective smokescreen. Training grenades were far better. Pull the pin, let go of the fly-off lever and smoke would begin pumping out of the end. By the end of the tour we had used in excess of 550 smoke grenades. On some jobs five or six were used to complete the task.

By late August 2009, Brimstone 42 had spent more days in FOB Keenan than any other Counter-IED team. From a purely operational viewpoint, we should have been rotated out because we ran the risk of setting patterns. It had been an intense period and it often seemed like there wasn't a road, track or alleyway that hadn't been targeted. There were times when we honestly felt that for every bomb we'd clear another two went into the ground.

During that period we became so familiar with the work of

the Taliban in the area that we managed to discover their patterns. They were laying bombs all the time and so they needed to have some sort of map or visual markers to prevent getting blown up by one of their own IEDs. After a couple of weeks it became clear that the Taliban would nearly always place the battery pack at the base of a tree, while the pressure plate and the main charge would be positioned within a ten metre radius. Once the plate had been located it was left alone – it was the danger zone. Next I'd conduct a detailed examination of the area looking for ground-sign or other potential markers that could have been used. Only then, when nothing else was found, would I start to clear the ground around the pressure plate.

On one routine day in Keenan, Brimstone 42 was despatched to deal with a pressure plate found during a morning foot patrol. I carried out my normal drills and during the detailed search discovered that the battery pack had been buried around five metres away from the pressure plate at the base of a tree, an obvious marker. It was only after I had cleared about five devices that it became obvious the same bomb team had planted all of the IEDs. The battery pack for each device was buried next to a tree. Initially I thought: 'Great, I've got this fucker sussed.' Find the pressure plate and then look for a tree, find the battery, cut the wire, job done. Then I realised I was potentially setting a pattern and my actions could have been picked up in a matter of days, and in some cases hours, by the enemy. I had to consider that this was all part of an elaborate plan to lull my team into a trap. The feeling that we were possibly being targeted was reinforced a few days later at the end of a long day in the sun.

My Brimstone team had been pulling bombs out of the ground until the late afternoon and were heading back to

Keenan for a shower and an ice-cold Mountain Dew. The team, along with a platoon of soldiers from Keenan who had spent the day watching our backs, were slowly walking in single file along a track that would eventually lead back to the base when a local Afghan civilian approached us. Almost as one we all brought our weapons up to our shoulders fixing him in our sights.

Most of the military bases across Helmand were located near small hamlets or villages, containing a bazaar with a few run-down shops or stalls selling everything from chillies to radio parts. Troops going on patrol might stop and chat to locals if they were heading through the bazaar and likewise the locals would chat – if they spoke English – or approach the Terp (interpreter), sometimes just to say hello but more often than not to have a whinge, usually about the corrupt Afghan police. But out in the countryside the Afghans left you alone, probably concerned that if they approached ISAF troops they might be mistaken as Taliban.

As the Afghan came closer the Terp ordered him to stand still and lift up his clothing to show that he wasn't wearing a suicide vest. Two soldiers gingerly walked forward and searched him, one patting him down all over his body while the other aimed his rifle at the guy's face. It was an undignified experience for anyone and you could see the contempt in the man's eyes. He had the chiselled face of a Pashtun warrior. He wore a biblical beard and his skin was a rich brown colour and heavily lined from a lifetime in the Helmand sun.

'He's clean,' one of the young soldiers said and Ali, the Terp, and the infantry commander moved forward and began speaking to him, asking what he wanted. Everyone was wary. Soldiers had recently been killed by suicide bombs in almost identical circumstances.

After a few minutes chatting, the infantry sergeant turned to me and said, 'We've got an IED find.'

Ali was still talking to the man, being quite stern and kept asking him where the device was and how he knew it was there.

'I think he's telling the truth,' he said to the sergeant, 'but he's either stupid or hiding something. I'm not sure he's a local. He could be a foreign fighter or from another area but he looks like a Pashtun. He could be Taliban. You should be careful.'

The sergeant turned to me: 'You up for this? It's been a long day.'

'Yeah. Let's get it done. Better now than having to come back out. Whereabouts is it?'

The Afghan indicated that the device was along a track about sixty metres away from our position. The infantry sergeant radioed back to Keenan and got the necessary clearance for us to disarm the device. We were led along the track that ran parallel to a field up to a small irrigation ditch, where there was a massive marijuana field, at least ten acres in size and full of five-foot-high plants. The field was immaculate, a deep, rich green against the surrounding sandy-brown desert and was almost certainly owned by the Taliban. The IED, according to the Afghan, was just a few steps into the field, positioned at an obvious crossing point.

The infantry went into all-round defence, pushing deeper into the crops and securing areas that the Taliban might attempt to use as firing points. I had a quick look at where the Afghan said the IED was and could immediately see some ground-sign, suggesting that a device was buried there.

Within minutes of arriving, the local population disappeared and something inside me was saying that this picture wasn't right. It was partly to do with the reaction of the Terp, who was openly suspicious of the local, and the location of a compound about a hundred metres away, where large holes had been cut in the wall.

'Murder holes?' I said to Dave, pointing at the compound wall.

'Possibly,' he responded.

I went through the normal process of getting Dave into position before searching my way down to the target and got a metal hit on the metal detector as soon as I stepped over the irrigation ditch. I popped some smoke to screen off my position from the compound and got to work, sweeping the sand away, expecting to find a corner of a pressure plate. But instead I uncovered the edge of a cylindrical metal container, about an inch and a half in diameter. As I continued flicking away, the empty casing of a handheld parachute flare with a red wire tied to the end of the case began to emerge.

It had all the hallmarks of a possible anti-lift device. Pull the case out of the ground and the wire causes a victim-operated switch to fire, so best left alone. I popped another couple of smoke grenades and then decided to try and 'attack' the device from a different angle.

Everything was going according to plan until one of the soldiers in the cordon shouted to me that the Terp was picking up ICOM chatter from the Taliban. The ICOM is a handheld VHF radio used by the Taliban as their main means of communication and luckily for us we could also listen in to their conversations.

'The Terp says the Taliban can see you!' he shouted from about twenty metres away.

'What do you mean "they can see me"?' But the soldier shrugged his shoulders as if to say, 'Don't ask me.'

Back at the ICP, the Terp explained that the Taliban were

watching everything I did or at least trying to. The smoke was working to some degree but the Taliban appeared to be watching from several different locations.

'If they're over there,' I said pointing at the compound, 'they'll be able to see my legs and possibly my upper half.'

I threw another smoke grenade to screen off the entire compound and within about thirty seconds the ICOM receiver crackled into life. The Terp, providing a real-time translation of what the Taliban were saying, said, 'He's now saying: "Yeah, yeah. He's back, he's back. But his legs have disappeared."'

Dave and I threw another four or five smoke grenades into the field, creating an impenetrable blue wall. I headed back to the device and, although knowing the Taliban were in the area was slightly unnerving, I was pretty sure they weren't going to open fire unless they had an identifiable target.

Digging away again I uncovered an empty yellow three-litre palm oil container with a piece of red wire running from the oil container's handle to the base of the empty flare. I'd never come across anything like this before and assumed that possibly, just possibly, another bomb was buried underneath, but a quick sweep with the metal detector indicated that the ground was clear.

While all this was going on there was constant ICOM chatter with the Terp reporting that the Taliban were constantly moving their position to get eyes on me. It was almost like a game of chess. Every time the Taliban said they were going to move to the left or the right I would tell the infantry to push left or right and deploy smoke. The 'bomb' was extracted from the ground using a hook and line. As I assumed, there was nothing underneath, it wasn't booby-trapped and it wasn't an IED. Then it dawned on me that the Taliban had been monitoring us from the moment we had been approached by the Afghan. It was part of an elaborate plan to see how my team operated, what pattern we worked to, what tactics we used. They were looking for weaknesses. They had drawn us into an area where they could observe us but fortunately our lavish use of smoke had poured piss on their plans.

In a moment of clarity it all came together: the Afghan turning up out of the blue, the Terp being extremely cautious, and the Taliban constantly monitoring my movements. Just before we pulled out, the owner of the field turned up and began complaining about how our smoke had damaged so much of his field. Given that he was growing drugs for the Taliban and that he must have known about the hoax device, I told the Terp to tell him to go fuck himself.

After we returned to Keenan, I gave Sandy a full breakdown of what had happened and how the Counter-IED teams needed to be aware they were now being specifically targeted by the Taliban.

A few days later my team was pulled out of the base but before leaving I gave a comprehensive brief to Captain Dan Reid, who was coming into the area. Nothing was left uncovered – from how the local bomb team were using trees as markers to how on my last job I had decided to approach the device walking through an irrigation ditch full of shit. Being a good Counter-IED team wasn't just about finding and defusing bombs – it was also about conducting a detailed threat assessment and liaising with all the other troops in the area to ensure that you weren't setting yourself up for a fall. Honesty and integrity were key. Your survival was reliant not just on your skills but on what others told you. In some cases, attempting to clear a device can become a complete head-fuck because every avenue has been closed down completely. You can't do Plan A because another operator has done it, Plan B has been ruined by the infantry doing something similar in the area, and Plan C is out for some other reason and so you're left with plan 'suck it up and get on with it', which amounts to the best of all the worst case options. I was never quite sure whether the Taliban wanted to kill me personally or just any Counter-IED Operator. We were certainly priority targets. But if they were after me then I take that as a personal compliment. The game of cat and mouse was ever-evolving and only time would tell who would come out on top.

22

Last Job?

The day had finally arrived – 18 September 2009. After six gruelling months, Brimstone 42 had finally completed its last mission – a few random, not very memorable IEDs in FOB Keenan's area of operations. Bread and butter stuff – basic high-metal-content pressure plates that had probably been in the ground for a few months. By mid-afternoon the team was back behind Keenan's high secure walls and, as the rest of the lads began conducting their post-op admin, I headed over to the Ops Room to get an update on our planned move back to Bastion.

Operation Herrick 9 was drawing to a close and the RIP had already begun. A few lucky members of the EOD Task Force were already at home shagging their wives and girlfriends or on a beach in Cyprus, undergoing their twenty-four-hour period of decompression, where they could get shitfaced, finger-poke the chain of command about anything that had pissed them off over the last six months, and have a fight in a confined area without upsetting the locals.

The satphone in Bastion Ops Room rang twice before it was answered.

'Hi, it's Staff Hughes. Is the SAT about?'

Sandy answered: 'Kim. Good day?'

'Yeah – straightforward enough. Five pressure plates, no dramas. You'll have my report in an hour or so. Just checking in.'

'No rush, mate. You're offline. That's you and your team complete. There will be a chopper coming in for you tomorrow. Finish the report when you get back here and tell your team you should be back home by the end of the week.'

'Mega' – exactly what I wanted to hear.

For the first time in six months I felt a sense of relief surge through my body. Apart from losing Sam early on through a freak accident (the news on his condition was limited but he appeared to be making good progress), the team had survived Afghan unscathed. In 2009, that simple fact alone was remarkable, given the number of casualties being taken in the EOD Task Force.

As well as surviving, Brimstone 42 had done a brilliant job and developed a reputation for being one of the best IEDD teams in theatre. But at that moment I couldn't care about that. My team were alive and were going back home to grateful wives, girlfriends and families. No more tears, no knocks on the door in the early hours, no funerals, no more hospital visits for us. Right at that moment I couldn't have given a fuck about Afghan, its future, the Taliban or Al-Qaeda. I just wanted to get home and see my son.

The search element of my IEDD team had been pulled out a few weeks earlier. The increased workload of the summer fighting season meant that their R & R had slipped repeatedly. By the time they were due to get their break they were basically told by the OC of the EOD Task Force not to return and for the past few days I'd been breaking in a new search team. Like us, they too wanted to get back to Bastion so they could team up with a fresh ATO – they'd heard enough of our war stories and were now ready to fight their own war.

'Brilliant news,' I said to Sandy before hanging up. I suddenly felt unburdened of worry as I bounded over to our accommodation to break the news to the team. No longer would I lie awake at night wondering if a member of my team was going to be killed or wounded and I found myself smiling, properly smiling for the first time in months.

I pushed open the large, flapping white door of the tent. The team looked at me and I paused for a few seconds. No one spoke.

'We are done,' I said.

'Thank fuck for that,' Lewis said smiling. 'That's the best news ever – nothing is going to be better than that.'

Dave simply fell back onto his bed saying, 'Yes – going home.' There was no real American-style whooping or cheering. Just relief – total and utter relief.

'Right, let's get our kit sorted together. There's a chopper coming in at 0800 hrs tomorrow and we need to be on the HLS at 0745 hrs.'

That afternoon I made a quick tour of the camp saying my goodbyes to the soldiers we had grown close to over the last six months. I wished them luck and told them to stay safe. I shook hands and promised to meet up with just about everyone when they got back to the UK.

Later that evening in our tent, as we packed away our kit, Lewis, Dave and I joked and laughed as we retold the stories of the tour. The mistakes and the near misses. We concentrated on the light-hearted stuff. No one really wanted to talk about those who were killed or injured. The new search team looked on and chuckled. They were a good bunch of lads but they hadn't had our war, they hadn't shared our fears and the distance between us was unbridgeable. I slept like a baby that night and for the first time in ages I woke refreshed and invigorated. The constant tiredness that had dogged the entire team for the last few weeks felt as though it had disappeared.

At the HLS, the team said goodbye to Major Plant, as he shook each one of us by the hand. He was a good officer and had treated us as if we were part of his squadron.

'Thanks for looking after us, sir. Couldn't have asked for more,' I said.

'You were stars. Your boys saved a lot of lives. My lads included. I'm sure our paths will cross again.'

The distinctive thump, thump, thump of a Chinook's twin rotor blades signalled that our lift back to Bastion was inbound.

Within a few seconds the Chinook had landed and I took one last look at the camp before the RAF tail-gunner, one hand permanently fixed on his chain-gun, beckoned us forward. Each man weighed down by a heavy pack, some almost bent double, clambered on board, found a seat, turned their rifle's barrel towards the floor and strapped themselves in.

As was my ritual, I was the last on board. A quick head count and I gave the thumbs-up to the loadmaster. The Chinook was barely on the ground for two minutes before we were airborne, flying due south towards Bastion. Engine noise combined with a vicious crosswind made any form of conversation impossible. I sank into my seat, plugged in my iPod and breathed deeply. The tour was over. I felt like my world had suddenly expanded and there was now something to look forward to beyond the next IED and restless nights of death visiting my dreams.

The Chinook had been airborne for around fifteen minutes when the loadmaster was called forward by the co-pilot for what was clearly some sort of briefing. The loadmaster kept glancing and pointing into the cabin and then began writing down a message on a plastic arm panel on the inside of his forearm.

My gut told me something wasn't right and my concern grew as he began to head down the centre of the Chinook, stumbling over packs and equipment. He reached Dave and shouted something in his ear. Dave, looking serious, pointed at me. Whatever was happening wasn't good. It was like being punched in slow motion. I could see it coming but there was nothing I could do about it. I waited for the body blow.

The loadie reached me and mouthed the word 'ATO' and as I nodded he pointed to the plastic panel on his right forearm upon which was written: 'IED FIND. DIVERTING TO NEW GRID'. I lifted my hands in protest and said, 'What are you on about?'

But he shrugged as if to say 'Not my problem' and of course it wasn't. He patted me on the shoulder, smiled and headed back to the cockpit.

Never had I felt more gutted. Did the camp rats back in the Ops Room have any idea what they'd done? We'd been messed around before, too many times; it was part of life on ops. But this was different. They were fucking with our lives.

I angrily scribbled down the same message in my notebook and passed it along to the soldier next to me. One by one the smiles fell from their faces. I didn't blame them for looking miserable. Someone had just pissed all over our chips and we weren't happy.

Just as I was wallowing in my own self-pity, I was hit by the realisation that I had completely stripped out my equipment.

The previous evening had been largely spent breaking down my kit so that it could be handed in to the various stores in Bastion. Normally my Bergen would be packed with my ops kit on top – and my rations, sleeping bag and other bits and pieces at the bottom. My day-sack would contain explosives, ammo and my man bag.

Just at that moment the loadmaster reappeared with another message: '45 MINS LANDING IN BABAJI'. Babaji was a shithole, even for Helmand. The area was riddled with IEDs and outside of the FOB and PBs, the ground was effectively controlled by the Taliban.

'Great,' I thought, 'tell us that we're being pulled out so that our heads are full of beer and shagging and then send us into Terry country.'

I grabbed my day-sack, dragged it towards me and pulled out my man bag swearing loudly at the messed-up situation. I began filling it with explosives, making sure I had my EOD weapon packed along with all the other bits and pieces I would need. Dave and Lewis were doing the same. While my team were completely gutted, the search team, by contrast, were hugely excited. For them it was wartime – they were going to find a bomb.

As we approached the target, the tail-gunner gave us the countdown – five minutes out, then four, then three. One minute to land and my heart was thumping. I clocked the LZ through the Chinook's tailgate and it was basically in the middle of the desert.

The chopper landed heavily, rear wheels hitting the ground first. A thick cloud of dust was forced inside the cabin from the downdraught. My mouth filled with dirt, a nauseating mixture of dust and dried shit. I spat while pulling my goggles down and held my breath.

The tail-gunner gave me the thumbs-up and I staggered off the back of the chopper stumbling under the weight of my Bergen before dropping down to one knee. I brought my rifle up to the aim and signalled to the team to move into all-round defence until we could work out what was going on. Seconds later the Chinook was airborne and banking steeply to the right. Our ticket home was gone.

As the dust settled I stood up and scanned the barren, featureless desert. The sun was beating down on my back like a hammer and the feeling of disorientation was almost overwhelming. No patrol bases, no soldiers, no vehicles, just empty desert. I wasn't even sure whether we had landed in the right location until someone spotted a small, armoured convoy heading our way. The convoy halted in a cloud of dust. Soldiers providing top cover menacingly trained their heavy machine guns out towards the edge of the Green Zone in the far distance. The door of the lead vehicle opened and a US sergeant jumped down and introduced himself as George, a member of the US Army Police Mentoring Team, a bit like our RMPs.

George was a bear of a man, friendly, smiling and insisted on calling everyone 'buddy'. He was chewing tobacco and spat gobs of black saliva every few seconds. My mood worsened when a dishevelled group of Afghan National Police emerged from another vehicle. I was always wary of the ANP. They had an appalling reputation in Afghan and were largely despised by the locals. Many were drug addicts and most were corrupt. This bunch seemed to be particularly wired, smiling widely and wanting to shake hands with all of us. George explained, in a southern states drawl, that an ANP call sign had found a remote-controlled IED (RCIED) and in their inimitable way had pulled it out of the ground. The bomb was now lying on a roadside waiting to be cleared. I tried to get some sense of what was going on via a Terp, who was part of the US team, but the Afghan commander kept saying that the bomb was now safe, which clearly it wasn't.

'Is it an intact IED?' I asked George and then the Terp.

The Afghan commander gave a lengthy reply but the Terp simply said: 'He doesn't know.'

I turned to George. 'OK. I think it's best if we just go and have a look. Not really getting any sense here, are we?'

He nodded in agreement while the Afghan commander added, 'Go, yes, go.' Possibly the only English he knew.

The IED was sitting on a small bank, similar to a bund you might see in the English countryside, seemingly in the middle of nowhere. RCIEDs need to be monitored by the enemy so that they could be detonated when a target entered the killing zone – but this one obviously wasn't.

The ANA had literally dug it out of the ground, probably with their hands, and left it in the open. Whenever possible we tried to tell the ANA that if they found an IED to leave it alone and call for a bomb disposal team. But they rarely did. Dozens of Afghan police and soldiers had been killed or maimed pulling bombs out – but they carried on regardless, almost as if it were a slight on their manhood to ask for help.

There was no immediate threat so I quickly got to work, hoping that the sooner we got the job done the quicker we would get back to Bastion. I recovered the RC pack and blew up the main charge – technically it was a straightforward job, taking around thirty minutes to clear.

Once completed I turned to George. 'Right, job done. Now what?'

'Well, buddy, we're going to get a vehicle to come and collect you.'

'To take us where?' I responded impatiently.

'To Lashkar Gah. The vehicles are coming from Lash and they'll take you back there for a nice cool shower and some chow,' he said smiling.

'You're kidding, right? It's going to take the rest of the day to get back to Lash.'

I couldn't believe it. We were minutes from landing in Bastion, living the dream, looking forward to a cold smoothie in the Green Bean Cafe and now we were going to trundle across the Helmand desert for the rest of the day.

It took another two hours before the vehicles arrived and another three hours before we arrived, hot, tired and pissed off in Lashkar Gah, the provincial capital of Helmand, and the HQ of all British forces in southern Afghanistan. It was brimming with top brass and not the place any soldier wanted to be for too long. It was now around 2000 hrs, although I had lost all sense of time, and I made an immediate beeline for the Ops Room to get an update on what was happening.

I asked, actually demanded, to use a secure line to call the Ops Room in Bastion: 'Staff Hughes here. My call sign is in Lash. Can you give me an update on our extraction?'

'You're to wait out until a decision has been made on what we're going to do with you,' said an anonymous watch-keeper.

I could barely control my anger. 'What do you mean by "what we're going to do with you"? The decision should be how are you going to get us out of here so we can strip our kit out ready for the move back to the UK.'

But the watch-keeper was only passing on the message. I spent the rest of the evening going backwards and forwards to the Ops Room gradually pissing off everyone with my continual requests for a flight out. It was only after the third visit that the Lash Operations Officer turned to me and said: 'Your aircraft is inbound. You are going back to Keenan.'

My morale hit the floor. If I hadn't been so pissed off it would have been funny.

'No, that can't be right. We've just come from Keenan. We're finished, we're heading home.'

The team had been waiting patiently for a couple of hours, sitting on the floor near to the HLS in the hope that we'd be returning to Bastion. They had showered and got dressed into their clean kit. I had stripped out my man bag and repacked my day-sack.

Later the Operations Warrant Officer called and confirmed our worst fears. Brimstone 42 was heading back to Keenan to provide cover for the third phase of an ongoing operation.

'Bad news, guys. We're being extended out on the ground. We're heading back to Keenan.'

If someone had burst into tears at that moment or thrown a major tantrum, I wouldn't have blamed them. Everyone took it badly for different reasons and I could see by the look on Dave's face that he was very frustrated. But no one complained. Everyone nodded and accepted the situation. The following morning the team flew back to Keenan where Major Plant was waiting for us.

'Seriously, what are you doing here?' he asked, genuinely confused.

'Being fucked around, sir. We're going to be your IEDD team for the next few days.'

He looked slightly embarrassed and asked me to come into the Ops Room where we discussed the next phase of the operation.

'It's going to be busy. And it could get a bit cheeky,' he said slightly apologetically and he wasn't wrong.

23

Is that a Fucking Rubber Dinghy?

Six days after Brimstone 42's tour was supposed to be over, the team was back on operations providing EOD support for a joint ISAF and Afghan National Army operation code-named Tufaan Dakoo. The operation was an attempt to close down the Taliban's freedom of movement in a large chunk of the Green Zone where the ground had become laced with IEDs.

The cruel heat of the Afghan summer was slowly ebbing away as the first signs of autumn began to appear but the days were still long and sleepy hot. It was day two of the operation and the plan was to close all of the Taliban's routes into an area of five square kilometres. Every road, bridge and track was physically blocked and guarded by ISAF British and Danish troops. But one route was left open. Ideally, the enemy would enter the area over the course of a few days, plant their IEDs and withdraw. ISAF would then use an Unmanned Aerial Vehicle (UAV) such as a Reaper to track the Taliban back to their bomb factories. But rather than go after the guy planting the IED we'd smash the lot of them once we knew where they were based. At least that was the plan.

It was 23 September and the entire Brimstone 42 team was relaxing in a secure area close to a bridge code-named 'Mickey', one of several crossing points over a fast-flowing tributary of the Helmand river. Our role was to react to any IED finds and given that our tour was meant to be over we were all hoping for a quiet day.

Mickey was a bridge typical to the area. It was wide enough to take a standard saloon car with a couple of feet to spare and about forty feet in length. A simple construction of steel girders and concrete, it had possibly been made by British engineers a few years earlier. It had been blocked off with a large Hesco chunk and coils of razor wire that should have made using the bridge impossible. But a Taliban bomb team had managed to booby-trap the bridge with a command-pull IED.

At sometime during the previous evening when darkness had fallen, a Taliban IED team swam across the river and buried a main charge, battery pack and firing switch almost at the foot of the main barricade. They had also managed to dig in a long piece of kite string that would act as the command wire without being seen. Once in place they swam back to the other side and ran the kite string off into the distance to a position that allowed them to monitor the bridge.

The following morning, a Danish major, in charge of the operation, accompanied by Major Sam Plant, the officer commanding FOB Keenan, went to inspect the engineering works on the bridge. The route up to the Hesco barricade on the bridge had been searched earlier for IEDs by Danish engineers and declared clear. So the two officers confidently marched up to the bridge while around twenty soldiers secured the area.

All seemed quite normal until the ground in front of them began to move. A member of the Taliban was trying to initiate the main charge buried beneath the officers' feet by tugging on the kite string. The two officers momentarily froze before performing a quick about-turn and took cover behind a bank.

Although not known at the time, the main charge was a 105mm artillery shell packed with home-made explosives. Quite how such a huge lump of metal could be missed by soldiers searching for IEDs remains something of a mystery. The command-pull initiation failed because the kite string became entangled in the razor wire.

Minutes later Brimstone 42 were told to get their collective arses up to bridge Mickey.

Major Plant was waiting to brief me. 'Staff – morning. Bit of a funny one this. I was carrying out an inspection of the bridge when the ground began moving. There's a piece of string running along the bridge and into the distance, possibly into that compound close to the tree line approximately three hundred metres away. Whoever was on the end gave it a few good tugs and has exposed part of the IED. We beat a hasty retreat back here.'

'OK, sir, no dramas. Give me a few minutes and I'll give you a plan of action. We're going to establish an ICP in this area but my REST will need to clear the area first.'

The ICP was positioned around a hundred metres from the bridge on one side of a small embankment, which provided cover from the enemy's side of the river. As I surveyed the area my gut told me this wasn't going to be a straightforward job. A track ran over the bridge into the distance and another track hand-railed the river on the far side of the bank. The kite string attached to the IED ran over the bridge and disappeared, probably into a large, abandoned compound around three hundred metres directly ahead and left of the bridge. Either side of the track, on the other side of the river, were two large fields growing a mixture of crops, including maize, wheat and poppy. Over on the far right, but slightly closer to the river, was another abandoned compound, almost directly opposite where the ICP had been established. The whole area was flat and open with plenty of potential enemy firing points. It was a perfect ambush position for the Taliban and we were now slap bang in the middle.

With the ICP marked and cleared, the new team RESA, a young thrusting lieutenant, and I began to plan how we were going to smash the task. As we chatted through the various options an infantry sergeant known as 'Trees', probably because he was over six foot five, appeared with a broad smile across his face. I had grown friendly with Trees – I never knew his real name – over that summer and every time our paths crossed he asked me the same two questions.

'How many bombs, Kim?'

I looked up and I saw Trees' smiling face. 'Fuck knows, mate. Lost count but well over a hundred.'

'You going out dressed as a Dane or one of us?'

I laughed out loud. 'As you see me.'

I had spent so much time with the Danes and trashed so much of my own kit that I had developed a bit of a reputation for wearing mixed dress – Danish combat trousers and a British camouflage jacket. The Danish combats were a deep-green camouflage material, ideal for the Green Zone and made of rip-stop material. It was mega kit, much better than our own. Desert camouflage was pretty good in the desert but once you went into an area where crops were being cultivated it was useless – you were dressed in light sandy-brown gear when all around you was green.

Trees gave me a breakdown of the situation as he pointed at the bridge: 'If you look really carefully you'll be able to see the string running back over the bridge and beyond into the distance.'

'I can't see anything,' I said, squinting into the distance.

Trees was a sniper and was carrying some pretty Gucci kit. He pulled out a laser rangefinder and said, 'Try this.'

And there was the string as clear as day.

'I'll swap you my best set of Danish combats for this,' I said to him, hanging on to his rangefinder.

'Fuck off,' he said, smiling and snatching it back.

The IED was in a sort of limbo. The Taliban couldn't detonate it but that didn't mean it was safe. Another tug on the kite string might work so the IED had to be treated as if it was in a dangerous state.

Back with the rest of the team I began to run through the various options. Firstly, a wider search of the general area needed to be conducted, which entailed crossing the river, cutting the string and taking control of the device away from the Taliban. Then the river would have to be recrossed ensuring there were no other command wires coming into the area. The river was the obvious hurdle. Anyone crossing it would be completely exposed and although there was no sign of enemy activity it had to be assumed that the Taliban were watching. No one would want to be in the middle of the river if a firefight kicked off.

There was a collective rubbing of heads as we brainstormed the problem. Jake, who was now the new search team commander, quickly pointed out that the river was fast-flowing and an unknown depth. Anyone attempting to cross it would have to ditch their body armour, helmet and most of their kit.

More suggestions were put forward, some bordering on the insane, when out of the blue one of the Danish soldiers, who was listening to our conversation, said, 'We've got a rubber dinghy.'

I hadn't quite understood what he said and initially dismissed his comments with a 'Yeah, nice one, mate.'

The brainstorming session continued for the next ten minutes or so but we were getting nowhere fast and I could see that Major Plant wanted to get a move on. I was on the verge of thinking that the job was potentially too dangerous when a Danish armoured vehicle appeared on the track and began heading towards our position. As the vehicle got closer I could see what looked like a boat strapped to its roof.

I stood up, walked over to the now stationary vehicle and found myself standing next to the same Danish soldier who had mentioned something about a boat a little earlier.

'Is that a fucking rubber dinghy?' I said.

The Danish soldier looked at me and laughing said, 'That's what I was trying to tell you.'

As I walked around the vehicle wondering whether this was the solution to our problem, a couple of Danish soldiers lifted it from the roof. It was about seven feet long and three feet wide, black in colour and similar to a rigid inflatable boat (RIB).

I turned to the Dane again: 'What have you got a rubber dinghy in Afghan for?'

'For river crossings,' he responded, amazed that I was even asking the question.

None of us had ever used a boat before on a Counter-IED task and our boat-handling skills were pretty non-existent. But within a few minutes we'd come up with what can loosely be described as a plan. The search team would clear a path while carrying the dinghy up and over the embankment and down to the water's edge. We'd paddle across the river, conduct a search of the area, disabling the device in the process, then climb back into the boat and return while being protected by the Danish and British soldiers who had already occupied defensive positions on the friendly side of the river. I briefed Major Plant on our plan and he gave us the green light to execute.

Tiggs, the new search team's youngest member, led the way clearing the path, swinging his metal detector from side to side, Jake followed and I brought up the rear along with another member of the team, called Smudge. We moved over the embankment and down towards the river. It was all going as planned until what seemed like the entire Taliban army opened up with sniper and automatic fire from a compound almost thirty metres directly opposite on the other side of the river.

The bullets whizzed past just above us, so close that we could almost feel the crack above our heads. Volleys of AK47 rounds tattooed the ground around our feet, spitting up dirt as they struck home. The entire area where the four of us were trying to launch the dinghy was lacerated by machine-gun fire, just like in one of those old Second World War movies. RPG rockets were flying overhead and thumping into the embankment behind. I turned to see where the fire was coming from, thinking I might be able to engage some of the enemy, but all I could see were muzzle flashes coming from the compound opposite.

Everyone froze for a split second before all four of us scrambled up the bank and hurled ourselves over the other side. I somersaulted over the bank and Jake dived head first and landed on top of me with Tiggs and Smudge bringing up the rear. As we rolled down the other side of the bank we began to laugh uncontrollably. Somehow we had escaped being killed or wounded and our response was group hysteria. A few seconds later the British and Danish soldiers securing the friendly side of the bank opened fire with a vengeance. The compound opposite disappeared in a cloud of dust as the bullets struck the outer walls. Chunks of masonry, possibly centuries old, began to crumble. As the gunfire intensified so did our hysteria. I looked over at Trees and he was firing his sniper rifle shotgun-style because he was too close to the target to use his high-powered telescopic sight. Beyond Trees, through the noise and confusion of battle, a young soldier was preparing to fire his 40mm grenade launcher.

'What's he going to do with that?' I thought to myself.

The overeager soldier pulled the trigger and fired a red phosphorus grenade directly into the bank on the opposite side of the river. The grenade exploded on impact but showered most of the British and Danish troops with small pieces of burning red phosphorus. Phosphorus will set alight and burn through almost anything. Fortunately the damage was minimal but Trees was less than impressed. He put his rifle down, grabbed the young soldier by the helmet straps and gave him a major battlefield bollocking. The firefight died down after a couple of minutes and my team, using the embankment as cover, moved into a large, unoccupied compound adjacent to the ICP.

The team gathered in one corner. 'Right, we need to

reformulate the plan,' I said, still slightly amazed that we were all still alive. 'We've still got a job to do. Somehow we've got to get across that river and disarm the device. Everyone start thinking – I don't care how stupid you think the plan is, let's hear it. Let's work out the solution.'

After about ten minutes of deep thinking and running through a series of increasingly mad plans, I had a light-bulb moment. 'I'll ditch my body armour and helmet and swim across the river on my own,' I told the guys who were now looking at me with deep suspicion. 'I'll keep my pistol and tie a metal detector to my back. I'll only need my firing device and det-cord to take control of this. The soldiers on the roof should be able to provide enough covering fire if needed. Once across, I will search my way up the bank and over to the string, set up my firing device, search my way back, fire the device and then swim back across the river. I just need to avoid drowning, getting shot or blown up by the Taliban. In theory it should work, with a bit of luck.'

But even as I was speaking I realised it sounded as if I had a death wish.

Lewis looked at me and said, 'What are you talking about, you lunatic?'

Given the obvious dangers of the task, I needed to refer the mission back to the EOD headquarters to get the SAT's authorisation. Using the satphone rather than the radio I got through immediately and a young private soldier answered: 'Sorry, Staff, everyone's at lunch.'

I looked at my watch. It was 1230 hrs. I couldn't help but laugh.

'OK. No worries. Send a runner to the cookhouse and get the SAT back in the Ops Room. Tell him that I need to speak to him urgently and I will call back in ten minutes.'

As I waited for the Ops Room to respond, I ran over some points of the plan again, really voicing my concerns.

'I need to take control of the device away from Terry before I defuse the bomb, hence the need to swim across the river,' I said to the team. 'Although if the Taliban can't see the bridge I could just go straight to the IED and deal with it. Saves getting wet.' The latter option seemed to be gaining a bit more traction than the earlier plan.

'I can sort that for you,' one of the infantry corporals said smiling. I looked at him slightly confused.

'I can get you close to the bridge without being seen,' he said again. 'I'm the Mortar Fire Controller [MFC]. You tell me where you want it and I'll drop smoke. The enemy won't have any idea what's going on.'

The MFC and I climbed onto the roof of the compound and took cover behind a small wall. A sniper scanned the area where the Taliban were located and gave us the nod to sit up enough so we could look across the battlefield. I pointed to a field between the large compound believed to be occupied by the Taliban and the bridge.

'Can you fill that field with white phos?' I asked.

'Yeah, no problem. The mortar team back at FOB Keenan already have our grid reference. All I need to do is adjust it onto the target. I can put it anywhere you want.'

'So you could screen off Terry's line of sight and I could move forward on this side of the bank to the device, place a needle and move back.'

The corporal gave a nod of approval.

'Right, that's our second option,' I said.

We dropped back down inside the compound and Major Plant appeared, wanting to know how the problem was going to be fixed.

'Right, sir, there are two options to this. One, I swim over the river, cut the string and swim back . . .'

The major began shaking his head. 'Staff, I admire your enthusiasm but the last thing I need now is a dead ATO.'

'Or,' I added quickly, 'the MFC screens off the bridge using white phos. I move forward and place a weapon on the device. The enemy will still have control of the IED but he won't know I'm on target.'

It was clear that the OC preferred the second option and before he could change his mind I turned to the MFC. 'Right, you need to get your team squared away. Get all your grid references sorted and anything else you need. I want to get moving on this. How long do you need?'

'Give me ten minutes and we should be good to go,' he said.

While I waited, I called Sandy, explained the situation and briefed him on both plans. After about a second's thought Sandy simply said, 'Option two,' and the call ended.

Eight minutes later, mortars began crashing on their target, sending out a thick curtain of white smoke as the phosphorus reacted with the air and burned furiously. The smokescreen was good but I felt it needed to be closer to the bridge to have a real effect so I told the MFC to drop the mortars closer, but not so close that I was at risk of being fragged by a piece of bursting mortar round.

The mortars came raining down again, in salvos of three or four bombs, but they were landing either too close or too far away from where I wanted them.

Major Plant, who was getting increasingly frustrated, gave the MFC a roasting. 'Get a grip. Get those mortars on fucking target and do your job. You've only got one job to do, now do it properly,' he told the corporal.

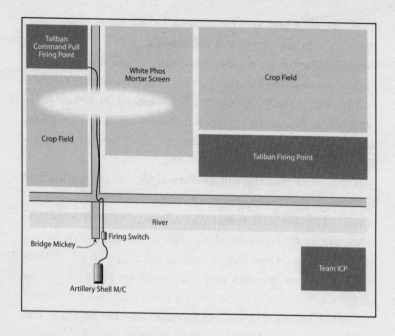

It was the first time I had really seen the major angry but it worked. Within a few minutes the smoke had completely screened off the opposite side of the bank. I set off clearing a path towards the bridge with Dave following close behind.

The battery pack and the firing switch, which consisted of two metal washers with bare wires twisted around each one, had been pulled out of the ground at the first attempt at detonation leaving the IED in a highly unstable state. Worse still, the two contacts, which would cause the bomb to explode if they came together, were a gnat's chuff away from touching each other. I took a deep breath, my eyes fixed on the contacts, and carefully inched my way forward. The wind caught the string and it blew in the breeze. My heart missed a beat and I waited for the explosion, which fortunately never came. I was now at the mercy of the elements and, for a brief moment, considered turning back. But if it wasn't me, someone else would have to deal with the device.

I placed my needle and flying scalpel against one of the exposed wires before withdrawing quick-time back to Dave and then into the safety of the compound, where the rest of the team were waiting. Every five minutes or so a mortar would land with a thump across the other side of the river ensuring that the smokescreen remained in place.

After firing the needle, Dave and I checked our equipment before heading back to the bridge. I taped up the cut wires and pulled the battery pack and firing switch out of the ground using the hook and line.

On the third approach I found the main charge packed inside the 105mm artillery shell, which had probably been fired by a British unit a few years earlier. I used my trowel and paintbrush to dig and sweep away the dirt so that I had enough room to tie a loop around the casing.

Every now and then I looked up to ensure the smokescreen was still effective. Over in the compound I could see some of the soldiers looking anxious, almost as if they were waiting for the Taliban to start shooting through the smoke. With the loop secure I returned to the compound, trailing the line so that it didn't snag on any rocks or stones.

As I approached the compound I saw Major Plant standing in the doorway. 'Sir, can you just explain to me where you were standing when you saw the ground move.'

He pointed to a piece of scrubby ground about ten metres away from the Hesco block at the foot of the bridge and just as he finished speaking I gave the line a tug and the artillery shell popped out of the ground, virtually in the same spot where the two officers had been standing. His face dropped and he was momentarily speechless. He turned and looked at the Danish searchers who had supposedly cleared the area with a face that said, 'You wankers.'

The main charge was destroyed in a controlled explosion while anything forensically useful was placed in plastic bags. With the device now cleared I approached the two majors as they chatted.

'Sirs, had the bomb exploded, I doubt we'd be having this conversation.' They realised how close they had come to a very messy death. As a souvenir I gave each of them a piece of wire with a metal washer attached – the two halves of the firing switch. 'You can keep those as good luck charms,' I added.

The rest of the day was punctuated with sporadic firefights, causing some of my team to grab their helmets and take cover while urging me to do the same. 'I'm all right,' I'd tell them. 'Terry isn't going to get me today.'

Some members of my team joined the infantry on the roof, ready to take on the Taliban. Lewis was like a man possessed – as if he was in his very own 'Call of Duty' game – letting rip with his SA80 big time. Down below, Dave was filling magazines of ammunition and throwing them up to Tiggs on the roof, who handed them to Lewis who in turn was passing empty ones back down.

I turned to Dave. 'Why don't you get up there and smash them too?'

'Not interested, Kim. If I fire my weapon I'll have to clean it later. Lewis is gonna be cleaning his rifle for about a week the way he's going.'

'You lazy fucker,' I said laughing before closing my eyes and plugging myself into my iPod.

Later that evening we were back in FOB Keenan with its comfy, pristine tents, warm showers and fresh, delicious food. That was Afghan. One minute you were inches away from death, the next you could be safely relaxing in relative comfort, looking forward to a good night's sleep.

Brimstone 42 remained operational in FOB Keenan until 29 September, when we finally received notification from the EOD Task Force headquarters that it would be another three days before we eventually arrived back in Bastion and were finally taken offline.

24

Pissing off Politicians

Brimstone 42 finally arrived back in Camp Bastion on the morning of 4 October 2009. The frustration of being sent back into the fight after being told our war was over was forgotten. The last few days in Keenan had been long and arduous with sleep at a premium. Inevitably the return to Bastion was a bit of an anticlimax. Everyone was tired, not just physically but mentally. And all we wanted was to get out of Afghan and return home.

After landing just as dawn was breaking, when the air was still cool, the team trooped back to our tented homes while I headed for the Ops Room unshaven, dirty, stinking after having turned my underwear inside out twice. The Ops Room staff were as usual dressed in pristine, freshly laundered uniforms, clean-shaven and slightly tanned. In general they looked fit and healthy – the contrast between them and us was never so great.

'Staff Hughes. Call sign Brimstone 42. That's us off the ground,' I told one of the Ops Room staff whose pasty, untanned skin suggested he was a relatively new arrival.

'Sorry, what was your name?' he said, eyes fixed on his computer screen.

'It's "Staff" when you talk to me, dickhead. My name is Staff Sergeant Hughes. Call sign Brimstone 42.'

Sandy appeared from behind a computer screen: 'Right, Kim. Good to see you. I need your team to get their shit squared away. You are going to be doing a demo for a VIP visit.'

'Yeah, right. Nice one,' I thought. Good old Sandy, always one for a wind-up. But he was being serious.

'You are having a laugh.'

'No. I need you shit, showered, shaved and ready in clean kit. We need you to be ready to brief the Defence Secretary, Bob Ainsworth. He landed about an hour ago and he's interested in what we do here.'

'Sandy, the boys are licked and our kit is in a shit state. There must be someone else who can do this. We've just walked in off the ground after six months plus an extra eleven days.'

'Actually no,' Sandy said. 'There are teams here but they are fresh and ready to deploy. We need a seasoned team who can speak with the experience of a six-month tour under their belt and that's you.'

Sandy was in an unenviable position. Brimstone 42 was the obvious choice for the job and I would have done exactly the same if I were him. But that didn't make it any easier for me. Back at the accommodation, I explained that we were required to put on a Counter-IED demonstration for the Defence Secretary, Bob Ainsworth, along with other members of the unit, on how an IED would be found and cleared. It would be a simple task out on the Bastion training area, I explained, exactly the same sort of demo we'd done dozens of times before during pre-deployment training for new soldiers.

'It's the same deal,' I said. 'No dramas except this time the audience will be the Defence Secretary and a few hangers-on. He might ask a few questions so just be prepared for some fast balls.'

The British public had grown tired of the war in Afghan. Support for the war, if there was any, was falling by the day. Casualties were mounting, mainly from IEDs, and politicians were getting worried. The visit was the Defence Secretary's second in a year so I assumed he'd have a reasonable understanding of what had been going down over the last few months.

The Bastion training area was outside the wire but, supposedly, secure. Soldiers arriving for their six-month tour would spend about a week zeroing their weapons, carrying out exercises, practising drills and, crucially, being briefed on the latest IEDs being used against them. Counter-IED teams would put incoming battalions and regiments through a series of tough exercises, explaining what to do to avoid making fatal mistakes.

Each element of the EOD Task Force had a stand displaying the equipment taken into the field – almost like a barracks 'open day'. The idea was that Bob Ainsworth could wander around, have a look, ask a question or two and get those all-important publicity shots for the TV and newspapers.

Down on the training area, I carefully laid out my pristine unused bomb suit and prepared my kit while Lewis tested his robot, even though we'd only ever used it once before it got put back into storage, and the search team rehearsed their bit. The demo was a pain in the arse but we had to be professional. Get this wrong and we'd give the EOD Task Force a bad name.

As we were getting ready, Sandy appeared. 'Look, Kim, if you get the opportunity, and he asks you what you need, push the fact that we need light scale equipment. Don't overdo it but it is an opportunity for us to put down a marker for what we need. Usually works on occasions like this.' Light scale equipment was identical to the stuff we already used but was composed of titanium and carbon fibre rather than steel. It was a fraction of the weight but much more expensive. The kit we were using was designed to be carried around in an EOD truck, not on the backs of the ATO and his No.2.

After Sandy, other members of the Task Force were almost queuing up to offer advice on what I should say if asked a question.

'Don't forget to mention helicopters. We need more of them. Ask him if he's aware that the armoured vehicles we have aren't great.' The list went on and on. And all the grievances were genuine. The Army had been in Helmand for three years but at times it felt as if it was still on the back foot. Britain was part of one of the most powerful military alliances in the history of warfare – the Taliban had AK47s, home-made bombs and flip-flops – and yet NATO certainly wasn't winning. I was given a five-minute warning and we stood in line, at ease, waiting for Bob Ainsworth to appear.

Then, almost out of nowhere, Ainsworth and his entourage of senior officers and ministerial aides appeared, followed by a massive pack of newspaper reporters and television news teams and at that point it began to occur to me that this was actually quite a big deal – not for me but for Her Majesty's Government.

Sandy reappeared again: 'Kim, by the way, he's got the Home Secretary, Alan Johnson, with him as well.'

As well as the politicians there was the head of the armed forces, and seemingly dozens of military and political aides. In fact I had never seen so many top brass at one single event.

The engineers began the brief, explaining how searches were conducted and the type of devices now being used by the Taliban. They showed him their specialist equipment and gave a breakdown of their skills. Ainsworth and Johnson were given a metal detector to play with and had a go at trying to find an IED. By the time they arrived at my stand, they seemed quite relaxed and happy, although a little hot.

I was slightly surprised at how ordinary they looked. Dressed in a sky-blue shirt and sand-coloured chinos and wearing glasses, Ainsworth looked like a bank manager out for a weekend stroll. He sported a small, scruffy moustache and the belly of a man not used to exercise, but he seemed decent enough. He smiled and chatted with the troops and appeared genuinely interested in the work being carried out by EOD teams.

'Hello,' he said smiling, while shaking my hand. 'My name's Bob Ainsworth, I'm the Defence Secretary. Who do we have here?'

'Hello, sir. I'm Staff Sergeant Kim Hughes. I'm an Ammunition Technician and this is my Counter-IED team.'

I introduced each member of the team who put on false smiles and tried to show some interest. Senior officers would often come to visit the troops, no doubt hoping to boost morale without realising what a massive balls-ache VIP visits are for everyone involved. Troops, bored beyond imagination, would spend hours cleaning the camp, picking up pieces of litter and making sure everything looked clean and in perfect working order. The VIPs would depart relaxed in the knowledge that everything was fine and dandy, when often the reverse was true. It occurred to me that if senior officers, politicians or any other VIPs really wanted to find out what life was like they should arrive without any notice and demand to spend a day and night in a FOB or PB, where half the troops were ill with the shits and where clouds of mosquitoes invaded at dusk and dawn. Only then would they get a true impression of what life was like on operations.

Ainsworth was sweating profusely. His shirt was covered with dark, damp patches and his hair was slick with sweat. Even in October the Afghan heat could be oppressive for the uninitiated.

'This is the equipment we use on a day-to-day basis. But not the bomb suit, that's too heavy and too hot,' I added with a smile.

He seemed to get the joke. 'I can believe that,' he said, wiping his brow with a clean handkerchief.

I went through some of the more interesting bits and pieces for five to ten minutes, trying to keep it informative but brief and pausing just long enough for questions.

At the end of my little brief he turned to me and said: 'Right, Staff, you've been at the coalface for six months. You've had a busy tour, from what I understand. What do you need or more pertinently what will be needed by those taking over from you?'

I thought for a few seconds and felt the eyes of the senior officers burning into me. The press were poised with pens and notebooks in hand and the TV crews and photographers massed behind him, presumably looking for the money shot that was going to make their editors back in London happy. Even Sandy was there in the background almost willing me to say 'lightweight kit'. But as I thought about the answer in those few brief seconds I realised it wasn't just the kit, it was troop numbers, too.

'More men on the ground, sir.' Now I don't know what answer he was expecting or whether he had been briefed that I would talk about the need for more advanced kit but he certainly wasn't expecting that answer. Possibly for just a fraction of a second I think his world stopped spinning. No one spoke, no one moved. Nothing. It was a real tumbleweed moment. Then the shit well and truly hit the fan.

His face dropped and the press moved forward as one, suddenly engulfing us. I gave him a look as if to say: 'Well you did ask.'

'Err . . . OK,' he said stuttering. 'Can you explain that?'

Filled with confidence that my comments seemed to hit home, I was now on a roll: 'With more men on the front line, we could do more. Secure more areas and have a greater presence on the ground. At the end of the day we haven't got enough manpower physically on the ground. For example, the infantry will clear an area from the Taliban, either simply by being there or after a series of costly battles. The Counter-IED teams will then come in and clear the area of IEDs but we can't hold that ground because the infantry have to go elsewhere and clear more areas, or we do, and the Taliban move back in and reclaim the area and rebury the devices. Sir, I'm not just saying this. This has happened to a colleague of mine. He had cleared an area, a device had been pulled out of the ground. The cordon that was securing the area collapsed and the infantry returned to their patrol base. As the troops left, the last man periodically turned around to check the rear. When they were about three hundred yards away they saw someone planting another device in the same hole they had just pulled one out of.'

Bob Ainsworth was nodding as I spoke and was genuinely interested but the senior officers and my bosses were less than impressed.

Undeterred, I continued: 'And this is why I say, sir, that

we don't have enough people. This is happening all the time. Senior officers call it mowing the lawn – we go out and clear the Taliban, can't hold the ground, withdraw and the Taliban come back in and the whole cycle repeats itself a few weeks later, with a few more of our lads dying or getting their legs blown off. The Taliban are putting bombs back in the ground as quickly as we are taking them out. And on the equipment front we need more helicopters and we need light scale equipment.'

But the damage had been done. I looked up and could see almost unconstrained glee across the faces of the press while the faces of senior officers revealed a different story. I caught Sandy's eye and could see him shaking his head in despair.

Bob Ainsworth was quickly ushered away by his aides, no doubt in fear of what I was going to say next but not before thanking me for my frank comments and shaking my hand.

I took a breath, turned to my team, and said, 'Well . . . that went well.'

Lewis looked at me as if to say: 'You've just fucked yourself.'

Sandy appeared and wasn't impressed. 'One thing, Kim. We asked you to say one thing. Mention light scale equipment and you've come out with that.'

'Hang on,' I said in protest, 'what I said wasn't wrong. I told him the truth. If they wanted someone to lie to him they probably shouldn't have asked a soldier.'

I could sense Sandy was pissed off but we all knew I was right. We had often spoken about why no one ever told politicians and senior officers how life is at the coalface. This was an opportunity and I took it.

Sandy took a deep breath. 'You're right,' he said with a smile and patted me on the shoulder. 'See you later.'

Once the mass of top brass and the VIPs had left, some of

the other soldiers also giving presentations began packing up their kit and heading back to the main camp but, unknown to me at the time, some of the press were still hanging around.

As I was packing away the bomb suit, a member of the Task Force came over for a chat. 'Fucking hell, Kim, do you think you should have said that? Do you think you'll be in the shit? Telling the Defence Secretary that we need more troops on the ground. You've got some balls.'

I couldn't see the big deal and without checking to see if anyone was in earshot, I said: 'You know what? What's he going to do – send me home?'

My mate chuckled before saying, 'Yeah, fair one.'

I thought nothing more of the whole event until the following day when I was walking into the Ops Room and noticed that the place was almost empty and those who were at work were looking at me with a mixture of amusement and concern. 'Where is everyone?' I thought to myself as I sat behind a desk and logged on to my Facebook account to see what had been happening in the weeks I had been out on the ground.

I opened a message from a friend back in the UK that read: 'LOL. What's he going to do, send me home – nice one mate.'

As I was trying to make sense of what the message meant, another ATO came over to me and said, 'Kim, you're a legend.'

'What are you on about?' He then flicked to Sky News on the TV in the Ops Room 'chill out' area and the main story running was my brief Q and A with Bob Ainsworth, along with the headline: 'Bomb disposal expert challenges the defence secretary' along with 'Soldier says: "We need more men."' I was surprised but not overly concerned given that everyone present at the event had heard what I said. That was until another picture of me appeared on the screen with the words: 'After the confrontation Staff Sergeant Hughes was undeterred and added: "What's he going to do? Send me home?"'

I closed my eyes in the vain hope that what I had just seen was some sort of dream or event that hadn't really happened. My heart began to beat faster as I realised I was now in a world of shit.

'You are joking,' I said out loud, now possibly more worried about my immediate future than at any time in the last six months. I had visions of being dragged in front of senior commanders for a major bollocking and sent home in disgrace.

It then emerged that the reason why the Ops Room was empty was because all of the senior officers had been called into a meeting with the Helmand Task Force commander, as part of a damage limitation operation. I sat down and went over the previous day's events at the demo. I thought about what I had said and then realised that one of the reporters who'd been hanging around at the end had probably overheard my conversation. I might have spoken out of turn, I thought, but had I really said anything that bad? Was I wrong? Ultimately it didn't matter what I thought.

About half an hour later Sandy and the OC returned to the Ops Room and before they could say anything I stopped them in the doorway: 'Look, I don't even know when or how that happened. Am I in the shit?'

'Don't worry about it. The commander was pretty relaxed. His attitude was what do you expect? A politician asking a SNCO a straight question. He said he hoped a SNCO would always give a straight answer.'

The sense of relief was almost overwhelming and it was nice to know that the chain of command was backing the troops. The spin being placed on the whole episode was that the Defence Secretary should have known better than to ask a soldier who had been on the front line for his honest opinion. The drama and the noise created by a brief and honest conversation between two adults died away after a few days. But it did make me question why the Army was seemingly so worried about soldiers speaking their minds. Everyone in Helmand knew we didn't have enough men, so presumably every senior officer back in the UK knew that was the case so why the fuss? The whole experience did leave me wondering whether anyone in the military was really giving the politicians the hard facts about life on the front line in Afghan.

25

Going Home

It was over. Brimstone 42 was finally offline. I'd always assumed I'd be really happy, ecstatic almost, doing cart-wheels, laughing, joking. But the reality was very different. It was a massive anticlimax, brought about by the constant, unremitting weariness of war. I felt conflicted. I was relieved that my part in the mission was over but I also felt almost empty and disappointed.

Afghan was now in my blood. It had given me a direction and purpose, possibly for the first time in my life. I had spent the last six months riding a wave of adrenalin, dodging death every day, pitting my wits against the Taliban and saving lives. Soldiers in Afghan had a saying: 'Living the dream'. It was an ironic take, I suppose, on the various life choices that had taken them to the front line but I really was 'living the dream', I just hadn't realised it.

Tours of duty in Afghan don't just end. It's never a case of 'Right, you're finished – pack up your kit and get on that plane.' There's a whole river of bullshit admin you have to wade through before you step foot on the flight and the first part of that was the arduous process of de-kitting and handing back all the equipment we'd been using every day for the last six months. Everything from weapons to radios, including all of my bomb disposal gear, the ECM equipment, the robots and IED weapons, all had to be cleaned and handed back into the stores – it was a real balls-ache.

After de-kitting we had one final job to complete before we could relax. All new Brimstone teams coming into theatre had to go through Role Specific Training (RST) – it was basically a last chance to iron out any issues and be brought up to date with the latest Taliban tactics and IEDs. Brimstone 42 had gone through the same process six months earlier and it was a bit of an awkward transition. As the new team you just wanted to get out on the ground and do your job and not have to listen to people constantly pointing out the errors in your drills. Everyone tried to be professional but the clenching of jaws and biting of lips was always a giveaway.

The new ATO coming into theatre was Staff Sergeant Paddy Read. He knew the score and was only too willing to scoop up every bit of knowledge on offer. Each member of my team sat down with their opposite number and basically gave them a breakdown of the type of missions undertaken over the last six months – it was a full-scale intelligence brief on how the threat had changed and how Taliban tactics had evolved. Next, out on the training area, Paddy's team were put through a series of scenarios they could expect to encounter once they were online and operational. It was a fairly intense couple of days and by the end of the week his team were ready for action.

With Paddy's team ready to go, Brimstone 42 was moved out of its tent and into transit accommodation as we waited for information on our flight home. Bastion was now in the full throes of the 'relief in place' (RIP), when a new brigade is coming in and another going home. Over the six-week period from the end of August to the middle of October, 14,000 troops were on the move, 7,000 coming in and 7,000 going out of Bastion, and it only took one mistake to throw the whole system into chaos.

I was never quite sure whether it was one of the flights out of Bastion that went tits up or whether the RAF crews hadn't managed to get their beauty sleep, but our flight was delayed by at least forty-eight hours. Morale plummeted. It didn't seem to matter that we were going home – or home via Cyprus for twenty-four hours' decompression – the mood among the blokes was grim. It was as if the entire military system was working against us, fucking us around until the very last minute.

Bastion wasn't the sort of place you hung about in unless you had to. There were only so many times you could go to the NAAFI, or the gym, before the days began to drag miserably. The prospect of spending twenty-four hours in Cyprus having a few beers before flying back to the UK didn't do much for our morale either. As far as we were concerned it was just another delay.

On 8 October, at around 1000 hrs, I was heading over to the Ops Room to see if there was any news on our flights when the sound of a massive explosion rumbled through Bastion. I knew immediately that it was an IED. Had the Taliban got inside the camp and planted a bomb? My pace quickened and pushing open the door of the Ops Room I headed straight for the watch-keeper.

'What's going on? That was an IED. It sounded like it was inside the wire.' I was dressed in a T-shirt, shorts and flip-flops. 'My team just need to re-kit. Use us.' Although I had no real idea what was going on, I still wanted to be part of it.

The Taliban had managed to sneak onto the training area – the same place I had been earlier in the week putting Paddy's team through their paces – and plant an IED on one of the ranges. The whole training area was beyond the wire and a series of manned watchtowers were supposed to provide over-watch to prevent any incursions by the Taliban.

The 1st Battalion, Coldstream Guards had been going through their RST on the ranges when Lance Corporal James Hill, a soldier from Surrey, who was planning to get married at the end of the tour, was killed. One of his mates, Guardsman Jack Davies, was severely injured, losing a leg and suffering spinal injuries. It was a major fuck-up. A year earlier an officer had sent a report up through the chain of command stating that he believed the shooting ranges were unsafe but it seemed that the report had been lost.

Clearing the ranges could take up to four hours but the demands on getting soldiers through their training meant that on that particular day the range had been cleared in just forty-five minutes. The ranges were like a magnet to the local Afghan population. They would walk onto them at night and collect the empty bullet cases to sell on as scrap. The Taliban had obviously clocked that the area was insecure and dug an IED into one of the firing points on the range. Lance Corporal Hill was just twenty-three. He had been in Afghan less than a week. Soldiers know operations carry risk, they know they can get killed in battle – that was part of the deal, but being blown up in an area meant to be safe was unacceptable.

I was desperate to get back out on the ground for one last job and just when I was hoping Sandy might change his mind,

Paddy walked in looking serious and focused. As well as the casualties, there were a couple of hundred soldiers out on the different ranges, who had been ordered to stay exactly where they were until the area had been cleared.

I had to stop myself from getting involved and took a step back. I wished Paddy and his team good luck, before heading back to the transit accommodation and spent the rest of the morning lying on my bed feeling useless. Paddy and his team did a great job. The casualties were recovered and there were no further injuries.

Later that afternoon the word came through that we'd be flying out to Cyprus for twenty-four hours' 'decompression' in four days' time. Decompression consisted of a one-day stopover in Akrotiri where troops were supposedly allowed to blow off steam and get pissed in a controlled environment. Frankly I thought it was a load of bollocks. I simply didn't like the idea of being told to have fun. I was a bit too long in the tooth for that kind of bullshit, especially after six months of being smashed in Afghan. Now that my tour was over, I just wanted to get home and face the music and deal with my marriage.

The next four days dragged like fuck. Each day that passed we all lost a little bit more of our sense of humour. When our departure date finally came, we dropped our kit off at the airhead where hundreds of Bergens were loaded onto pallets before being moved inside the C-17's massive cargo hold, which was large enough to carry a tank halfway around the world.

Then later that evening, after spending what seemed like an eternity drinking coffee and watching comedy repeats in the NAAFI, the order came to board. The Afghan sun had slowly slipped beneath the distant snow-capped mountains and as I climbed the steep metal stairs up to the giant transport aircraft, I paused briefly for one last look. Bastion was lit up like a football stadium on match night – it was huge, the size of a small town. The hospital was bright and busy with helicopters still bringing in the dead and wounded.

Looking back down at the single file of soldiers stretching across the runway I smiled and gave Afghan the finger one last time. Inside the main cabin, soldiers were strapping themselves into rows of seats. The atmosphere was end of term with jokes and smiles from soldiers no longer young. Everyone carried the signs of loss and war either physically or mentally. They were the lucky ones, the soldiers who had made it. Six months older than when they had arrived but most had witnessed and experienced enough death and gore to last a lifetime.

Every single one of us on that flight had been touched by tragedy and I believe that none of us gave a fuck about Afghan. Not the people or the country. Was the sacrifice worth it? Absolutely not. Unquestionably, some things in life are worth dying for: family, friends, but Afghan didn't fall into that category. It was a fucked-up country when I arrived and it was just as fucked up when I left – the only difference was that more blood had been spilled.

The aircraft began to fill and soldiers began putting on body armour and helmets in preparation for departure. I plugged myself into my iPod, closed my eyes and forty minutes later the C-17 climbed effortlessly into the velvety black sky. The sense of relief in the aircraft was palpable. The pilot's announcement that it was safe to remove our body armour and helmets was greeted with a raucous cheer. It really did start to feel as if we were going home. I dozed fitfully during the two-hour flight into Al Minhad, the military air base in the United Arab Emirates, and from there it was another four hours on board a charter airline to Cyprus.

The aircraft arrived at RAF Akrotiri early the following morning. The sky was aqua-blue and the airfield was immaculate, with green manicured lawns and palm trees gently swaying in the Mediterranean breeze. It felt as if we'd landed on another planet.

As the soldiers trooped off the aircraft with stale breath in creased, sweat-soaked uniforms, two PTIs dressed in shorts and pristine polo shirts were waiting to brief us. Standing in my stinking desert uniform just hours after leaving a war zone, I wanted to tell them to go and fuck themselves. I held them both in utter contempt. 'All you do is sunbathe all day and fuck around doing water sports while we were fighting and dying in the world's biggest shithole,' I thought but kept it to myself.

'Right, lads, this is what's going to happen. Strip off now and get into your shorts and T-shirts. Put your uniform into a laundry bag with your name on and we'll get it back to you cleaned and pressed for the morning. From here you'll be bussed down to the beach where you'll have fun.'

I hadn't really bought into the enforced joviality of 'decompression' and I certainly didn't want to be told by a couple of gym queens that 'I was going to have fun'. But I was actually pleasantly surprised.

Everyone who'd been on the flight was loaded onto a bus and driven to a private beach, where water sports, ice cream, food and fizzy pop were freely available. It was like an all-inclusive holiday. The atmosphere was chilled and fun. The more we laughed the further Afghan drifted away. We got our hands on some kayaks and inflatable waterslides and as the hours ticked by I suppose we learned to enjoy ourselves again. My team chatted about the tour, the things that went wrong, about what happened to Sam and those members of the Task Force who didn't make it.

As the sun began to slip slowly beneath the horizon, we headed back to the transit camp to a barbecue and a couple of beers, our first drink in months, all rounded off with a bit of a show with singers and a comedian. After a few beers, maybe four, most of the soldiers were pissed and ready for a few hours' kip and a chance to dream about other things rather than their own death.

Morning greeted us with a cooked breakfast and clean uniforms, as promised. Later that morning we boarded the five-hour flight back to RAF Brize Norton. That last leg home was oddly surreal. Afghan felt like a million miles away and the last six months could have almost been a dream. I don't know whether that was the point of decompression, but if it was, the idea certainly worked.

It was a typically British autumn day. The sky was gunmetal grey and an icy wind barrelled across the runway. One by one, in a sort of single file, the soldiers made their way into the arrivals hall, through customs to the waiting wives, husbands, children and families. The air was filled with a mixture of relief and excitement. Everyone had a loved one to hug, to welcome them home – except me. As we collected our bags, my team began to say goodbye to each other and one by one they departed. We'd spent the last six months living closer than brothers and now it was all over. There were man-hugs and promises to stay in touch. Stu Dickson and Lee Ridgway, my two pals who had picked me up at the start of my R & R, were once again waiting for me.

I clocked their faces among the waiting families and was lifted by their smiles. They immediately went into the relentless piss-taking mode once again, my weight or lack of it being the main point of attack. I knew they were trying to give my morale a bump but to be honest the impending reunion with my wife weighed too heavily on my mind.

I loaded my bags into the boot of Lee's car and placed my body armour on top. The vest still had all of my Afghan insignia attached – the Velcro badges identifying me as a member of the EOD Task Force, my ATO tabs and blood group. It was stained with sweat and the blood of those whose broken and traumatised bodies I helped to recover.

Pausing for a few seconds, I wondered if and when I would ever return to Afghan. The feeling was indescribable, as though you were saying goodbye to something you had grown to depend on. Afghan takes something from everyone – if you're unlucky, it's your life, or possibly an arm or a leg or some sort of horrendous mental wound, like PTSD. I suppose I had lost what I craved most, a job I had loved. Afghan defined me and now it was gone, possibly forever and I felt empty and lost. I had spent the last six months living a dream I didn't want to end.

'Come on, Kim!' Lee shouted. 'You do want to get home?' he added laughing.

The next couple of hours passed in a bit of a blur as we chatted about what was going on in Afghan and about how Paddy had only been in theatre for two minutes before he was thrown into the cluster fuck on the training area. As we drove along country lanes and through small quintessential English villages, Stu and Lee brought me up to speed with what was happening back at the Bomb School. They also confirmed that I would be joining the High Threat team as an instructor – it was a brilliant job and the one I wanted, but my mind was elsewhere.

Inevitably the conversation slowly edged towards my disaster of a marriage.

'So what's happening, Kim? Are you two going to sort your shit out?' Lee asked.

'Nothing's changed. I called home once a week while I was in Afghan, mainly to check on my son. More often than not there was no answer and I just left a message. But it's over. We're done and nothing's happened which is going to change that. She's gonna let me stay at the house for a few days to get my shit sorted.'

'Then what? The Mess?' Stu asked.

'Yeah, I suppose so.' And the conversation ended. The Warrant Officers' and Sergeants' Mess was full of single soldiers, or those whose families lived in other parts of the country and people like me – the few whose marriage couldn't withstand the pressures of service life. I knew then that the moment I walked into the Mess I would be greeted as a casualty of war – another soldier who'd sacrificed his marriage for the job. There is a saying in our trade that EOD actually stands for 'everyone's divorced'. Looking back, my marriage was probably doomed from day one – married too young, too busy with work, wanting more than just slippers, a family and the easy life. It wasn't my wife's fault – actually far from it, she was great. I just wasn't ready for it.

The car turned slowly into the married quarters at Marlborough Barracks in Kineton and my heart began to beat faster. I was just hoping there wouldn't be a scene on the doorstep, not in front of my mates. The car came to a slow stop at the back of my house. Stu and Lee offered to help with my gear but I told them not to bother and that I'd catch up with them later. Both of them lived on the same patch and part of me wondered whether I would be knocking on their doors in the next ten minutes or so asking for a bed for the night. As the car pulled away I headed up the garden path and hesitantly knocked on the door.

'Come in, Kim,' my wife sang from the kitchen. I opened the door and she greeted me with a smile, a hug and a kiss, but on the cheek. It was good to see her again.

My son appeared from the sitting room. He looked older but was the same smiley little boy with happy blue eyes and light-brown scruffy hair. I dropped to my knees and he ran into my open arms shouting: 'Daddy, Daddy, Daddy!' I buried my face into the space between his neck and shoulder and hugged him tightly.

My eyes filled with tears. 'Hello, son.' It was the best feeling in the world and I was overcome by the emotion of the moment. I had feared that my son wouldn't recognise me but my wife had been brilliant. Despite our differences and the fact that the marriage was over she had ensured that he knew who I was. Suddenly, and completely unexpectedly, I felt exhausted – almost as if I had been ambushed by the mental trauma of serving six months in Afghan. For him to hug and recognise me was probably one of the highlights of my life. He had changed massively from when I was on R & R and although my wife had sent pictures of him to me he was not the boy I had left behind. Over the next couple of hours I played with him just like any father and son who had been separated for months while at the same time forcing myself not to think of the immediate future. My wife sat back with a brew watching us play and I would occasionally catch her staring, looking sad and perhaps wondering what might have been.

For the next few days, I spent as much time as I could with my son but I also got acquainted with my new role at the

Bomb School. Going into the office was part of a normal-isation process to allow families to get used to seeing each other again. It is meant to ease that often fraught period when soldiers return home after so long away. Then once a couple have got used to one another again, the soldier will go on his post-operational leave.

During that first week I spent a couple of hours a day in the office sorting out the boring, mundane things in life like seeing the chief clerk to make sure you get your post-operational bonus sorted, booking back into the Mess so they know you'll be coming in for lunch – or in my case living in – and handing in and withdrawing kit from the stores.

At home, I was sleeping in the spare room, preparing myself for moving out of the family house and into the Mess. I wished it could have been different, that we could have been a happy family like everyone else, but it was not to be. Our son was going to grow up with divorced parents. My rela-tionship with him wouldn't be like most other dads, and that hurt more than I ever thought possible. Eventually, the day came for me to move out. I packed up my car and drove the 150 yards or so to the Sergeants' Mess, picked up my room key and headed for the annexe.

'Jesus,' I mumbled to myself as I opened the door. I hadn't expected much but I was still shocked by the state of my room. It was dark and gloomy with a single dirty window, moth-bitten curtains and a smell of damp. It measured just seven by six feet and felt more like a cell than a bedroom. It had a sink in the corner that had probably been pissed in more than washed in – a hot and cold running urinal.

There was barely room for me, let alone my kit. I sat on the bed and put my head in my hands. 'I survived Afghan, came home, my marriage is over and now this. A shitty little room for how long? Two years?' It felt like a punishment and I hadn't felt so low in months. Worst of all, I now had a month of post-operational leave to fill.

After about an hour of being utterly miserable I slapped myself around the face, figuratively speaking, and got my shit together. I called my wife and said that I would like to see as much of my son as possible over the next month and she was more than happy.

Within a week I had been given a bigger room in the Mess, which meant that my son could come and stay. In the evenings I met up with pals I hadn't seen in months and slowly my morale began to improve.

Towards the end of October, Lee, Stu, another pal called Simmo and I decided to get away for a lads' weekend. The four of us grabbed some clothes, our passports, filled our wallets with cash and headed to Birmingham International Airport and the enquiries desk. The deal was we would just rock up and get the first available flight out of the UK, no matter where it was. 'I can offer you Amsterdam,' said a very attractive sales assistant.

The weekend away was just what was needed – almost a continuation of decompression. It was carnage. I got so drunk I ended up getting a tattoo on the inside of my left arm. It was an image of praying hands with rosary beads. The nights were spent in a city-centre hostel and our room was reminiscent of something from a Russian labour camp, with steel bunk beds and rubberised mattresses. The walls were made of breeze blocks and the floor was raw concrete with a drain in the middle, presumably to allow the owner to hose the room down after his customers had puked and pissed all over the place. I'd stayed in better accommodation in war zones, but the hostel served its purpose.

Just being with three good mates helped me get some perspective back on my life. A group decision was made to isolate ourselves from Kineton and the Army during the weekend so phones were switched off, there were no calls home and emails went unchecked.

On the Sunday we headed back to the airport, nursing hangovers and all of us feeling that we needed another break to get over the one we'd just had. As we moved through passport control looking like death and stinking of booze, Lee turned his phone on. Almost immediately it began to bleep furiously with a deluge of text messages.

Lee stopped, his face went white, he looked up and said, 'Oz has been killed.'

He was referring to Staff Sergeant Olaf Schmid, known to everyone in the EOD world as Oz.

'What?' I said, convinced that Lee had made a mistake. 'I was with him a few weeks ago. He's fine.'

But Lee shook his head and showed us the text. It seemed impossible. Just a week ago Oz was being his normal larger-than-life self and now he was gone. It was difficult to believe. I felt numb, sick and angry all at the same time.

The flight home was spent in a depressing silence. We all felt guilty that we had been having a great time on the piss without knowing that Oz had died. As the plane began to descend through the clouds into a gloomy-looking Birmingham, I began to ask myself how did I manage to survive Afghanistan? My team had pulled more bombs out of the ground than Oz's because we had been in Afghan longer, yet we had survived virtually unscathed. It didn't make sense. It seemed to prove the old adage that when your time is up, your time is up.

Disbelief that Oz had gone was soon replaced with acceptance. Death and bomb disposal often go hand in hand. Every bomb disposal operator who'd been deployed to Afghanistan had come close to death and, as harsh as it may sound, there was no point dwelling on it; Oz definitely wouldn't have wanted that.

I spent the rest of my leave spending as much time with my son as possible and preparing to go back to work. My relationship with my estranged wife was about as good as could be expected. We both knew that our marriage had run its course and there was no mutual, lasting animosity. By the time my leave was over my life was back on track. Oz had been buried and there was a rumour that he was going to be awarded a posthumous George Cross. A few weeks later, all members of the Counter-IED Task Force who served on Herrick 10 were reunited at a medals parade at Carver Barracks, Wimbish, in Essex, the home of 33 Engineer Regiment (EOD). It was great to see soldiers and families celebrating the end of a gruelling six months. Sam had also managed to make the parade; he had only been given a 20 per cent chance of surviving his wounds so his recovery was remarkable. He'd lost an eye and suffered a brain injury and had been told that, in all likelihood, he faced being medically discharged. But his spirits were high. He wanted to get fit and reassess his future.

By mid-November, I was ready to get back to work. My life felt as though it had come full circle. A year earlier I was a keen-eyed student on the High Threat course feeling as though I was out of my depth and now I was an A-Team instructor, training the next generation of High Threat bomb disposal operators.

I arrived at the Felix Centre early on Monday 16 November 2009, clean-shaven, combats pressed and hair cut to regulation length. One by one the students – some officers but mainly SNCOs (some faces were familiar but most weren't) – trooped into the classroom and waited for me to tell them to sit down. I scanned the room looking at their faces and remembered those in the EOD world who hadn't returned.

'Gentlemen, welcome to the High Threat course. We are now going to spend the next eight weeks teaching you how to survive Afghanistan. Firstly, the most important piece of equipment you will need is this . . . a paintbrush.'

Epilogue

January 2017

It's almost two years since the British Army left Helmand and the Western world's focus has shifted once again to Iraq and the conflict against the Islamic State terrorist group. Improvised explosive devices remain the primary weapon of the majority of terrorist groups around the world and people like me – bomb disposal experts – are right now, as I write, on standby across Britain ready to react and to put their lives on the line to keep the country safe.

I'm now a Warrant Officer Class 1 serving in 11 EOD Regiment RLC. I can't tell you what I do except to say that the soldiers under my command train every day in a bid to keep one step ahead of the terrorist. The work is often difficult and dangerous but every one of my soldiers would willingly lay down his life to keep members of the British public safe from the threat of terrorist IEDs.

My time in the Army is almost over. I've had a fantastic career but it hasn't been without its difficulties and frustrations – what would you expect – it's the Army. But learning recently that the Taliban are still causing issues in parts of Lashkar Gah, Helmand's provincial capital – and before that it was Sangin, Musa Qala and Nawzad, all areas where hundreds of British soldiers were killed and injured – was very difficult to accept. The Taliban were often quoted as saying, 'You have the watches but we have the time.'

So I'm left asking myself the question: was it worth it? It's a very difficult question to answer and soldiers who served in Helmand, who killed and watched their mates being killed, will have their own opinions. I'm not sure yet whether the war was worth the cost in lives or the billions of pounds of taxpayers' money that funded the conflict. But I will say this: I enjoyed almost every minute of the challenge and the reward. I got to do what I had been trained to do in one of the most dangerous countries in the world. But I was lucky. I survived six months of pulling bombs out of the ground almost without a scratch. But for those who were killed and injured – it's probably a different story.

Appendix

Staff Sergeant Kim Hughes's
George Cross Citation

On 16 Aug 2009, Staff Sergeant Hughes, a High Threat Improvised Explosive Device Disposal (IEDD) operator, along with a Royal Engineers Search Team (REST), was tasked to provide close support to the 2 RIFLES Battlegroup during an operation to clear a route, south west of Sangin.

In preparation for the operation, elements of A Company deployed early to secure an Emergency Helicopter Landing Site and isolate compounds to the south of the route as part of the inner cordon.

Whilst conducting these preliminary moves the point section initiated a Victim Operated IED (VOIED) resulting in a very serious casualty.

During the casualty recovery that followed, the stretcher-bearers initiated a second VOIED that resulted in two personnel being killed outright and four other very serious casualties, one of whom later died from his wounds.

The area was effectively an IED minefield, over-watched

by the enemy and the section were stranded within it. Hughes and his team were called into this harrowing and chaotic situation to extract the casualties and recover the bodies.

Speed was absolutely essential if further lives were not to be lost.

Without specialist protective clothing in order to save time, Hughes set about clearing a path to the injured, providing constant reassurance that help was on its way.

On reaching the first badly injured soldier he discovered a further VOIED within one metre of the casualty that, given their proximity, constituted a grave and immediate threat to the lives of all the casualties.

Without knowing the location of the power source, but acutely attuned to the lethal danger he was facing and the overriding need to get medical attention to the casualties rapidly, Hughes calmly carried out manual neutralisation of the device; any error would have proved instantly fatal.

This was a 'Category A' action only conducted in one of two circumstances: a hostage scenario where explosives have been strapped to an innocent individual and a mass casualty event where not taking action is certain to result in further casualties.

Both place the emphasis on saving other people's lives even, if necessary, at the expense of the operator. It was an extraordinary act. With shots keeping the enemy at bay, Hughes coolly turned his attention to reaching the remaining casualties and retrieving the dead.

Clearing a path forward he discovered two further VOIEDs and, twice more, carried out manual neutralisation. His utterly selfless action enabled all the casualties to be extracted and the bodies recovered.

Even at this stage Hughes's task was not finished. The Royal Engineers Search Team (REST) had detected a further four VOIEDs in the immediate area and stoically, like he has on over eighty other occasions in the last five months, he set about disposing of them too.

Dealing with any form of IED is dangerous; to deal with seven VOIEDs linked in a single circuit, in a mass casualty scenario, using manual neutralisation techniques once, never mind three times, is the single most outstanding act of explosive ordnance disposal ever recorded in Afghanistan.

That he did it without the security of specialist protective clothing serves even more to demonstrate his outstanding gallantry. Hughes is unequivocally deserving of the highest level of public recognition.

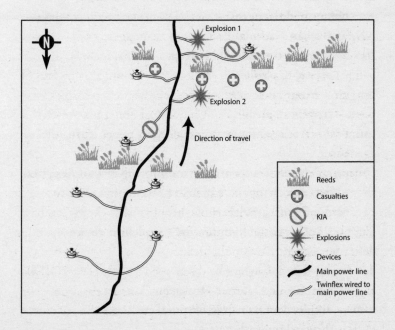

Glossary

AH – attack helicopter

AK47 – Kalashnikov automatic rifle

ANA – Afghan National Army

ANFO – ammonium nitrate and fuel oil – form of
home-made explosive

ANP – Afghan National Police

APC – armoured personnel carrier

bang – plastic explosive

Bergen – Army rucksack

C-17 – transport plane

camp rat – Army slang for someone who never leaves the
base

collapsing circuit – a secondary monitoring circuit designed
to detect a change in a primary circuit and then to
respond with an electrical output.

Counter-IED – counter-improvised explosive device

det – detonator

det-cord – detonating cord

ECM – Electronic Counter Measures

EOD – Explosive Ordnance Disposal

FOB – forward operating base

helo/heli – helicopter

Hercules – RAF transport aircraft

Hesco – wire-mesh containers filled with sand, soil or gravel that may be stacked up to form a wall

High-metal pressure plate – a pressure plate consisting of high-metal-content electrical contacts such as hacksaw blades. Easily located with an in-service metal detector

HLS – helicopter landing site

HME – home-made explosive

Hoodlum – handheld metal detector

HQ – headquarters

ICP – incident control point

IED – improvised explosive device

IEDD – Improvised Explosive Device Disposal

ISAF – International Security and Assistance Force

KIA – killed in action

Low-metal pressure plate – a pressure plate consisting of low-metal-content electrical contacts such as bare wire. A device that proved challenging to detect with an in-service metal detector

Mastiff – armoured vehicle

MERT – Mobile Emergency Response Team

MFC – mortar fire controller

needle – EOD weapon used to cut wires

No.2 – second-in-command of the Counter-IED team – usually a corporal

OC – officer commanding

PB – patrol base

PE – plastic explosive

PP – pressure plate

PPIED – pressure-plate IED

PTI – physical training instructor

QRF – Quick Reaction Force

RC – remote control

REMF – rear echelon motherfucker – Army slang for someone not in the front line

RESA – Royal Engineer Search Advisor

REST – Royal Engineer Search Team

R & R – rest and recuperation

RIP – relief in place

RMP – Royal Military Police

RPG – rocket-propelled grenade

RST – Role Specific Training

SA80 – standard issue British Army rifle

SAT – Senior Ammunition Technician

snips – pliers

SOP – standard operating procedure

SSgt – staff sergeant

STT – Specific to Theatre Training

Terp – interpreter

Terry – Army slang for Taliban

UXO – unexploded ordnance

watch-keeper – NCO or officer who monitors the radio within an HQ

WIS – Weapons Intelligence Section

WO – warrant officer, can be Class 1 (WO1) or Class 2 (WO2)

Acknowledgements

A friend of mine told me a while back that writing a book is like running a marathon – you're excited at the start but towards the end you just want it over. I ran a marathon last year and have written a book this year, and completely agree, with an added similarity of the emotional roller coaster in the middle. When I was awarded the George Cross, I was approached on a number of occasions to write a book, to put pen to paper and talk about my life and what I had experienced. Back then, I was relatively young and felt that I had nothing to say, nor thought for one minute that anyone would want to read about it. I was also not a writer, a fundamental part of the whole process – don't get me wrong, I can talk shit like the best of them, but the time wasn't right.

Almost seven years on, and here I am doing something I never thought I would. But this isn't something I've just pulled out of a hat – it's taken time, effort and a hell of a lot of patience, and I'm not talking about mine. I wouldn't have been able to do this without the help of some great people.

Firstly, Sean Rayment, a fantastic chap who's helped me understand what it means to be a writer, the complexities in describing the most simple of things and the ridiculous amount of time it takes to get it right.

Julian Alexander, my agent, the fount of all knowledge – the experience and guidance he has provided has been second to none. My random phone calls, often late into the night, were always met with calm, reassuring advice.

Iain MacGregor and the team at Simon & Schuster have been ultimate professionals. The gap between military life and the civilian world often seems unbridgeable, however they have made this experience a relatively easy and enjoyable one.

Sal and my family, for being my sounding board and support as I revisited some of the darkest moments of my life.

The 'Circle', my closest friends, who have stood by my decision to push through and get this done, embracing my endless chat about 'this chapter here' and 'that chapter there'.

Finally, my mum – her continued support throughout my life and through some of her toughest years has been unwavering. She is my rock and my best friend.